Maurice Fluegel

Spirit of the Biblical legislations

In parallel with Talmud, moralists, casuists, New Testament, ancient and modern

law

Maurice Fluegel

Spirit of the Biblical legislations
In parallel with Talmud, moralists, casuists, New Testament, ancient and modern law

ISBN/EAN: 9783337134723

Printed in Europe, USA, Canada, Australia, Japan

Cover: Foto ©Lupo / pixelio.de

More available books at **www.hansebooks.com**

SPIRIT

OF THE

Biblical Legislation,

IN PARALLEL WITH

TALMUD, MORALISTS, CASUISTS, NEW TESTAMENT,
ANCIENT AND MODERN LAW; ESPECIALLY
THE SOCIAL AND POLITICAL
INSTITUTIONS.

BY

REV. MAURICE FLUEGEL,

LECTURER IN BALTIMORE, MD.

AUTHOR OF "RELIGIOUS RITES AND VIEWS;" "DIET AND HYGIENE;"
"REPLY TO PROFESSOR FR. DELITZSCH;" "GERMANY," ETC.

———————

BALTIMORE:
PRESS OF THE SUN BOOK AND JOB PRINTING OFFICE.
1893.

CONTENTS.

Part I.

Part II.

PART III.

PART IV.

Spirit of the Biblical Legislation.

PART I.

SCOPE OF THE BOOK.

In delivering over this volume to a kind public, the author does not presume to convey the idea of offering hereby a full tableau and a complete discussion of all the Biblical institutions, statutes and laws. Such is not his scope; he aims rather at elucidating the *spirit* of the law; to examine not the matter and the details, but the principles animating and pervading it; to search for, and, if possible, to point out the objects of the legislator in framing the code. This conscientious examination the reader will find here, and by way of illustration, a large part of the leading groups of the law, too, carefully analyzed and set forth.

For nearly a quarter of a century, having had it as my calling to publicly interpret the Bible and its commentaries; fully well aware, with the best expounders, that part of its prescriptions belong to ages and circumstances in which they were originated; whilst part of them were framed for later centuries, some even for times yet to come,—I tried to elucidate here, not so much the matter thereof, as rather their final, social, political and ethical objects in view.

Part of the results of these modest endeavors are laid down in the following pages, on purpose and intentionally denominated: *"Spirit of the Biblical Legislation."*

The reader will, therefore, be so kind as not to look here for a work as that of Michaeli's *"Laws of Moses,"* or Salvador's *"Institutions de Moïse,"* or the Hebrew (*"Taamai Ha-Mizvoth"*) *"Reasons for the Bible Commandments,"* but rather as Montesquieu's *"Esprit des Lois."* As that French writer took, especially, the Roman Law for his starting point and, at the hand thereof, discussed many of the modern legal codes, in nearly the same manner did I treat here of the Biblical Legislation in constant parallel with modern laws and institutions.

Particularly do these pages endeavor to find out the original Mosaic aims, ideas and ideals concerning the political and social status of the people to be constituted; the State, the Church, the Society, and the Economic conditions that legislation was intended for.

Whilst thus expressly stating that this volume is not a rendition of the entire and full Biblical code, the reader will find that, by way of illustration and as examples of the theories brought forward, I have especially treated in these pages a salient portion of the Biblical code, viz: those most important enactments bearing on State, society, civil, criminal and economic laws, family and church, contained in the chapters 21 to 24 of Exodus, conjointly with their wide ramifications, numerous expoundings and qualifications, scattered throughout the entire Pentateuch and the Bible.

These chapters are denominated *"Laws and Ordinances,"* *"Judgments,"* *"Mishpatim,"* par excellence, in sacred writ. As these appear to have been the nucleus around which the Biblical legislation clustered and from which it slowly developed, they form the centre of this volume.

Around this centre of laws and conjointly with them, find here full room and consideration their later elaborations in the Talmud, *Halachah* and *Agadah*, the New Testament, ofen, too, their parallels in Roman law, Zend Avesta and Koran, and especially their paramount influence upon the State, the society and the laws of to-day.

The result of these investigations seems to me to be that most of the political aspirations of our own contemporaries, of our truest statesmen and noblest philanthropists, that most, if not all, of the objects of our present democracy, have had their forerunner, their initiator, their first warm advocate in the Legislator of Sinai; that our American democracy found its first enthusiastic expression in the Pentateuch, repeated and inculcated over and over by the Biblical prophets; that modern democracy is simply the evolution of the Biblical Democracy.

As a practical law, the *great book* undoubtedly made its concessions to the rude conditions it originated in and emerged from. But, as is the case with all extraordinary productions of divine mind, the Biblical legislation was essentially non-sectarian ; that it finally aimed at universal justice, tempered with charity, for universal mankind, children of the one universal Parent; that though admitting special forms for a special people and country, it taught but universal doctrines; that Israel was but a nucleus of the one human race, and Canaan or Judæa but an epitomized United States of the World.

Every one knows the prejudices the Bible has been, and is as yet, the object of. To some it is the incarnate, all-absorbing, crystallized, last and final word of God, authoritative for all times and all circumstances. To others it is an archæological mosaic, a compound of divers elements and heterogeneous suggestions, by different schools and centuries, for various objects in view. The following pages, examining into its leading principles and institutions, not prejudiced by any bias of sect, doctrine or theology, reverently abstaining from all inquiry into the supernatural and miraculous, taking the Bible as a positive legislation and as extant before our eyes, studying it in the light of reason and fairness, in connection with the contemporaneous and subsequent history of ethical and political human development, for these last three thousand years, they result in the following conclusion! The Bible represents a well digested and admirable whole, an elaborate system for an ever-developing, homogeneous human kind, progressing under struggle, vice and error, towards the ideal of "*a kingdom of priests and a holy nation*," a humanity, united by justice, reason and sympathy, with the same rights and duties and aspirations; "no longer learning war;" "breaking their swords into implements of husbandry;" following up the divine law of justice and eternal fitness, and establishing slowly "a kingdom of Heaven on earth," the dominion of truth, peace and love among harmonized and reconciled mankind.

This highest ideal concerning State and Society, aspired to by present democracy, by modern humane economists and philanthropists, is identically the same as the one held up in the Pentateuch; of course with the necessary developments and complements answering our contemporaneous conditions. That type and ideal first dawned and loomed up in the Pentateuchal Institutions. It developed with the Judæan seers and the non-Judæan sages. It is taking definite shape and form with Adam Smith and John Stuart Mill, with Karl Marx and Herbert Spencer. It is being slowly realized in our present State and Society. It is all along but one chain of evolving, philanthropic thought about human amelioration, from Sinai to Washington, from Abraham to Lincoln and Cleveland. That book is therefore one of the grandest monuments extant for the contemplation and the study of man. It is not simply a book; it is the book; it is the Bible. It is underlying human civilization. It is not the property of this nation and that country, but of mankind, of the world, the study and the profit of ages yet to come.

In 1888, at the publication of my "*Thoughts on Religious Rites and Views*," that small volume was the object of many kind comments and appreciations by some of the best and most learned men of both hemispheres; as by the hoary, English leader, the Right Hon. W. E. Gladstone; the renowned Professors, Franz Delitzsch and W. Wundt, of Leipsic; N. Bruell, of Frankfurt; H. Gratz, of Breslau; A. Neubauer, of Oxford; Presidents Day, of Yale, and Green, of Princeton Universities; Fredrich v Bodenstedt, the poet, etc., etc. In different words they kindly declared "the little book to contain much food for reflection, and a real contribution to science." (Delitzsch). Such kind encouragement made me continue my modest efforts, and these leaves are part of the result thereof.

Go ye forth then, as a respectful greeting to these eminent men, my noble seniors and kind teachers, objects of my veneration and my emulation, bearers of solace and cheer to me in the sharp and intense "struggle for existence;" you great and good men, some of you resting already, your work nobly finished, and some yet leading on the "*Wars of Jahveh*," in the service of humanity! May these leaves be grateful to you, and may they prove as interesting and useful to the kind public at large.

THE AUTHOR.

BALTIMORE, August, 1893.

THE BIBLICAL LEGISLATION.

The Biblical statutes on State and Society, on civil, criminal and economic legislation have, no doubt, their root and *raison d' être* in the hoary Ten Commandments. That truly Sinaitic *Magna Charta* dates back to the great lawgiver. It bears on its face all the marks of original legislation. All hypercritical cavelling is impotent to impugn that fact. It is the organic law of the Biblical Commonwealth. The Decalogue establishes the State and its people on the immovable basis of God, as omnipotent Ruler and all-wise Providence; on a sanctified humanity,—the Sabbath or day of culture; on the family, with filial piety; on the sacredness of life, property and chastity; on the inviolability of our word and the purity of our feelings. On such a basis the Biblical Society could rise to the ideal of a "kingdom of priests and holy nation"—a "kingdom of Heaven upon earth"—a society of educated, free and duty-bound men and women.

SINAI.

From that Sinaic root slowly grew up the tree and developed the branches and the fruit of the Mosaic Legislation, as extant in "Laws and Ordinances," "*Mishpatim*," in II. M. 21, etc.; successively supplemented and enlarged in Pentateuch and Bible, elaborated in Talmud, slowly rising to a fairly complete legislation, civil and criminal, agrarian and religious; political, social and ecclesiastical. With rare exceptions, they are nearly all worked out in the same spirit, all bear the stamp of the same divine genius, as the splendid rays, the bright emanations from the same flaming

Horeb, the wisdom and the benevolence of the "great Moses, standing upon Sinai as his footstool." ([1])

THE CARDINAL PRINCIPLES.

Four cardinal principles appear to underlie that entire code. These four principles are but in our present century fully being appreciated and slowly realized. They have first clearly loomed up before the Biblical Lawgiver, more than 3,000 years ago! These are: Individual liberty, Social equality, Equal distribution of the national wealth, and Community of interests, or Solidarity. Let us illustrate these four principles:

I. *Individual Liberty.*—In ancient, and even in modern, times the State consisted of dominant races and of subjugated ones. The latter were not free, and the first neither. Only the State was free, its leaders, the prince, the Senate, the nobles, the high ecclesiastics, etc. Whilst the bulk of the people, the rank and file of even the dominant race, had no personal freedom. The individual, his life, his family, his property, his work, all belonged to the State. His rights were measured by the good pleasure of the rulers.

The Bible first put forth the axiom: Every Ebrew inhabitant of the country is personally free; the man, woman and child; the poor, the weak, the criminal, cannot lose their original character of free agents. All yield to the State just what is necessary for their own protection. None are born to rule, none to serve. God and law are alone natural rulers. Even laws had to be accepted by the people, in covenant with God.

The later kings were elected and had a Constitution. Thus the claim that personal liberty came into the world with free Greece, or Patrician Rome, or the Anglo-Saxons, or with the English *Charta Magna*, or with Calvin of

---

(1) Heine.

Geneva, or with Holland and Switzerland, or with Rousseau
and Voltaire, or the American and French revolutions,—
that claim is unfounded. Personal freedom dawned upon
history with the Code as extant in II. Moses, 21, called
"*Mishpatim*," over 3,000 years ago. That blessed seed of
the principle of human freedom may be as old as the
Adamite or Biblical era of civilization. It was propagated
by Abraham with the doctrine of Monotheism as the creed
of the people: Whereas the Egyptian Mysteries may have
taught both as the privilege of the few. The idea of
human freedom thus entered with the patriarchs Jacob and
Joseph into the splendid and powerful, yet despotically-
governed Egypt; and crushed by the Pharaohs, the Raamses
and Menephtas of the eighteenth dynasty, freedom went
forth triumphant, with Moses, to assert itself in eternal
legislation slowly embracing mankind.

II. *Social Equality.*—The ancient society was a hierarchy
of different gradations and strata; a monarch, descendant
from and representative of the gods; a nobility by the same
claim, his companions and satellites; a military clan, his
supporters and tools; an ecclesiastical aristocracy, his coad-
jutors; the trades and crafts, and lastly the serfs, remnants
of all the vanquished tribes. Hence, were the inhabitants
divided up into privileged classes and disfranchised ones—
in born ruling, and in born serving social strata. The Bible
conceived another polity; a commonwealth without a hierarchy, a State without king, nobility or military class, with
absolutely equal civic rights and duties, burdens and emoluments for all. This social equality was the necessary result
of the personal liberty underlying the Biblical republic in
federation. Later, monarchy and aristocracy crept in, yet
democracy remained paramount. Its sense of equality has
remained to *this day* as a salient feature of the Hebrew
people.

III. *Equal distribution of the national wealth among the members of the Ebrew nationality.* This is the next concomitant of the axiom of individual liberty. The inequality of wealth is the supreme cause of the deterioration of civil freedom and equality. The exorbitantly and hereditarily wealthy will soon buy off those rights from the chronically poor and weak ones. You remember the constant commotions among these classes in Athens and Rome. You remember how Draco and Lycurgus tried to avoid these difficulties by even more dangerous social monstrosities. The Mosaic lawgiver succeeded better in that attempt at economical average equality, by infinitely more moral and more humane means. He divided his country's soil, per capita, in equal portions, into family lots, and declared them inalienable, just as the citizen's personal liberty. Commerce and enriching wars were discountenanced. A new economic feature of the grandest dimensions, periodically renovating the social physiognomy and restoring the equality of property, was introduced into the State, forever prohibiting plutocracy, proletariat and pauperism ; same justice to all ; privilege and drawback to none; hence all had the same chances in the arena of existence.

IV. *Solidarity or Community of Interests.*—The Biblical legislator endeavors by positive laws, religious doctrines and moral persuasions, to impress his fellow-citizens with a sense of mutual interest in each other, the deep consciousness of altruism, side by side with the other necessary instinct of egoism. "Live and let live." " Love thy neighbor as thyself." Thine interest is not antagonistic to his. It is rather intimately bound up with his and that of the entire community.

HERBERT SPENCER'S CRITICISM.

When Herbert Spencer points out[1] the flagrant contradiction of the two dominant religions, viz: *Selfishness* and *Self-sacrifice*, the first in practice, the latter in theory, the one in the State, the other in the Church, this may be true with the State and the Church, now, as extant. The present society practices egoism; the Church teaches "Love thy neighbor—yea, love thy enemy—as thyself." We must not forget that the present State and the present Church derive from divers sources: the State from Diocletian and Constantine the Great, the Church from Jesus and Paul—vastly different characters! The first two acting from selfishness, the others from self-sacrifice, and hence the flagrant discrepancy, so pointedly and vividly remarked by Herbert Spencer, J. J. Rousseau and others. Not so in the *Biblical polity.* There stand State and Church upon the harmonious co-workings of *egoism and altruism combined.* Self-preservation requires the preservation of our fellows. Our interests go hand in hand with those of our neighbors. The aim is: *"Look that there should be no chronic pauper class among you."* (V. M. 15, 4.) There will always be, sporadically, poor ones. Let them not become permanent, hereditary, socially doomed proletarians.

Hence is *charity with the Pentateuch,* not an ideal, a sermon, but a commandment, *a positive duty.* Help the poor so as never more to need thy help. Lend him even on a slender security. So in Pentateuch, Talmud and Casuists (Joreh Deah, 246, 9.) Take no interest nor increase of him. He must pay his debts, even by six years labor, but the *seventh year* cancels them. He cannot be sold nor imprisoned for such. In Athens and Rome he could,—even be mutilated, too. There his family also could be taken from him. The Pentateuch levies a host of imposts upon the farmer in favor of the poor, the stranger, the widow and the

---

[1] Data of Ethics.

orphan, the State and the temple; not as alms, but as a stern duty of solidarity.

MAN'S PERSONAL FREEDOM.

Having glanced at the four cardinal principles of the Biblical legislation, let us analyze some passages of that code, following the chapters and verses designated as *Laws and Ordinances* in II. M. 21, etc., called "*Mishpatim*" in the text.

The universal feature of the ancient State and Society being serfdom, the woman, the child, the poor, the conquered, the foreigner, as also the mass of the people being unfree, the lawgiver begins with the declaration of the personal freedom of each and every citizen (II. M. 21,2.)

" When thou wilt buy an Ebrew servant (slave or working man) for six years he shall serve, and in the seventh he shall go free without redemption money." That verse means plainly that an Ebrew can never be a slave. He can be hired out for some years, but his liberty is inalienable.

Indeed, from II. M. 22,2, the Talmud gathers that the above took place forcibly, that the Ebrew was sold by the courts for theft, and nevertheless the quality of a freeman could not be wrested from him, as a criminal either. Hence is personal liberty inherent. To be an Ebrew is to be free. The principle was, "To me are the children of Israel servants (III. M., 25,55), God's servants; man's never."

FREEDOM A BIBLICAL DOCTRINE.

Remembering this to have been enacted over three thousand years ago,—those chapters in form and substance pointing to a primitive condition of ancient Israel,—that is truly grand! It points to the fact that the personal freedom idea did not come with the Saxons or the Huguenots, or classical Greece, or the American and French Revolutions, but that mankind owes it to the Bible.

(II. M. 21,3.) "*If the Ebrew servant be a husband, his wife leaves with him.*" During his servitude the master was bound to support her, justly remarked the Rabbis.— (Ibid., verse 4.) "But if the master gave him a (slave) wife, she and her children remain with the master." Here we find the clashing, hard concessions to the social conditions, stronger than the laws of nature and State.—(Ibid., verses 5 and 6.) "*But if the servant declare to prefer his affection for his master and family* to his freedom, then let the rogue be branded as a slave." "*His master shall bring him to the Courts* and nail his ear to the public gate, and then he shall serve for ever." "Why bore the ear?" says a witty expounder. The ear that heard, but did not listen to, at Sinai, "*thou shalt not steal,*" not be lazy, not be wasteful, etc., shall be bored for having neglected the lesson. Historically, the boring of the ear was the mark of slavery among ancient nations. Our ladies' ear-rings are yet a sparkling reminiscence thereof. The clause, "*He shall serve for ever,*" received later by the Rabbis the interpretation of: He shall serve till the coming *jubilee*, or until his master's death; thus forcing the letter of Holy Writ in favor of the spirit thereof; the biblical law is thus consecrating the inviolability principle, good for every Ebrew inhabitant, that personal liberty is inalienable, even with the criminal and the coward, not admitting even the possibility of absolute loss of freedom. Let us not overlook the moral and psychological features of that passage: A vicious freemen is given to theft; he lapses unto serfdom; he marries a slave; he begets slave children; he has to choose between these and his free citizenship; and yielding to his natural yearnings, he must bear the mark of infamy. "One sin brings another one" and "Misfortune never comes alone."

Status of Woman in the Bible.

With even greater care does the lawgiver screen the freedom, the dignity. the delicacy of woman. Woman, the *"mother of all living,"* is the rudiment of society. Not an hour could she alienate her freedom. A free person, wife and mother, her children, too, were free. Hence was so the entire people. You remember the myth of *Pandora*, the toy, drudge, and the Circe of the Greek world. The Ebrew *Eve* represents woman as the very opposite thereof. She is the wife, help-meet and blessing of man. Hence the noble legislation concerning her station in II. M. 21, 7 to 12. She could not be enslaved for one single moment. From her father or brother she had to pass to none else but her husband. It was, therefore, a natural presumption that her master would make her his wife. If he did not, she was considered as ill-used ; something not far from the modern *breach of promise.* Her lord was morally bound to marry her, he or his son in his stead. If not, he has lost his money, and *she shall leave him.* A Ebrew woman shall be a wife and a mother, never a slave! Israel shall be a nation of free men and free women. Thus the law states, *" When she displeased her master to whom she was destined,* he shall free her." Or give her to his son, and then she must be treated as an honorable girl. The natural presumption being that her master was acquiring her to make her his legitimate wife, he was fairly expected to fulfill her expectations. Yet he could not be compelled to do so. The legislator supposed that she had displeased him. Some other reasons, less charitable, he would not accept. If this poor girl did not appear to the master to be good enough for his wife, he could not alienate, speculate nor trifle with her, the modern part of *Gretchen* or *Clarchen* being unknown to Mosaism.

What, then, was the reparation, the honorable amends due to her? His son was to marry her, or he had to free and endow her; assist her to a new establishment. The master not consenting to be her spouse, could not be her lord either; and she could not stay under his roof with her modesty unprotected. What noble championship of woman's rights! As in those barbarous times, one loop-hole was open yet to avarice and lust, as the master might contrive to pass her away to somebody else, in order to get rid of her shrieks and her claims, the legislator stopped up that loop-hole. In just indignation he exclaims: "He is not allowed to sell her to a stranger. He having been faithless to her, she shall leave him; she is free!"

By one of the Hermeneutic rules that Hillel I, and especially later, R. Ismael and R. Jose, the Galilean, had contrived in order to enact new laws opportune for the times, tradition curtailed that parental right to sell one's own daughter, viz., limiting it to her puberty. If at that time, about twelve and a-half years old, she had not been betrothed to her master, she could leave him and dispose of herself at full liberty. So, too, was she free, even within the six years' servitude, if her master died. In Hindostan, and even elsewhere, she had to ascend with him to the funeral pile and serve him—in Hades.

EVE AND PANDORA.

Yet you will hear time and again the claim that the Bible has created the prejudice of the inferiority of woman, and this in the known legend of the temptation of the first couple by the serpent (I. M. 3). The vulgar is misrepresenting the sense of that Oriental allegory and overlooking the real views of the sacred writer, plainly expressed in the history of the creation of woman. There she is declared and emphasized upon, as the noble companion of man—in contradistinction with the Greek Pandora, created for the destruction of man. Indeed, womankind always was aware of the high plane the Bible placed them upon; they willingly exchanged the position of *Pandora* for that of *Eve;* that of a drudge, or a paramour, or a toy, for that of a free and equal help-meet of man. The sex always felt a strong leaning towards the Ebrew Bible, as the earliest advocate of their human rights. The Greek poets imagined woman a bewitching she-devil; even Klytemnestra, Penelopeia and Phædra are not shown to much advantage. The Romans relegated her into the *Atrium*, as the drudge or the nurse of the children. The Spartans imagined her the fit prize for the strongest warrior. The Teuton gambled her away, in lieu of something else. The Slav made her the beast of burden of the household.

The Biblical Moralist alone thought her the free, equal and dutiful companion of man; and before him the legislator had declared that no circumstances, however humble, can rob her of the position of an honorable citizen, at the level of king and high priest.

CHRISTIANITY AND WOMAN.

Hence Josephus narrates, that 1800 years ago the best women of the proudest capitals of his time felt much inclined to Judaism; because they justly appreciated the position which the Bible had given them, and this was the good chance of Christianity. Christianity was the necessary outcome of the moral and religious conditions of the, then, Gentile world. The faith in the gods and their government was broken down, and the world turned to Judaism, its God—idea, morals, family, justice and purity. But the Gentiles were not ready for the Judaic ceremonies and observances. The then Talmudical Jews could not and dared not separate the two to accommodate the world. They had not the courage to give the Gentiles the first alone and drop the latter, and what they did not dare, Paul

did. And thus came out Christianity; it sprung from seeds
left unharvested. Christianity gathered in what the Bible
and the times had matured. It arose from the leading elements of the Biblical structure, with a strong Græco-Egyp-
tian drapery. It is simply an abridged form of Judaism,
adapted to the state of mind of the then Gentile world.
Now the position of woman, not as a toy or a drudge, but
as the companion of man in his struggle for existence, shar-
ing in his burdens and his triumphs,—that position the Bible
gave to woman. Woman seized upon the opportunity,
gaining through that book the throne in the household,
and in her turn helped the book to conquer the world.
Rome feeling her sword failing, enlisted both book and
woman, and saved her dominion for a new lease of centuries.
Slowly mankind enlisted Bible, woman and Rome, and
gained by that its own emancipation, for right engenders
right, and freedom, freedom. Wrong has no future.

CIVIL FREEDOM LAWS.

Let us now recapitulate the leading traits of the Mosaic
civil freedom laws, sketched more than 3,000 years ago.
They solemnly guarantee the liberty of each and every
inhabitant of the land. The citizen's liberty is an inherent
right, and hence inalienable. The criminal or the insolvent
man may, in punishment, be sold, for six years' labor, but
not beyond that term, guaranteeing him all the rights of a
free man, especially protection against over-hard work or
harsh treatment, or abuse of his helpless family. That law
declares woman to belong to her family ; never to a master.
It tolerates no illegitimate sexual connections. That is the
sense of the Talmudical axiom—a striking instance of a
noble and rigid moral sense. ([1]) "Any sexual union is naturally presumed to be on legitimate grounds." It screens the
woman from the ill-usage of the libertine, the wealthy or

---

(1) חזקה אין אדם עושה, בעילתו בעילת זנות.

the rough. Whoever thinks her too bad for his wife, is too mean to be her lord. The Bible declared woman the equal companion of man. (Genesis, 1:26). It yielded to the times in making her subordinate to him, but on express condition that their relations are those of love, not of lordship; those of husband and wife, not master and slave. That law, too, protects her children against the avarice of an unnatural or even an unjust father. Ever presuming and treating mother and children as legitimate, both to enjoy their full rights as wife and heirs; not to be alienated, or sold, or sent to a foundling house. Compare those laws with other legislations, yea, even with some of modern times, where to marry an ignoble person was considered a crime, whilst at the same time public justice was indifferent to all irregular, domestic intercourse, deaf and blind to the shrieks and tears of helpless women and children— make this comparison, and you will find out, why many old statute-books are buried in the dust of oblivion; why others again have been wiped out in a pool of blood and fire. Read of the long and bloody wars of Rome and Byzantium grappling with the Teutonic invaders, under the most violent commotions of social conflagrations, whilst the Mosaic law of 3500 years ago is yet alive, is continually spreading to all races and climes, is preserved and revered as the embodiment of divine wisdom. Because it is not the law for the strong, the crafty, the highborn, the rich, the learned; it is not the law of the classes, but of the masses ; not the privilege of this or that race or people or clime, but the natural equity, the rule of conduct for all races, nations and times. It is the nearest expression of the inherent fitness of things, and hence bearing on its face the divine seal of eternal truth. This is scientific revelation.

2

THE BIBLICAL STATE AND CITIZENSHIP.

The personal liberty Mosaism guarantees to its citizens, the human dignity it vindicates to each and every inhabitant, modified entirely and radically its conception of the State in relation to the individual. Through all antiquity and until recent times, the State was all, the individual but the cipher; the first the unit, the latter the zero; the first counted for a thousand, a million, etc., according to the number of its inhabitants, the latter reckoned for little or nothing. The State was the aim, the inhabitants the means; the first was the real sovereign, the other the subject; the commonwealth owned the soil, the laborer had the drudgery; the government or prince was lawmaker, and yet above the law; the subject had blindly to obey; his life, his work, his opinion, his property, his family belonged to his country and its chiefs. The legislator aimed at the security, the greatness, the welfare thereof; whilst the inhabitants were rarely taken into consideration.

The American and the French Revolutions, only one century ago, had yet to struggle against such an all-absorbing State and Prince. The American Colonies were simply sacrificed to the interests of Old England. They existed in order to buy English manufactures, and to produce for the English markets. They existed as the flock—for the good of the shepherds. When the French Premier, Necker, in 1789, convoked the Nobles, the Clergy and the Tiers-Etats (the people) to remedy France's impending bankruptcy, the liberal leaders felt that they had to contend against that State—*Moloch*. A pamphlet appeared then which gave the *clue* to the awful situation, in its very first lines. "*Qu'est-ce qu' est le Tiers-Etats?*" (What is the people). "*Rien!*" (Nothing). "*Que-veut-il être? Tout!*" (What will it be? All). This was Cæsar's march over the Rubicon. It plainly stated the bitter conflict between the old and the new society. When, a little earlier, in 1661, Louis XIV of France entered parliament, whip in hand, and ordered the venerable assembly to register his edicts, he frowned down their hesitations by his superb *"L'Etat c'est moi."* "The State am I!" The people individually are nothing, the State is all, and is incarnated in the prince. Such it was everywhere and through all times, until the dawn of this very century, except in the Biblical Society.

THE STATE ELSEWHERE.

The boastful, free Greek Republics of old were not a whit above that crude relation between State and citizen. Remember the ruinous intrigues between Athens, Sparta and Thebes. Think of those of Rome and its provinces; how and by what means she subjugated Italy and the world. Ponder over the policy of the Roman and the Byzantine emperors. Ever and ever there is the question of the welfare and the glory of the State, that means the vanity of the rulers. Never is there the question of the masses. From Charlemagne to Louis XIV, from the Napoleons to the present ruling dynasties, the same reckless policy prevailed. When Madame de Stael asked Napoleon I. "Which is the greatest woman?"—"She who rears the most soldiers for the army," was his ominous reply. "What are the people for?" the same was asked, and he replied as categorically, "To pay taxes and be food for the cannon." Machiavelli, in his famous book "The Prince," put it into doctrine: "Everything is good that increases the power of the Prince; the Prince is the State."

So it was from the dawn of history until our own times, except in Mosaism, except in the Biblical Society. Three thousand years ago, in Judæa, the inhabitant was declared a citizen, not a subject; endowed with freedom and rights, which no misfortune could wrest from him, not even crime; there he was the aim of all legislation; he was there the sovereign and absolute owner, obeying but God and law, whom every one was bound to obey, the State and the governors, too; none were born to rule, none to obey; his human dignity, his liberty were inalienable. The State and the princes had what he, what the democratic law, chose to yield to them; they were for his welfare, not he for theirs. The tithes were moral, free gifts, not taxation in our sense. His conscience, his work, property, family, life were his; no privileges and no drawbacks; no aristocracy and no pariahs; the rulers were elected, and obeyed as long as they fulfilled their duty. The right of demonstration and rebellion against tyranny was reserved and often exercised. Thus, the modern democratic free State, as aspired at and slowly unfolding in America and Western Europe, was first attempted in the Biblical Society of yore.

The Biblical Democracy.

There were there later a king, an aristocracy, a priesthood, with the same pretensions as their later confreres elsewhere, but their roots were slender; democracy could not be overturned by them. The priests had the privilege of serving in the national sanctuary, but their emoluments were small; they had but the voluntary sacrifices of the people, ("God is their inheritance," *id est.*, the sanctuary and its offerings. V. M., 10, 8.) As the *poets* in Schiller's "Division of the Earth," they had but the spiritual domain and could never become dangerous; whilst the ancient *Magi* were really the political masters; the Druidic priests possessed most of the soil; the Catholic and Greek clergy owned one-third part of their respective countries until of late. The Popes claimed the sovereignty of the globe; the Hebrew priesthood remained poor; they and the Rabbis later constituted but a spiritual aristocracy. The nobility of mind will never be abolished, because it is the reward of personal merit, and for the good of the people, and can never become dangerous.

There was, too, in Judæa a king with a retinue of satellites and nobles, but their tenure of office was precarious; they rooted in an essentially democratic soil; they were apparently a later concession to the new political constellations and emergencies. Compare I. Samuel, Chapter 8; analyze the circumstances, the popular murmurings, the hesitations, the picture of priestly corruption and of bold royalty there. Compare that with V. M., 17, 15, etc., and you will see how democracy fastened its constitutional fetters around the new monarch. He shall not be a foreign dynast, no blue blood, no descendant from the gods, but an humble mortal, a *brother* among his *brethren*; no assumed superiority, no exorbitant wealth is allowed; no harem and no standing army. He shall study the *Law* all his lifetime and not depart from it, but fear God and rule according to that law. Then he will keep his office. If not, the natural right of rebellion was reserved, and later but too often exercised. This is quite another prince than that of Egypt, Assyria or Babylonia, themselves gods and descendants of gods. In Judæa God alone continued king. A mortal king was and remained half a rebel. When the Ebrew people asked a king of Samuel, God appeased him with the words: "It is not thee, but *Me*, they have rejected from ruling over them." (I. Samuel, 8, 7.) Saul was deposed by the prophet; so was Rehoboam by popular secession; so were many other princes, in the kingdom of Israel especially. You see in spite of royalty and priesthood, the Mosaic democracy remained unbroken.

DEMOCRACY, PROPHETS AND TRIBUNES.

Nowhere is the spirit of democracy so conspicuous as in the extraordinary part of the Biblical Prophets. Here we see men without any public office or any artificial authority, assume such a formidable sway and wield it with such *éclat*, such indomitable perseverance, for such a length of time, and with such stupendous results. The prophetic role is quite unique in the history of mankind; the only key to it is: first, that original democratic spirit, and next, the exalted purity and disinterestedness which characterized those truly holy personages, by far superior to the tribunes of Rome. Men sprung from the lowly ranks of the people, with the thunder of Jahveh vibrating upon their lips, boldly tearing off the mask from king, grandee and priest, in the name of God, honesty and truth, whose lightnings burn in their bosoms. Did you ever realize the magnanimity of Nathan addressing the conqueror David, on a most delicate occasion, with *"Thou art the man?"* Or Elijah's defiance of the Kings and Queens of Israel? Or Jeremiah's denunciation of the iniquities of Jerusalem? We admire the courage of a Demosthenes or Cicero, of a Schiller, Lessing or Victor Hugo, boldly affronting the wrath of mob and prince. They cannot compare with the self-sacrifice of the Hebrew prophets. Now the source of their sublimity and virtue is to be found in the Mosaic democracy. Democracy alone inspires the citizen with such unselfishness, such heroism. Democracy alone breathes into us true and pure love for our fellows. There alone we feel patriotism and self-interest fused into one; for there alone our fellows are our family. We toil and sacrifice for them, as our brothers and kinsmen. We feel, work and hoard for our dearest; not for a cold-hearted tyrant. Monarchies produce brilliant courtiers; Democracies create great patriots and prophets.

Leaders and Orators Elsewhere.

The great orators and tribunes of Greece and Rome have often been compared to the Ebrew prophets. But, supernaturalism not considered now, looked upon from the purely human standpoint, we must give the palm of victory to the biblical prophets, not to the tribunes of Rome or

Athens. Ten to one, these latter ones were demagogues, brilliant rhetoricians and ambitious politicians, who harangued for office, money and self-aggrandizement. For one Aristides, Demosthenes and Epaminondas you will find a hundred venal orators. For one or two *Gracchi* you will find scores of Catalines and Antonios. Even with the best of them was not absolute right and purity the aim, but the interest of their State, viz., their caste. The overlauded Cato hired out his fair slaves to the highest bidder. He was ever ready with his *Carthago delenda est*, without reflecting whether she had not as much right to exist as Rome herself; and/when his caste was beaten, he suicided. I can see there no special sublimity in the *sublimized* Cato. Nor can the Homeric nor the Virgilian soothsayers and sibyllas hold out any comparison. I could never get serious at the frantic outpourings of the heathen *mantis* and *vates*. They strongly savor of nonsense and deceit. They were the tools of kingcraft and priestcraft. So was the Greek Calchas, so Valeda the German. Otherwise are the biblical prophets, tribunes of the people indeed. Whether you believe or not, you cannot help being thrilled with deep emotion and sympathy at the burden of their message. You feel they are inspired by the true interests of the people; by justice and right universal; by truth, purity and goodness. Do they speak for themselves, or even for their caste and class? No; they often harangue against their personal interests; against the masters, and against the majority. They live on roots; sleep on stones; hide in the wilderness; at the mercy of wind and wave, with hunger and death staring into their faces; but they yield not, hide not, hush not up. They bring the message of truth, or of warning, or of consolation, to those needing it. Read the harangues of Moses, Isaiah, Micha, Jeremiah. "Listen, O ye heavens, hear, O earth, for God speaks! Children, I have reared and exalted —but they rebelled. Listen, O ye princes of Sodom. What

for to me your many sacrifices? I have enough of your burnt
offerings. Bring no more of your falsehood—gifts and
hypocrisy—incense. . . . Do away with your wicked
deeds; learn to do good; search for truth and justice;
encourage the oppressed, plead for the orphan and the
widow. If willing and obeying, you shall enjoy the fat of
the land; if not, the sword is ready for you . . . Thus
speaks Jahveh." (Isaiah I.) The Bible contains a thousand such addresses. They ring from the deep recesses of
a heart, brimful with truth, purity and sympathy. Now,
such men, such words, such holiness, could grow only in the
soil of genuine democracy.

THE BIBLICAL AND THE NON-BIBLICAL STATE.

This striking contrast between the biblical State and the
non-biblical one is easily explained by looking at the ethical
basis of each. The first was built upon Monotheism; the
last upon Polytheism. The one has as its foundation an all-
just and benign God, hence is *right* and *benevolence* the
rule of the State and the ideal of the citizen; the other
has force and interest for its pedestal, hence the individual,
the woman, child, foreigner, weak, conquered, etc., are
without rights. The State alone is strong, and to him
belongs all. The prince there is free, is infallible. What
serves his advantage is right; he can never be wrong—as
long as he is strong. So taught Machiavelli: "Everything
is permissible to the prince, if advantageous." So is arson,
poison, treachery, perjury, unjust wars, breach of word,
incest, assassination—all. Upon that basis acted the Tiberias,
the Neros, the Borgias of old and modern times. As to the
subject of the ancient State, he had but one virtue, one merit
and one distinction, viz., *patriotism*. His conscience, feelings and thoughts were absorbed by patriotism; to contribute
to the greatness of the State, or prince, was his only merit;
that was superseding all other virtue and morality. The

Bible, on the contrary, basing upon right, exacted justice from people, State, prince and noble, and, if neglected, let loose upon them the flaming tongue of its prophets, its orators, its leading priests.

THE ROMAN AND THE JUDÆAN CITIZEN.

A few well-known facts from history will illustrate this difference of the Mosaic State from the Pagan one. A Spartan mother loses her three sons on the battlefield, and repudiates the fourth, because he had lost his buckler, with his three brothers.—Brutus the elder delivers over his sons to death, because of their suspected intrigues with the banished king—*i. e.* the State deadens a parent's heart, the citizen stifles a parent's feelings.—The three pairs of the Horaces and Curiaces fight the mortal battle of their respective countries. The last Horacius, victorious, murders his sister for bewailing her betrothed Curiace—and receives the laurel wreath, notwithstanding.—Mucius Scævola burns his hand off on a slow coal-fire, in order to deceive the enemy into a precipitate retreat, for nature must be silent in presence of the State. Thus the Moloch, called the State, obtained the mastery over and the total sacrifice of all sympathetic feelings; over all morality and nature itself.

Another was the ideal of the Biblical Society. The object there was not a great State, but a great nation teeming with noble individuals. Not force, but goodness, was aimed at. The highest ideal was, therefore, duty, justice, conscience—the "*voice of God.*" For these the citizen must be ready to die. State interest could not stifle them. What an immense advance in the Mosaic Society over the most boasted ones of Persia, Greece and Rome! Compare the crooked ways and petty jealousies of the several leading cities and leading men of Greece in their fratricidal struggles for selfish hegemony. Compare the crooked policy of the leading patricians of Rome in their conquest of the world. Compare the aims and means of its later leaders and imperatores. For one honest Galba, Trajan or Julian, how many Neros and Caligulas and Ottos? Nay, Judæa was infinitely beyond Athens and Rome in true moral grandeur. So, our Franklins and Washingtons, Lafayettes and Neckers, Steins and Carnots, took their models in Jerusalem, not in Rome, nor Athens, nor in the Persian seraglio.

BIBLICAL PATRIOTISM.

Let us return to the biblical patriotism. The Judæan citizen cherished the State that protected himself, the ashes of his fathers and the cradle of his children. He would willingly die for it. Hundreds of thousands did die in the defense of the first Jewish empire; millions in that of the second one. They died fighting in Judæa, Parthia, Babylonia, Egypt, Africa, etc. They died since then on a thousand battlefields. The Judæan knew how to die, heroically, for the State that has well deserved of him. Yet patriotism is but one virtue out of a hundred equally sacred. The State does not absorb our being nor our moral sense. There is but one thing absolutely sacred: *that is duty.* You remember the family picture—Abraham, ready for the sacrifice of his son Isaac, hears the divine behest calling: *"Do not touch thy son, for I do know that thou wilt obey My voice."* The Ebrew gracefully yielded life when duty dictated. So teaches the Talmud: "For three things a man shall die and not trespass: Idolatry, murder and unchastity."

The nation and the citizen, not the State, being the aim of the biblical patriot, he would sometimes drop the latter to save the former. So did Jeremiah advise the Babylonian exiles to identify themselves with their new homes. (Jeremiah 29, 6). So did he repeatedly advise the Judæans to surrender to King Nebuchadnezzar, spare themselves and hope and wait for better times. So did, seven centuries later, Rabbi Johanan ben Sakkai steal away in a coffin from the tottering walls of Jerusalem, besieged by Titus, and save the nation by erecting his school at Jamnia. Whilst that grand, pathetic legend of the mother stoically witnessing the tortures of, and encouraging her seven sons in adhering to their inherited faith, shows us in strikingly lurid colors the Ebrew ideal of self-sacrifice for duty. Thus we recognize that the Bible has given to the world not alone Monotheism, but a phalanx of other ideas not less fruitful of human happiness. Among these are the principles of a free State and free citizenship, of human dignity, of individual freedom, of social equality, of man's equal rights and duties, of freedom of the woman, of charity as a *duty* to the poor, the weak, the stranger, the orphan and the widow—*basing society upon right and sympathy, not force and egoism.*

Strength of the Biblical Law.

Compare these laws with other legislations of even the proudest nations, and you will easily find out the cause why these latter have disappeared under the dust of ages, or have been wiped out in the collapse of decaying races; whilst the Bible is alive, silently gaining over and permeating mankind, *revered as the word of God.* For what is good now and thousands of years ago, good for all ages, countries and conditions—that is divine, that is dictated by the spirit of God, the universal mind.

We may further learn from the above that only what is *God's word*, what is just and holy, and good for all, not for the few, is lasting and enduring. Hence, that not chance, blind force or cunning prevail, but an all-wise law, a providential plan, as suggested by the Bible perhaps identical with evolution, governs and permeates human history. That is one of the grand traits of that great book, running through all of its parts and chapters and verses; through laws, moralists or historians, that not chance or force or cunning govern the world and man, but an all-wise Supreme Being, providing for the eternal fitness of things. In the long run only the just and the wise will be triumphant. The heathen view was the very opposite. The gods are not just and wise. Fate is stronger than even Zeus, and fate is blind accident, or at best brute force, a crushing necessity. Pre-ordained? Arranged? That is, distinctly, never stated. Eternal fitness of things is not fate. For neither human reason nor divine wisdom ever attempted to raise the veil of fate. Yet it is the supreme power, unscrutable and blind, in whose presence Zeus himself trembles. Now, that is a most desolate doctrine, not true, baffling all human effort and all wisdom. It is most dangerous to a virtuous, serene life. It is a theory for daring Prometheus, Alexander or Napoleon I. The Bible doctrine of a just, all-wise Providence is more favorable to both, to human virtue and human happiness. Hence more appropriate to underlie the foundations of a State.

PART II.

SOCIAL EQUALITY.

Have the ancient times not been cognizant of the principle of individual liberty and human dignity, much less did they know the other principle, the necessary complement thereof, viz., *social equality*. The equality as to rights and duties of the different members composing the community was entirely foreign to the ancient world.

Society was one great hierarchy, one great chain of subordination, where every link had its superior and its inferior link: the king, the high-priest, the general, the princes, the nobles, the soldiers, the officials, the proprietors, the mechanics, the peasants, the slaves. *This is the "militant social type."*[1]

In earlier times this hierarchy was not only personal; no, it descended from father to son and grandson. The

---

[1] Herbert Spencer.

entire number of inhabitants were divided into *castes* or sharply differentiated classes of people, and it was not permitted to pass from one class into another. If your father was a soldier, you would be but a soldier; if a tailor, your children had to be tailors, and nothing else. Nor was intermarriage allowed between different castes. Mosaism alone of all antiquity knows not of this hierarchy. Every one was as good as his neighbor. Every one could choose his own calling. Every one could cumulate or change his occupations, if he thought he could do so profitably. There was indeed an official priesthood belonging to a particular family, but they never ruled, as elsewhere. The judges, the soldiers, the generals, and later the kings, the teachers, the prophets, did not belong to any caste; they came from every class and every rank of the people, as part and parcel of the people. In the kingdom of Judæa the more conservative part of Israel, there did spring up a dynasty and an aristocracy, but it never degenerated into a caste. The different estates of nobles, priests, Levites and Israelites did always intermarry and occupy alike any position. The principle of social equality, of the same laws, same rights and same duties for all, was first recognized by Moses three thousand years ago. Thus individual liberty and social equality both mankind owes to the Bible.

MAN-SERVANT.

Which are the passages applying to social equality? Let us first review the verses mentioned above, but now considered from the social standpoint. (Exodus 21, 2). "When thou wilt buy an Ebrew servant, he shall serve for six years; in the seventh he shall go out free, without compensation." Why so? Because all Ebrews are and remain equal before the laws. Because manhood-rights and equality are original and fundamental principles.

We read in Levit. 25, 39: "When thy brother has impoverished and becomes thy servant, let him not do any slave work, treat him as a hired servant. With the *Jubilee* he shall go free and return to his family acre—"for my servants are the Israelites." To which *Rashi* adds: "Israel is God's servant, not the slave of slaves." How magnanimous! What a generous pride! The ancient state was one long chain of social inequality. First came the Pontifex Maximus, then the Emperor, the provincial ruler, the duke, the baron, the monk, the soldier, the burgher, at last the Jew, upon whom all trampled. "I defy all your hierarchy," shouted, proudly, Rashi, the great commentator, "I serve not burgher, soldier, monk, baron, king or pope; I obey none but God. You rob me of my rights, my honors, my share of the land, yea, of the warm sunlight and the fresh air, yet you can't make me a slave. The Ebrew is but God's servant." Thus spoke a Jewish writer in the eleventh century. This is the fruit of Mosaic social equality, viz., human dignity, elasticity of mind, energy under adverse circumstances. The mob was happy in feeling the Jew lower than themselves. The Jew proved free in his very chains. "I am the servant of God, freer than all your hierarchy, and am not the slave of slaves."

Woman-Servant.

(Exod. 21, 7.)—"When a man will sell his daughter—as a help—she shall not be treated as male servants, but the acquisition of her services imply the expectation of ultimate wedlock. If not, she leaves without compensating the master." Why so? Because the law guarantees the equality of man and woman; and more so because, as in our United States, Judæa allowed to woman even privileges. She being the weaker party, the law was especially solicitous for her. The ancient world allowed the father to sell his *child-daughter*. Yes, says the Mosaic law, he can sell, *i. e.*, deliver her to her husband, not to a master. The

Rabbis, in the same sense, add: "Woman rises with her husband, but never descends with him." (¹)

CRIME AND MURDER.

(Exod. 21, 12)—"Who smites a man, that dies by it, shall himself be put to death." No difference of rank, class or nativity, nor is a money compensation admitted. All other ancient legislators discriminated, whether patrician or plebeian, patron or client, native or alien, free-born or slave. They allowed compensation, which alone is a token of social inequality. (Exod. 21, 13)—"When the killing was not intentional, but accidental, then the innocent man-slayer shall have the chance and right of asylum. He shall not be the victim of blood-revenge at the hands of the relatives of the killed person." The blood-revenge, i. e., to avenge a relative killed, was universally acknowledged as the first duty of kinship. Social opinion was inexorable thereupon. Mosaism mitigated it. The intentional killing is murder, and can be expiated only by the death of the murderer. The accidental slaying was sufficiently atoned by exile; hence the right of asylum. Thus it states (Exod. 21, 14): "When a man will intentionally waylay his neighbor and kill him, then take him from my altar to die." The ancients abused the right of asylum, granting it indiscriminately even to the worst criminals, especially to powerful ones. The Mosaic law allowed the use and dis-carded the abuse, sheltering the innocent, never the guilty,—because of social equality.

RIGHT OF ASYLUM.

So the ancient world guaranteed immunity to criminals who succeeded in escaping to some famous temple. That of Diana, Apollo, Jupiter Ammon, etc., were such. There were in Christendom hundreds of places of refuge during

---

1) אישה עולת ולא יורדת עם בעלה.

the Middle Ages that screened the thief, the murderer, the political intriguer, from just punishment. Ecclesiastical Rome abounded in such holy asylums. Many churches and abbeys became thus the dens of all the outlaws and desperadoes, whilst criminal priests were never delivered to the arm of public justice. The Bible of three thousand years ago, on the contrary, ignored such privileges of places or persons. With awful rigor, it states : " From my altar take the criminal to his deserved punishment." Crime shall not be sheltered by the sanctity of place. Crime at the altar is doubly hateful. It defiles the altar, and cannot be purified by it. The Bible thus allows no compensation and no immunity to places or persons; no chicanery, no tricks, no asking, Who was the killer and who the killed one? whether the murderer belonged to a powerful or rich family? no quibbling about murder in "first or second degree"—the loopholes of trickery. Our criminal cases offer what dilemmas, monstrosities, surprises, as if justice were blind and deaf. If the jury had before their eyes these plain, lucid, unsophisticated verses, there would be no room for chicanery, bribery and venal oratory. They would see their way clear, wrong would be punished and innocence avenged, and the jury institution, one of the most glorious bulwarks of liberty, would not be so often discredited as it is. The lawyer triumphs when succeeding to whitewash a murderer, not caring for innocence unavenged, justice ashamed and lynch law calling for self-help.

PENAL LAWS.

" Who smites a man that dies, shall be killed." ([1]) (Exod. 21, 12 and 23). " Who kills shall be killed. Life for life." Even so the Talmud declares the death penalty for murder, as also for other capital crimes against the State and society, as will be ascertained in other places. Modern over-senti-

---

(1)   מכה איש ומת מות יומת, נפש תחת נפש.

mentality is against capital punishment. How to screen society against tigers in human shape? Why be sentimental to the criminal and callous to the innocent victim? How to deter from crime? That is not satisfactorily answered. Imprisonment for life, hard labor, deportation to Siberia or Cayenne is costly, probably more cruel and unsafe and not striking enough.

CAPITAL PUNISHMENT AND STRIKING EXAMPLES.

The Bible is practical. It aims at satisfying both, the wronged party as much as the public. The feeling of revenge, if moderated, is natural and wise. Its substratum is the instinct of self-defense. Every one feels the law of equity in his bosom, the wrong-doer and the wrong sufferer. The first feels deterred, the other encouraged by it. Hence is sentimentality for the murderer both wrong and foolish. Next is the punishment of crime the safeguard for society at large. Capital punishment reassures best outraged society, for it does it strikingly. Imprisonment, deportation does it not. An embezzler in a Canada hotel encourages thieves; in jail and in the criminal's jacket he deters. J. J. Rousseau narrates that in order to show his pupil "*Emile*," the consequences of lewdness, he called with him at a hospital of veneric diseases.—Will you make a young girl conscious of the dangers of gallantry, take her to a representation of Victor Hugo's "Rigoletto." There is nothing so effective as objective lessons, and quick punishment is the best object lesson. It is a powerful motive with the Bible in punishing, that "They shall hear and fear." (1) The defaulting bank cashier running away with his prey, is poor consolation to the depositors. To deter the evil propensities from crime, the punishment must be quick, striking, public, and serve as an example of rash acts followed by stern consequences. The fashion of newspapers lionizing a bold

(1) למען ישמעו ויראו.

criminal, reporting daily about him, as a hero, or a victim,
is most mischievous. *Guiteau*, the murderer of Garfield,
was quite as much talked about as that noble patriot himself. He was presented to the vulgar as a sensation, and all
the roughs and the idiots mistook it for glory. The only
tenderness the Talmud has for such a man is a quick death.
They say: "Love thy neighbor as thyself," means here:
"choose for him a proper death." ([1]).

In our times of huge standing armies, incessant dynastic
wars and crushing competition, where wealth goes to the
wealthy, and starvation to the poor, where plutocracy on
one hand, and pauperism on the other, have created the
most tremendous *Social question*, absorbing all other political dilemmas, in such an age, the biblical common sense
axiom of "Who kills shall be killed" is good enough. As
to the future, let it take care of itself. The future may
better provide against crime and too cruel punishment.

FILIAL DISRESPECT.

Exod. 21:15 and 17: "Whosoever smites his father and
mother, or even curses them, shall die." That law appears
to be of a draconic rigor. Yet in primitive, rude societies
it was just and salutary. Later traditions added their
accompanying qualifications. The Talmud requires (Sanhedrin 85[b]) in such cases, the majority of the culprit, a
solemn warning, in presence of witnesses, and a visible
wound inflicted. in presence of witnesses, and that in spite of
the express warning and the announcement of the resultant
punishment, as also many other restrictions fully answering
to the purpose. Now, when a grown person, in full reason,
in quiet temper, well forewarned, is so abundant and so
conscience-seared, so obdurate, and beastly, when no longer
needing the sustenance and help of a parent, to forget all the
tender and most sacred ties of blood, gratitude, reverence,

ואהבת לרעך כמוך, ברר לו מיתה יפה.   (1)

and to curse and smite a parent—that shows of the utmost depravity; and society has no interest in sparing such a monster. Modern times have been busily at work in undermining filial piety. I am afraid modern times have gone too far. Beware! American society especially, beware! The French philosopher Jules Simon, of late gave a sad picture of the reverence and filial piety in—America especially.

MAN-STEALING.

Exod. 21, 16.)—" Who kidnaps a person and sells him, or detains him in his power, shall die." Now, remember this law was enacted over three thousand years ago, at a time when slavery was universal, conquest legitimate, the right of the stronger fully acknowledged, equality unknown. At such a time the Mosaic legislator declared man stealing a capital crime. It may be caviled, he meant but stealing a fellow Ebrew, a free, civilized being, a grown person, a man—vir-*Ish* in Ebrew—not a child or woman, but that is caviling and belittling. The plain face of the verse is : " Whosoever kidnaps a person shall die." Should even the interpretation, by the standard of antiquity, restrict the range of the word *Ish*-vir, nevertheless the absolute sense thereof is universal, sweeping, covering all cases, persons, sexes and races, and thus be a solemn declaration against all kinds of man-stealing and enslaving. Let me here invoke on behalf of liberalism the current theory of *Inspiration.* I admit that ancient and more modern times did restrain the sense of that verse to prohibiting only the kidnapping of a fellow-citizen; but why should not the modern interpreter take the verse in a universal and absolute sense, befitting all times and cases and truly worthy of the Deity ?—

MALTREATING A SLAVE.

(Exod. 21, 20.)—"When a man will smite his male or female slave with a rod—not with a dangerous weapon—and they die under his hand, they shall be avenged." The Rabbinical tradition is: "The murderer shall suffer capital punishment by the sword." That slave is, of course, a non-Ebrew bondsman. For, as to the Ebrew servant, acquired but for six years' work, that needed no special law, his life was guaranteed by the previous general axiom.—(Exod. 21, 12): "Who kills shall be killed."—"But, if the slave, beaten by his master, remain alive and erect for a day or two, then—capital punishment, according to tradition—such avengement shall not take place, since the slave was his property and bought by him" (Exod. 21, 21), he losing his money anyhow. Here is a concession to social conditions. The master could buy bondsmen and hold them, hence he must be permitted to chastise them, when necessary, with a rod, not with a dangerous weapon. If, long afterwards, death ensues, he loses his property anyhow. Follows there no other punishment? Wait and read further: (Exod. 21, 26, 27,) "When a man knocks out the eye, or even the tooth of his slave, he shall let him go free in compensation for his eye or his tooth." Here is social equality. The Bible originally declared all men free and equal, all entitled to liberty and happiness, all made in the image of God, all offspring of the same parental couple (Gen. 1, 9), yet it *tolerated* the social institution of slavery, but tried by all means to safeguard the slave as much as it could. Of course, in those remote times master and slave were of the same physiological race. Spartan and Helot, Ebrew and Gibeonite belonged to the same stock and clime. That fierce antagonism, as between Caucasian or not, civilized and not civilized, etc., was not yet developed, and cannot be taken here into consideration. The non-Caucasian races were simply never contemplated in the Pentateuch.

EYE FOR EYE AND DEMOCRACY.

The democratic spirit of, and the high sense for rigid and equal justice of Mosaism, is particularly illustrated by the legal axiom expressed in Exod. 21, 24: "Eye for eye, tooth for tooth, (1) hand for hand, foot for foot, burn for burn, blow for blow, wound for wound." Here is the consecrated principle of retaliation, the legal formula of natural justice and equity, of original equality, as practiced by small societies living yet in a state of nature, following yet the unsophisticated dictates of unbiased conscience, prompted by the inborn instincts of talion, as deposited in our breast by the Author of all, before conquests and castes had robbed man of his pristine sense of self-preservation. That formula has been decried as barbarous and harsh. Yet it is but the strict logical, mathematical, legal expression of full and untempered equality and justice before the law, when dispassionately looked at. Consider: If one man is as good and valued as much as another man, then necessarily, one man's eye is as valuable as another one's eye. If one is equal to one, then one-tenth part, etc., is equal to another one-tenth part, etc. Whilst, if, instead of that Mosaic axiom, we shall put fines instead, or compensation, as a principle of law, then the natural equality of man is destroyed. For the rich can pay $100 easier than the poor can pay $10. Hence, punishment would be unequal. The rich would pay and laugh at it; the poor be ruined or oftener submit to loss of life or limb. In both ways is equality destroyed. To declare the value of each and every eye to be $100, would not be equal punishment, for the value of $100 is vastly different to the rich man and to the poor one. Compensation means, therefore, aristocracy. "Eye for eye" is democracy. Thus, "eye for eye and tooth for tooth," or *jus talionis*, is the legal measure of the biblical civil and criminal law. No doubt sympathy will have opportunities to demur. In practice we may have occasion to deviate from it, but as a legal, universal axiom, it can not be impugned. Justice alone is equitable to both parties; sympathy favors one party and wrongs the other.

It is claimed that in 1888, the noble-hearted, late Cardinal Manning demurred against that axiom on the following occasion: During a time of popular distress, he said that the law of *"Thou shalt not steal"* "does not apply to a hungry man stealing a loaf of bread." I admit that Cardinal Manning could not be condemned for heresy on that score. I acknowledge that decision does honor to his heart. Nevertheless, could we accept that sentiment as a principle of law? Where should we draw the boundary line? A poor man stealing a loaf is pardonable, and a poor man stealing a dime? stealing a dollar? stealing a winter coat? stealing $50 to pay his rent? $200 to start in business his daughter? steal an office to support his family? Some years ago Maxwell killed his friend, needing his diamonds. Guiteau murdered Garfield for having refused him a consulship, much needed. Please extend the line till you arrive at Cromwell and Napoleon taking a crown — much *needed* by them, too! . . . No doubt, in practice there is a vast difference between stealing a loaf and stealing a crown. In theory, *"eye for eye and tooth for tooth"* is alone a safe principle, and society must insist upon it.

COMPENSATION.

But it will be asked, "How can 'eye for eye' practically be carried out?" May not the offender die under his punishment? In a state of nature that would be no serious objection.

A scandalous author being asked by a witty judge, "why he writes such objectionable stuff," answered, "I must live, sir." And the judge replied: "I do not see the necessity thereof." Should the semi-murderer fully die, he could not much complain. Let the rogue bear the consequences of his viciousness. But it is true, its application is revolting to civilized society. Well, then, in civilized society the formula of *talion* remained but a formula, a theorem.

In practice the principle of compensation was ruling. The Rabbinical tradition was that, in practice, "eye for eye" meant the value of an eye, but with the important difference that equality, the democratic principle, nevertheless remained safe-guarded. For the fine was graded—not equal for poor and rich. The rich and the poor paid in proportion to their wealth and to the value of the eye to the offended party. Thus the legislator stated the rigid principle of retaliation, leaving to the judge the application of the law. The judge determined the amount of compensation, varying proportionately, always keeping in view the fact that $100 to the rich is no heavier than $10 to the poor, etc.

THE OLD AND NEW TESTAMENT.

A great deal of sentimentalism has been wasted on that subject. "Behold the harshness of the Old Testament in comparison with the New one." The one says: "Love thy neighbor as thyself;" the other, "Love thine enemy too." The one, "Take the criminal from mine altar to die;" the other, or rather, the Church, allowed him to escape into a sacred asylum or by vicarious atonement, in this world and hereafter. The one says, "Tooth for tooth;" the other, "If the wicked smites thee on the right cheek, offer him the left one too." The one, "The thief shall pay five oxen for the one stolen;" the other, "If he steals thy coat, give him thy mantle, too," etc. The answer is: The Old Dispensation is a code of laws, for men as they are, for a political State, a real, live society, with the actual, human passions and selfishness, and a very small stock of charity. Hence are rigid right and equity rule of conduct. The New Dispensation is ideal, for man as he might be; its principle is self-sacrifice, altruism, the very protest against man as he is. The Old Testament is practical law, enacted for the State as it is, and there rigid right with a small admixture of love and charity, can reasonably be asked. Or else every one will rely upon the charity of others, and act from sheer selfishness for himself. If the rich should work and give all to the poor, every one would prefer being poor, and receive all from the rich. Now, if all would stop work, whence should come the rich? And if all are poor and lazy, society will soon starve.

Other aims are pursued by the New Testament. It was intended for the kingdom of Heaven upon earth, with self-sacrifice as its leading principle, for beatitude in the hereafter as the final aim. This world is a vale of tears, tainted with original sin, the purgatory of the future Paradise. It aimed at a community of monastics (the Essenes), living in stoic simplicity and poverty (Ebionites), with community of property, and preferring celibacy to marriage. This world is doomed to destruction, and the kingdom of Heaven about to dawn.—Hence the discrepancies between the Old and the New Testament. Now look to the world in 1893. The interminable wars and huge standing armies—exorbitant taxations, with plutocracy, *soldateska*, pauperism, dynamite and constant social upheavals, eighteen centuries after the New Testament Era! Thus Herbert Spencer pointedly remarks that as yet, there exists no really Christian State in the world.

RABBINICAL PENAL CODE.

We have spoken of the leading principles underlying the Mosaic criminal jurisprudence. We have seen that spirit to be eminently practical; the emanation of a great lawgiver, truly inspired by the desire to found a strong society, capable of coping with the "evil inclinations," the bestiality and selfishness of man. He felt that law is for the protection of the innocent victim, not of the criminal transgressor. He gave the accused all chances of proving his innocence, if so; but none, or few, to profit by the intricate meshes of paragraphs, chicanery and subterfuge. We read (V. M. 19, 16): "By two or three witnesses charges shall be established." "Thou shalt examine and inquire diligently." "False testimony shall be rigorously punished." "But he insisted that wrong shall be removed." "Eye for eye, and tooth for tooth—whosoever shall spill blood, his blood shall be spilled." "Innocent blood cries to God, and that blood pollutes the land." "The unintentional manslayer was to flee to and hide in an asylum." The intentional murderer shall be seized and examined, condemned and executed by a regularly instituted court, not by lynch-law. Thus the leading traits of the Mosaic penal laws were dictated by the divine spirit of common sense, and with the pure aim of firmly establishing a civilized State and society, screening innocence, deterring crime, and giving the citizen as much security and happiness as the circumstances allow. This general outline of civil and criminal law is sound. Its principle lies deep in human nature, and hence it underlies the best of all penal codes extant. All build upon the principle of : (¹) "Whosoever spares the guilty, punishes the innocent."

Unfortunately, lay, and even professional, men are often liable to false sympathy. Seeing before them, not the murdered victim, but the person tried for his life, they think only of the possible wrong to him, and never of the certain wrong done by him. They pity him, forgetting that pity for him is cruelty to the victim and to society at large. Now, this charge of over-sentimentalism, which cannot be laid at the door of the Mosaic legislation, appears to me, to be

---

(1) Qui parcit nocentibus, innocentibus punit.

the burden of the Rabbinical penal code. The tendency
of the New Testament to put love in place of right, seems
to prevail in the Talmud, too. It appears, the rigid discip-
line of the Ten Words, the noble family influence, the refined
Monotheism and the deeply inculcated prophetic morality
had long ago educated the Teachers in Israel to such a high
idealism, that they knew crime but by hearsay, and legislated
upon it only theoretically, not to meet stern facts and protect society. Several large treatises discuss the Talmudical
penal laws. But they all bear the stamp of idealism, as if
they could never make up their minds that crime is actual
and must be restrained. They asked such proofs of guilt
that, a hundred to one, crime remained unpunished. It
would seem as if they were rather afraid of doing than of
restraining wrong. They started from the Mosaic law, but
interposed so many points and clauses and paragraphs as ever
to leave the case doubtful and give the criminal the benefit
of the doubt. They were implicitly trusting in miraculous,
providential interference that the guilty would be punished,
for heaven's sake.

ILLUSTRATIONS—SIMON BEN SHETAH.

Here is an illustration: In Babil. Sanhedrin 37a, the
leading treatise of the Rabbinical penal code, we read:
"How shall we overawe the witnesses?" They are to be
told: Perhaps do you speak only by guess, or by hearsay,
or by witness, even of an honest man? Remember, we, the
judges, shall closely examine you, for human life is therein
involved, . . . and future generations, . . . and
whosoever destroys a person is just as wicked as if he had
destroyed the world, . . . following up with a long
homily. Upon this Mishna comes the Rabbinical discussion: The witnesses are asked: Did you see the accused
running after a man, into a ruin, and you were after him,
whereupon you saw the accused with bloody sword in hand

and the murdered man weltering in his blood? If that is
what you saw, you have seen nothing! . . . We have
learned R. Simon ben Shetah (prince of the Sanhedrin)
said: So may I see consolation that once upon a time I saw
one running after a man, into a ruin, and I run after him, and
I saw a sword in his hand with blood trickling down from it
and the other man weltering on the ground. Whereupon I
exclaimed: "Bad man, who has killed this person? Either
I or you! But how can I help it; I cannot punish you,
because the *Thorah*—Law—has declared: 'By the mouth of
two witnesses he shall die.' (V. M. 19). 'He who examines
the thoughts shall punish thee for this murder!'" Indeed,
it was rumored that the murderer did not stir from the
place, "but expired from the bite of a serpent."—So for
Sanhedrin 37, *a* and *b*.

Now of that same Simon ben Shetah, it is told in another
place of the identical treatise, that he was a very energetic
man, fiercely striving to extirpate fraud and crime, to such
an extent that he had hanged eighty witches in one day, and
that once upon a time some aggrieved parties conspired
against him and accused his own son of some imaginary
crime, which son was actually condemned and executed,
though his accusers acknowledged, before the execution,
that they had slandered him; the Rabbinical law not
allowing witnesses to recant what they had testified to.
(Sanhedrin, 44 *b*, Rashi and elsewhere.)

The story is piquant enough and runs thus: " A ghost had
denounced in a dream the Synhedrial President, Simon ben
Shetah, for his tolerating Jewish witches in Askalon, a
neighboring Philistine city. Thereupon he surprised eighty
such witches ; he, followed by as many stout, young students,
who, on entering their conventicle by stratagem, raised them
from the ground to render their witchcraft impotent (¹)—the
known popular superstition.—They took them forcibly out

בשעה שתכנסו ינביה איש אחת מהן מן הארין, וישוב אין מכשבות שולטות (1
בכם, ואם לאו לא נוכל להן.

and at once hanged them. Thereupon their relatives
avenged them by accusing of a deadly crime the president's
own son, who was really executed, though the witnesses, in
time, confessed their slander." The legendary character of
the tale is palpable. A judge who abstained from punishing
a murderer upon the best circumstantial evidence, hanged
eighty women, in a foreign country, in one day, summarily,
upon the strength of their *own* confession, contrary to
Rabbinical law, for witchcraft, and had his son executed,
though his accusers confessed their mendacity! All of
these stories aim only at showing the eccentricities of
Simon ben Shetah, and say nothing more.

Of course, both these stories are legendary, yet they show
the spirit and drift of the Rabbinical statute. Let us give
here a cursory outline of its principles : Two witnesses, at
least, had to testify to the facts of the crime. Self-incrimi-
nation and confession was not tolerated ([1]) ; no torture was
ever used. No circumstantial evidence, even of a most certain
nature, was admitted ; only eye-witnesses, solidly testifying
to each and every item of the case, had a hearing. The
least contradiction was invalidating the testimony ; any
doubt was for the benefit of the defendant. The witnesses
were overawed and severely cross-examined, almost intimidated. ([2]) They were questioned about the major and the
minor circumstances, the surroundings, the hour, day,
month, year, Release year and Jubilee, the place, the clothing, the colors, etc., of the case. If several persons committed
one murder, *he alone* who gave the death blow was guilty of
murder ; hence again entangling questions. Above all, the
witness must have *given forewarning* to the would-be
aggressor, and this *just before the act*, with mentioning of
punishment, etc, which delinquent must have expressly
acknowledged. Each of the witnesses must be an eye-

---

(1) ‫חזקה אין אדם משים עצמו רשע.‬

2 ‫מאיימין.‬

witness of the *entire* crime; one part thereof supplemented by another witness was not sufficient. The accused must be of age, which majority varies *from puberty to full manhood.*

Carefully surveying the Rabbinical penal code, it would seem as if it had never been practically carried out; and that even from beginning, it was but a speculative study. The *Mishna* may yet represent practical law. The *Gemara* is but theory and speculation. The early Mishna-doctors, mostly, were yet judges; but after Hillel, and especially with the second century after C., they were but students of the law. For then Rome held the government with the administration of criminal justice. The Sanhedrin was no longer occupied with either; it was but the high religious court, presiding over the congregation and the civil justice, as in the *diaspora.* It is very possible that under the Persians, the Seleucidæ and the Ptolemeans, the Judæans had not, either, their own, full, criminal jurisdiction, and hence had but very little opportunity to work out a practical penal code. They were pre-occupied with two grand ideas—the preservation of the national religion and with watching the opportunities of restoration. Everything else they wisely left to the political masters.

In the meantime, to occupy usefully their minds, they expounded Bible and Mishna, preparing everything for the coming restoration. As to the penal laws of the Pentateuch, they seemed to have thought them too severe, and fell into the other extreme of being too lenient. They appear to have aimed at the abolition of capital punishment, probably also of all corporeal punishment, reserving it only for such extreme cases where the lawgiver had pronounced the curse of *excision* ([1]), or "elimination from among the people." There is much talk about the thirty-nine stripes, yet they may never have been administered. A very ideal way of thinking was that; unfortunately not

כרת. (1)

strong enough for this real world, as it is. In peaceful times the moral sense of the nation may have been sufficient; not so during civil commotions. Hence, the Roman's complaint about the "*sicarians*."

THE NEW TESTAMENT.

It is interesting to remark that the New Testament moved in parallel lines. It abolished corporeal and capital punishments. You remember Jesus dismissing the adulteress with, " Go and sin no more," and " Whosoever is better may throw the first stone," etc. It made even a trial at abolishing all kinds of punishment, pecuniary, too, suggesting: "Who steals thy coat, give him thy mantle, too," abiding by love, reason and persuasion for human improvement. There was a rich flood of ideality streaming in Judæa, coming from the heights of Sinai, which inspired her leading minds with so much hopefulness for human amelioration. Fifteen centuries have since passed over New Testament and Talmud, and those hopes have not yet been fulfilled. The Mosaic penal code, mainly, is yet the criminal law of nations; the ideals of apostles and rabbis are yet ideals. We are now in 1893, the epoch of Bismarck, the age of the " blood and iron " policy, of dynamite, and of anti-Semitism. How slow the masses move! . . . Beware, ye generous enthusiasts!—And yet these very dreamers and idealogists of to-day, are the models and ideals of the far-off future. In the age of the *blood and iron policy* we warm our hearts and cheer our souls with the hope that once man will make these ideals real, and we dream of the time when capital punishment and all punishment, will be abolished; when reason and sympathy alone will render man amenable to justice and kindness. And such dreams are worth more than many a reality. They are the leaven of progress, the quickening dew of human advance.

NATIVE AND ALIEN.

The equality before the biblical law has no restriction as to race, or creed or original country. The *Guer*, alien in blood, creed and origin, if he but renounced the grossest forms of heathenism, the cruel and licentious worship of Baal, Astaroth, etc., if he had but adopted the seven *Noachidic* commandments, which we would term the universal moral law, such an alien immigrant, called *Guer toshabh*, was entitled to the same civil rights and privileges as the indigenous Judæan of the creed and seed of Abraham. So we read in Exod. 12, 49, and Numb. 15, 17 and 29: "There is but one law, and one right for native and for immigrant." Realistic and sober as the Mosaic legislation is, in comparison with the idealism of the later New Testamentary development, it is most magnanimous compared with all other contemporaneous codices. Over three thousand years ago it did not discriminate against aliens, whilst our to-day's legislations are brimful of such discriminations. Europe has invented its Pan-Latinism—Slavism—Germanism, anti-Polism and anti-Semitism. No one can compete but the native, if of the dominant Church. There are in our America cropping up biases of the same nature and in the same direction, lurking among the vulgar, those having no other virtue to boast of, putting an embargo upon mind, protecting one's own indolence behind the Chinese wall of a protective tariff, prohibiting foreign-born talent and science from competing, in order the easier to barter off one's own incapacity, thus expecting civilization to come from Africa or Arizona. I hope every clear-sighted American, every thoughtful citizen of this broad land, will remember that we or our parents, have come hither in search of freedom, home and bread, coupled with the best part of European civilization. We did not come here to live in laziness and sink down into Indian barbarism. And that will be the result should we

exclude European mind, science and art from competing
and stimulating our rising generations. I hope this pitiful
addition to European craze, viz., "Pan-Americanism," that
new edition of old *knownothingism*, under the hypocritical
mask of assumed patriotism, in reality a screen for ignorance, will never become the polity of this great country,
the hope of liberated mankind.—Now the biblical law
alone among ancient States, declared for the equality of the
immigrant. For not only among barbarians, but even in
refined Greece and Rome, there was a' vast distinction made
between native and stranger, free-born and slave, patron
and client. Here is a trait of truly divine impartiality.
The modern equality of man was consecrated, at least in
principle, over three thousand years ago.

CIVIL JURISPRUDENCE.

The biblical civil jurisprudence, too, is built upon the
principle of rigid equality. In pecuniary matters, too, is
"eye for eye" the measure. But whilst that principle
made criminal punishment severer there than in our modern
sentimental times, it treated offenses against property much
milder than we do. We, in modern times, term fraud, theft
and robbery a penal, criminal offense, and punish them with
stripes, imprisonment, and even *death*. The Mosaic law
does not. Even in our America, the judge does condemn to
prison and stripes for theft. In Europe, now, it is mostly
punished with imprisonment and fines besides. In Eastern
Europe theft used to be punished by lopping off hands.
In Hungary formerly, they used to hang to the first tree
every unfortunate wretch robbing twenty-five kreutzer (eight
cents) on the public road. Undoubtedly such harsh treatment
is against equality. How can we punish bodily an offense
against property? The principle of "eye for eye" screens
the Biblical law from such barbarities. Any attack upon
property is there punished with loss of property and no-

more; this is democracy; the other is plutocracy. Thus in the later non-biblical legislations, the noble and the rich were fined with money for offenses against limb and life of the poor; the poor with life and limb for offenses against the rich man's property. The Bible says: "Limb for limb, life for life, and dollar for dollar." This is democracy, this is divine equality. The limit of civil jurisprudence in Mosaism is somewhat more largely drawn than in modern law. All matters not involving life or limb are civil. Non-payment of debts, fraud, theft, robbery, embezzlement, etc., fall under this heading. The offender must pay, even with an additional fine. If he has not, the court can hire him out for six years labor, but never inflict imprisonment or stripes or death. Generally no two punishments for a crime are inflicted at the same time.

THEFT, FRAUD, ETC.

So we read (Exod. 21, 36): "When a man will steal an ox or a sheep, and kill or sell them, he shall restitute five oxen, or four sheep instead." The ox, the chief wealth of the Judæan farmer, the bread-giver, in primitive times, an object of worship (the Egyptian Apis, the *"golden calf"* of Israel), must be protected by all means—hence, it must be restituted five-fold instead. The sheep, comparatively less important, yielding milk to the family, was restituted fourfold. When yet found alive with the thief, and hence suggesting a possible restitution, the indemnification was but double. (Baba Kama. VII), (Maimonides Jad., see Treatise on Theft, I, 4). On returning the stolen object before sued for it, no fine was imposed. Any other movable property stolen, incurred double restitution. Defrauding the sanctuary entailed one-fifth part in addition, as punishment. (Levit. 5, 16).—The same one-fifth was for civil fraud and over-reaching (Idem 5, 24); he must pay or be sold unto six years' servitude. *According to Rabbinical tradition,* the selling

4

of a man for six years was only for the original value of the robbery. If he could not pay the fine, he was not sold, but remained indebted for it until he could.

The Rabbis found in the Pentateuch 365 prohibitory laws and 248 affirmative ones. The transgression of the former entailed, besides the money involved, if so, flagellation, too, or thirty-nine stripes; but this was hedged in with such legal requirements, as forewarning by two exact witnesses immediately before the commission of the act, with their naming of the crime and its punishment, &c., the acknowledgment, yea, acquiescence in, or affronting the law by the offender; then again, rigid examination of the witnesses, etc.; that the claim, in theory, of flagellation, besides the money punishment, is pretty nearly illusory, and next to impossible. Hence, it appears that the general rule of the Rabbinical court was to punish for each offense, but with one kind of chastisement, viz: the severer of the two; though the Pentateuch mentions occasionally a money fine *and* stripes in the case of a man slandering his own bride.

BURGLARY.

We have seen that thieving never incurred imprisonment nor death. Yet the text says (Exod. 22. 1): "When the thief is surprised in house-breaking, in the dark of night, and—fighting ensuing—he is killed, that killing is not considered a criminal act. But if the stealing takes place in broad daylight, killing the thief is manslaughter." This is the plain sense of the verse. Breaking in during the night constitutes danger of life for the people of the house, and killing the thief is but self-defense; whilst in broad daylight the thief shall be held to pay, but not killed. So expounded *Eben, Ezra* and *Rashbam.* Whilst tradition expounds: "Any house-breaking renders the killing of the thief legitimate defense, except when it is *clear as daylight* that he never intended murder (?). (Sanhedrin, 72, *a*,) and (Maimonides on Theft, IX, 7.)

New Testament on Theft.

No doubt the New Testament teaching: "Whosoever steals thy coat, give him thy mantle, too," is more ideal, and if followed up, would create a righteous society, needing no laws, judges, police, prisons and armies. Unfortunately, the kingdom of heaven is not yet come, and the State needs yet repressive laws to maintain society; hence, right and force.

It is, as said above, both odious and sheer folly to make any such comparisons. Moses claims to be a lawgiver. Jesus assumed the role of a divine Messiah. One legislates for this earth; the other for heaven. One for the State; the other for the Church. The one for the immediate present; the other for an ideal future. Their aims differ; hence so their views.

Status of the Stranger.

A solid test of the calibre of a statute-book, to know whether a lawgiver is animated by narrow zeal for his own clan and class, or by large-hearted humanity, aiming at the ultimate benefit of all classes and all fractions of the people, such a test is: what he legislates concerning the poor, the orphan, the widow, and more than that, concerning the *stranger*—he the most unbefriended, unprotected, helpless alien, for whom nobody cares, nobody has a feeling, a word—nobody, except the great heart of a true legislator, a philanthropic sage. Indeed, the test of a sound statute-book is not sympathy with the strong, the crafty, the bold, the criminal, but rather with the victims thereof. This test applied to Mosaism, that proves to be supremely humane and sympathetic. So it is with the weaker portion of humankind in general, and especially with the alien. Wherever we look among ancient legislations, we find but harshness for him. He was pretty much out of the pale of justice—a piece of public property. A stranger was synonymous with an enemy. In Roman times he had to accept some citizen as his patron. During the Middle Ages his property was confiscated on any pretense, especially when he died. When shipwrecked, he was pillaged and enslaved. Crimes against him were connived at. Crimes by him were punished with exceptional cruelty. So it was everywhere. In Germany, during the Middle Ages, the Jews were so treated. So they were in England, France and Spain until their expulsion. In Russia and Roumania this is as yet the case—in 1893. In holy Russia the Poles, the Germans, the Tartars, etc., though inhabitants of the country long before the Moscovite dominion, are treated as such aliens and cruelly discriminated against. Just now liberal, Western Europe is pretty exclusive concerning new immigrants. When poor, they are simply not allowed to stay. Even when talented or wealthy and allowed to naturalize, they are never perfectly put on equality with the natives. A piece of the alien's chain, as the string at the foot of the bird breaking from its cage, is ever dragging after him. He is a native in regard to duties; he is a stranger as to rights.

One God, One Law.

Mosaism, with its one God-idea as the corner-stone of the State, is inexorable concerning idolatrous worship, with its obscene, cruel and revolting rites. Save that exclusion, it is impartially just and merciful to the stranger. Nay, sometimes it seems as if the lawgiver is especially solicitous concerning him. We find in Sacred Scripture hundreds of passages to that point. Nay, one of the attributes of the Deity is: "He loves the stranger, the widow and the orphan;" which occurs time and again on the pages of the entire Bible. It very seldom occurred to Homer or Hesiod or Virgil, that that might be a befitting attribute of the Deity. We do find it as a compliment to the gods of certain descriptions. The gods there in reality and fact side with the

stronger and the victors. Success was there the only criterion
of merit and virtue. So much so, that even the etymologi-
cal origin and meaning of *virtue*, denotes force, bravery,
success, not moral goodness, righteousness or wisdom ; virtue
actually meaning manly strength

PROTECTION TO STRANGERS, WIDOWS AND ORPHANS.

Let us look at a few Biblical passages concerning the
stranger and its status. (Exod. 22, 20) : " The stranger thou
shalt not overreach nor oppress, for strangers ye were in
Egypt. Nor shall ye wrong the widow, nor the orphan, for
if ye do wrong him, and he cries unto me, I shall indeed
listen to the cry. And my ire will enkindle and I shall kill
ye by the sword (of war), and your wives shall be widows,
and your children orphans !" Reader, please search throughout the entire Græco-Roman fine literature, with all its
piety, prayers and sacrifices, litanies and eulogies, and see
whether you find a passage of such a ring, so thrilling, so
worthy the Deity, so effective to enforce right living and
justice.

PLIMSOL, M. P.

Some years ago the following interesting piece of news
run through the papers : In the British Parliament a hot
discussion arose concerning the discovery that certain
English merchant princes had sent out to sea unsafe
vessels with huge stocks of merchandise, well insured,
viz : the vessels and the goods were insured, the sailors not.
Of course the vessels were wrecked, the princely merchants
got their insurance and chuckled ; the sailors, drowned,
became the prey of the fishes, and their poor widows and
orphans cried in vain and were thrown upon the poor-rates
and the work-houses. One, very plain speaking Mr. Plimsol,
M. P., an honest old-fashioned Puritan, quoted, in the face
of the murderers : " Ye shall not wrong the widows and the

orphans, for they will cry unto me, and I shall kill you by the sword, and your wives shall be widows, and your children orphans!" That was very unparliamentary, but it was telling; the merchant princes found it shocking.—(Exod. 23, 9): "The stranger thou shalt not press, for ye know how he feels at heart. Ye were strangers in Egypt.—The crops of six years are thine, but that of the seventh, leave to the poor. For six days thou shalt work, but on the seventh, rest; that on it may rest, too, thy beast, thy slave and the stranger." (Levit. 19, 33)—"The stranger in thy land thou shalt not over-reach; treat him as a native, love him as thyself, for strangers ye were in Egypt."

(Levit. 24, 20-22): "Eye for eye, tooth for tooth. The murderer shall die. One right for stranger and native."

(Deut. 1, 16-17): "Render fair justice between a man, his neighbor and his stranger. Do not discriminate between humble and big people."—(Deut. 10, 17-19): "For Jahveh, your God, is above all the gods, omnipotent and awe-inspiring, accepting no bribes, nor favoring any person; who renders justice to the orphan, the widow, and loves the stranger to give him bread and raiment. Love the stranger, for strangers ye were in Egypt."

CREED AND DEED.

Mark here how the broad theology of Moses yields a broad morality; how religion is humanitarian; a universal God, a universal mankind, a universal right; the fatherhood of God, the brotherhood of man; including all races, sects, countries, tongues, sexes, stations, classes and masses. Look here how right creed yields right deed, as root and fruit, as principle and life.

Homer and Hesiod, Virgil and Ovid, teach scores and hundreds of gods, that means as many colliding forces, interests, creations, human races and dynasties of divine origin, feuds and wars fomented by the gods and their descendants, the earthly rulers. Polytheism in heaven means war on earth.

Remember those grand tragic poems, Homer's "Iliad" and "Odyssey," the siege and destruction of Troy by combined Greece, originated in the jealousy and the quarrels of the gods and goddesses. So is Virgil's "Æneid." See how a contemptible theology produces an execrable morality and becomes the source of a wretched society. The Monotheism of the Bible community is, therefore, justly accounted as its corner-stone. It is so of its entire legislation. It is the base of the doctrine, "One duty and one right for all;" and hence the status about the stranger, who is fully protected by the law, because he is included in large-hearted humanity—offspring of the one Deity.

HOSPITALITY AND PROTECTION.

Let us contemplate a few more verses of that nature. They are fully worthy of our consideration. Verses over three thousand years old, standing upon the large base of broad, universal right and justice, without asking the "*shibboleth*" of race, sect or origin, treating native and alien alike. Such verses, indeed, are refreshing in our age, our Bismarckian age of blood and iron, in 1893, in our boastful Western civilization, brimful with pan-Germanism, Latinism and Slavism, and permeated with so many bitter antagonisms under the pretext of race and church. Let us look to a few verses more, breathing the divine spirit of one large-hearted humankind.

(V. M., 23, 16): "Thou shalt not deliver a slave running away from his master; let him dwell with thee wherever he pleases; do not bring him to grief." What a noble verse! How far-reaching! A stranger, a slave, a fugitive, the most forlorn subject under the sun; yet is he a human being, yet born in the image of God, yet a fellow being. Over three thousand years ago Mosaism granted him the right of hospitality. In ancient times every citizen was at the despot's mercy. The proudest dignitary of to-day could to-morrow become a fugitive. The Bible granted him hospitality. Russia wants the United States to deny an asylum to her victims! Three thousand years ago the State rested upon the principle of force. The poor, runaway slave was the weakest of the weak, hence no one took his part ; his fate was as in the story of Androclus, the fugitive slave of a Roman proconsul in Africa, to be thrown in the amphitheatre to the wild beasts. Androclus' lion was yet more merciful than his master. The Old Testament alone advocated his cause and took him under its divine ægis : " Do not deliver poor Androclus to his master, nor to the beasts in the arena." And the New Testament, too, came to its rescue. and lovingly admitted him to the " kingdom of heaven."

PROTECTION AND BREAD, TOO.

But whereupon shall poor Androclus live ? Listen ! (Deut. 24, 10, etc.): " When thy neighbor owes thee a debt, do not penetrate into his house to pawn him ; remain outside and he will hand thee the pawn ; yet towards sunset return it to him, for he sleeps on it, and God will bless thee for thy charity." " Thou shalt not withhold the wages from the poor laborer, be he a brother Israelite or a stranger Gentile. On the very same day pay him his wages before sunset, for he is poor and is waiting for the hire ; he might cry to God and that will render thee sinful."—" Do not turn the scales of justice against the stranger, the orphan," etc. " Remember thou wast a stranger in Egypt and God has redeemed thee." " When thou reapest thy grain harvest, thy oil, thy wine, leave a small portion to the stranger, the orphan, the widow, for a stranger and poor thou wast in Egypt, therefore do I recommend thee to act in that way."

Here we see the lawgiver does not only allow the poor stranger an asylum, not simply air, light and water. No ;

he provides for him an humble source of subsistence; he puts him on the same footing with the native poor. More, he allows him to work, to earn wages, and be punctually paid, not over-reached, nor harshly treated if resorting to the pawnbroker; he allows him the right to glean and participate in the blessings of the wealthy citizen; he is no pauper, no drone, no outlaw; he gets the chance to work up, thrive and become an independent citizen.

THE LAWGIVER'S HEART.

Read and ponder over those passages. Don't you distinctly hear the heart of the lawgiver beating with sympathy; don't you see his frame quivering with compassion, writing down: "Allow a poor fellow-man to live with thee; a crust of bread, a kind word will make him happy, and earn for thee the blessing of thy soul, if thou hast one."

Read these verses over. They will bring you tears of fellow-feeling into your eyes, and thrill you through and through. Those verses touch deeper a feeling heart than all the laments of Here and Aphrodite, of Paris and Helena, of Achilles and Patroklus, with all the heroes of Homer and Virgil inclusive; because they are honest and sincere. They are taken from the eternal quarry of stern reality. They are pages from the tragedy of human, daily, woeful history, rehearsed since the days of Abraham and Nimrod ([1]) until our own. They are of hoary age and still fresh and acute as of yesterday. Look to suffering humanity and you find it mirrored in those verses.

The Mosaic lawgiver is no communist. He well distinguishes between mine and thine. Yet he commands part of the crops to go to the poor and the strangers.

So *Cardinal Manning*, mentioned above, correctly stated: "'Thou shalt commit no theft,' never applies to him who steals a loaf of bread for his children." Practically, he well

---

(1) Midrash legend.

understood the great heart of the Mosaic legislator. A hungry man is no thief for a loaf of bread. A poor man is entitled to his "gleanings," be he native or stranger, granted him three thousand years ago by the Ebrew law. Of course, in theory the Cardinal may not be infallible. In theory is stealing always wrong, but the sympathetic, noble prelate, on making that statement, was biased by his humane heart. So was the Arabo-Ebraic lawgiver, in pleading the cause of the run-away slave, in securing for him the right of asylum, and saving out a pittance for his subsistence. Not because Moses was a communist, but because he could not help siding with Androclus against the cruel proconsul, his master; he felt with the eternal victims of social wrong. Truly, great men have great hearts.

USURY, INTEREST AND PROFIT.

We read in Deut. 23, 20: "Thou shalt take no interest of thy brother on money or eatables or anything else. Of the foreigner thou canst take interest; of thy brother, not. That God may bless thee in all thy doings." This was claimed to be a strong instance of foreigner-hatred and national exclusiveness. But that charge is erroneous. It originated in misunderstanding, in plain ignorance. The word *Nochri* was mistaken as identical with *Guer*, alien, which is not the case. No doubt both mean the non-Ebrew, but with the vast difference that *Nochri* means a stranger residing in his own, non-Judæan country; *Guer* means a foreigner emigrated into, domiciled and naturalized in Judæa. A Gentile immigrant making Judæa his home, submitting to its public laws and assuming all its civic duties, was entitled to all its civic rights. Him the law recommended to the especial protection of the State; whilst a stranger hailing from a foreign land and traveling temporarily in Judæa on some business, was entitled to international rights, but not to the privileges of a citizen.

And such was the extra privilege of getting money and
goods without interest and profit. A Gentile naturalized
among the Ebrews was entitled to that privilege. So we
read (Levit. 25, 35): "If thy brother should impoverish
and decay, give him encouragement. Immigrant (*Guer*) or
inhabitant, let him live with thee. Take no interest on
money, or profit or eatables, of him. Be afraid of God;
let thy *brother*, native or alien, live with thee. I am thy
God who brought thee out of Egypt," etc. Here we see the
non-Jew domiciliated in Judæa, who, hence, is a *Guer*, but
not a *Nochri;* he is fully entitled to the privilege of a
loan without interest. We shall have in the sequel of
these pages more occasion for seeing why the lawgiver
allowed profit and interest when trading with foreign countries and deprecated it at home. This was not from racial
or sectarian prejudices, but from economical reasons. He
would not have any commerce and speculation at home; he
discouraged home traffic, but allowed international commerce. Hence, all business profit at home was interdicted,
and any loan was to be given purely as a neighborly
assistance. We shall later dilate on that Mosaic State
policy.

THE STRANGER IN GREECE.

For any person or anything not Greek or not Roman, both
these nations had a classic expression—"*barbaros!*" Barbarians they called the Persians, the Ebrews, the Egyptians,
the Gauls, the Germans, the Skythians; indeed, the entire
world, except themselves. Their slaves were, of course,
"*barbaros.*" Any other country than theirs was "*barbaros
gy.*" War with them was natural and always in order—
"*polemos barbaros.*" Intermarriage with them was a
stain and a reproach—"*lechos barbaros.*" The foreigner
was deemed half a savage, rude and uncultured. They
owed him no consideration; he was out of the pale of

justice. To make war upon him, subjugate and enslave
him, rob and destroy him, if too numerous and dangerous,
was natural right, not in the least immoral, and perfectly
compatible with the highest virtue, even in our sense of
the term. Cato had it for his current expression—*Carthago
delenda est* (Carthage must be destroyed), because she was
barbarian and in the way of Rome. The Scipios, carrying
out Cato's word, are famed as the most ideal heroes and
demi-gods. Nothing harmed Antonius so much, as the fact
that he was the husband of a barbarian—Cleopatra, the
Queen of Egypt, a Ptolemean princess, but a barbarian
anyhow. May be that great Cæsar, too, suffered at the
hands of Brutus and Cassius for the same crime. To be a
foreigner was unpardonable in Greece and Rome, the patterns of ancient civilization. (See Arist. Polit. I, 8; and
Plato Republ. 373 and 469.)

THE STRANGER IN THE BIBLE.

Nothing of the kind was in the Bible (V. M., 10, 17):
"Jahveh, your God, is the master of all masters, the Supreme
Power who favors no persons (classes and castes) and takes
no bribes (sacrifices), who pleads the cause of the widow and
the orphan, who loves the foreigner and gives him bread
and raiment. Love ye the stranger, for such ye were in
Egypt."

Here is quite another ideal of Deity, and hence another idea
of right and justice; here is the foreigner not an outcast and
a fit victim, but a brother, as the native, hence under the
same law and protection as he.

Curious it is that sometimes we find among the Greeks,
too, the idea of pity and benevolence as due to the stranger,
the poor and the unhappy one. The ancient poets had some
such ideal of the gods, at least of Zeus, the supreme *Dios*.

THE STRANGER IN HOMER.

But it was rare and sporadic and it never became a practical rule of conduct for man. So we read in Homer's Odyssey, VI, 207, (¹) where the poet pleads for his hero, Odysseus, to be taken care of, "because all foreigners and beggars are under the protection of Zeus;" and further, there, VII, 165: (²) "Let us spend to Zeus, who accompanies (and safeguards) the respectable strangers, invoking his assistance." But that is a mere poetical phrase. This exalted view is empty poetry. The Greek gods were usually modeled after the Greek princes and heroes. Justice and benevolence were not their leading traits. Agamemnon and Achilles, etc., undertook to punish Troy in order to avenge a kidnapped woman, the Spartan Helena, or, at least, her husband, Menelaus; but they for long years quarrel and neglect the war; they quarrel over what ? Over their own captive women, whom they distribute as concubines. These captive women are treated with inhumanity and shamelessness. At the end of the long war *Andromache* and *Cassandra* fall into their hands—about the only two persons having the reader's full sympathy—and they are treated with the utmost indignity by the Greeks, their cruel captors; far worse than ever was Helena by Paris. All the gods and Zeus himself take a hand in the war without compunction. To neither hero or god does it occur to "plead the cause of widow, orphan or stranger." We need not search long for proofs that the Greeks did not practically think strangers under the especial or any protection of the gods. The most bitter hatred and contempt for them was the rule, and but as an exception they made show of generosity. In the very next chapter after the above passages, (Odyssey, VII, 30,) Athene accompanies the hero to the Faieken and recommends him "to follow her quickly and

(1). τὸν νῦν χρὴ κομέειν· πρὸς γὰρ Διός εἰσιν ἅπαντες ξεῖνοί τε πτωχοί τε.

(2). .,. . . ἵνα καὶ Διὶ τερπικεραύνῳ σπείσομεν, ὅσθ' ἱκέτῃσιν ἅμ' αἰδοίοισιν ὀπηδεῖ..·

silently, and not to look at, nor speak to any passer-by, taking even the precaution of enveloping him in a thick cloud, so as to make him invisible to the natives, adding, 'for the people here do not much tolerate strangers, nor do they offer them hospitality.'" [1]

And yet that people are described as rather good natured and humane! The fact is, that throughout entire antiquity the stranger was an alien, not a guest; the alien was an enemy, and the enemy a brute, having no rights whatever. The Bible alone declared him a human being—a brother. Of course Odysseus followed up the advice of Athene, and makes his way without any accident. [2] Nevertheless, it strikingly shows the prevailing sentiment of the times. It needed an extra effort on the part of the great deity to screen the favorite hero from violence. Without a miracle, strangers among the Greeks, etc., were treated as enemies. And as to the claim of Zeus to be the protector of the alien, that was mere poetry. The Bible posits the doctrine, and many passages there prove that the doctrine condensed into fact but slowly.

JAHVEH AND ZEUS.

Nor were the conceptions of the classic peoples about Jupiter himself very sublime. All the gods, without exception, were thought to be hungry and thirsty, and dependent upon the gifts of mortals. Hence, the above-mentioned biblical statement that "Jahveh does not favor persons, nor does he take bribes," viz., by accepting gifts or sacrifices for favors to bestow. For as to the heathen gods, they did discriminate against some, and show favors to others, and all for bribes and sacrifices, for *"hecatombs."* Jupiter,

---

(1). μηδέ τιν' ἀνθρώπων προτιόσσεο μηδ' ἐρέεινε. οὐ γὰρ ξείνους οἵδε μάλ' ἀνθρώπους ἀνέχονται, οὐδ' ἀγαπαζόμενοι φιλέουσ' ὅς κ' ἀλλοθεν ἔλθη.

(2). τὸν δ' ἄρα Φαίηκες, ναυσικλυτοί οὐκ ἐνόησαν ἐρχόμενον κατὰ ἄστυ διὰ σφέας· οὐ γὰρ Ἀθήνη εἴα ἐϋπλόκαμος, δεινὴ θεός, ἡ ῥά οἱ ἀχλὺν θεσπεσίην κατέχευε φίλα φρονέουσ' ἐνὶ θυμῷ.—(Odyss. VII, 39.)

indeed, was specially called *Dios*, God, and surrounded by
much pomp and circumstance. At his nodding the Olympos and the Heavens, the earth and the ocean shook. But
withal he was depicted, but as a *Roi-fainéant*, with not
too much will-power, nor too much brain. He was constantly led and misled by Juno or Venus or Athene, etc.
What a doubtful role he played at the siege of Troy, or later,
in Odysseus' wanderings! He was for the Greeks and
against them, for and against the latter, ever *trimming*,
according to the stratagems of Athene, Heré, Aphrodité, or
Porseidón; not seldom quarreling with his illustrious
sister and wife, Saturnia, after having dethroned and
exiled his father; offering occasionally his dear spouse
something like blows, and throwing his son, Hefaistos-
Vulcan, headlong to the earth, for having taken sides with
his mother, and laming him for ever, etc., etc. Now it is
true that Socrates, Plato and Aristotle had a nobler conception of the Deity. But their idea was not the people's idea.
They were more or less considered as atheists. Nor was it
they who framed the State laws; it was the vulgar and
their leaders who did, as at all times. Fifteen centuries
later Virgil did not describe Jupiter under more sublime
colors. Æneas steering for Italy, is the play-ball of blind
fate and of jealousy. The gods and goddesses are divided
about his success, and Jupiter himself is not knowing his
own mind, either, whether to favor the Trojans or the
Latins. Behold how weak *mighty Jupiter* appears, (Æneis
IX, 801): "Sed manus e castris propere coit omnis in unum;
Nec contra vires audet Saturnia Juno sufficere: aeriam cœlo
nam Jupiter Irim demisit, germanæ haud mollia jussa
ferentem." Thus Jupiter is not very complimentary to
his spouse.

There is no denying, the divine ideals of Greeks and
Romans, poets and people, were not over refined, and their
notions about human rights and duties, the rights of the

strangers, the weak, the conquered, etc., were just as crude.
The Bible is therefore outstanding, sublime and alone, in
those remote ages, teaching: "For thy God is great and
powerful, and above all the gods, who favors no person and
accepts no bribes.   He loves the stranger and gives him
bread and raiment. He pleads for the widow and the orphan.
Love the stranger, for strangers ye were in Egypt." (V.
M. 10, 17).   The Bible alone starts from the firm rock of an
omnipotent and all-just God, who favors none and discrimi-
nates against none, and hence it arrives at the conclusion of
justice and kindness to the stranger and the helpless, to the
child and the woman.

THE BENJAMINITE WAR.

There, too, we find an analogy to the story of Helena and
Paris.   It is in Judges, 19.   Read and see what a difference
between the Biblical and the Homeric spirit.

In the Bible we find no exaggerations, no heaven-tower-
ing poetries, no embellishments; nothing but plain matters
of fact.   Man and woman, honesty and dishonesty, act and
speak without paint and hyperbole.   It is a picture of
nature;   no poetic lies.   Read and compare: A humble
Levite is returning home with his mistress after a pleasant
visit to her parents.   They arrive at a wicked place among
the tribe of Benjamin, and find some isolated, kind hospitality, but are roughly treated by the youth.   The poor
mistress is abused, and dies of that maltreatment.   The
entire nation is aroused over the indignity offered to a
forlorn woman.   A national war ensues, and that wicked
place and its surroundings, with the entire tribe, are nearly
extirpated, after a short but most bloody war.   The entire
nation, with their ecclesiastical and lay leaders, as one
man, fight that battle for purity and right owing to strangers
and to womanhood.   There is no wavering and hesitating,
no petty jealousies and backthoughts, as we find in the

Iliad, among the very leaders of the expedition. With different feelings do we rise from the reading of the Iliad and from that of Judges, chapter 19. The former leaves back a feeling of deep sadness; the other offers the consolation that wrong is righted, though at an immense cost. Why this difference? The cause is that the Ebrew leaders did not claim to be descendants from the gods, nor did they fable stupidities about them on a par with themselves. They had nobler conceptions of the Deity, and having a higher and purer idea of that, they had a nobler conception of the rights of man; of those of the poor and stranger, and of helpless womanhood. The mistress of the Levite was not the daughter of the gods, nor the wife of a king, nor a divine miracle of beauty, as Helena. She was a *pilegesh*, the semi-wife of a nameless Ebrew, journeying as a stranger. But he and she were fellow-citizens; he was a lowly man, she was a helpless woman, and the entire nation felt the insult and injustice done to these poor strangers, and the entire nation arose to punish and avenge that crime. There is no doubt, a nobler conception of God yields a better man, a nobler people, and, fairer justice to native and alien; and these ideas mankind owes to the Bible.

BIBLICAL EXPRESSIONS FOR FOREIGNER.

The biblical expressions for foreigner are manifold, viz: *Zor*, meaning one not belonging to the same tribe or caste. So the Israelite was a *Zor* opposite to the priest in the temple; to perform sacrificial service was in him usurpation and sacrilege. In the same sense was the Gentile a *Zor* opposite to the Israelite concerning privileged rites and observances. But *Zor* has not even the odor of *barbaros*, in regard to positive human rights and duties or benevolent feelings.

Next comes the expression *"Nochri,"* pretty nearly coming up to the modern word outlandish or foreigner. It

5

means a non-Ebrew living in a non-Judæan country of his
own speech and creed. He was entitled to human rights,
not to civic rights and privileges in Judæa. The Ebrew
could do with him any kind of business, of money or
goods, for mutual interest or profit. That was forbidden
among his fellows, where such was done only for kindness
sake and as a mutual assistance.

Next follows *"Guer,"* the immigrant, a Gentile passing
over into the biblical State; and when permanently domiciliated there, he was termed *Guer Toshab* or *Shaar*. He
could be naturalized when not practicing, publicly, idolatry
and living up to the universal moral law, without having
adopted the Mosaic creed proper. He then enjoyed all
civic rights and privileges; he was termed *brother;* he could
live there. work, earn wages, get rich, acquire property and
occupy office, except kingship and priesthood. When a
slave, he was not delivered up to his former master; when
poor, he was provided side by side with the Ebrew poor,
widows and orphans. Everywhere he is recommended
equally with them to the justice and tenderness of the
State. (Maleachi 3, 5; Zach. 7, 10.) In that solemn covenant
on Mounts Garisim and Ebal (V. M. 27, 19), the lawgiver
pronounces the curse of God "against whosoever will bend
the judgment of the stranger." When he adopted the
Mosaic creed he was termed *Guer Zedek*, or proselyte, and
was assimilated to Israel in a religious respect, too.

THE TALMUD ON STRANGERS.

In Mishna and Talmud we find, indeed, expressions which
occasionally seem to smell of the Greek word *barbaros*,
though never going so far as to declare him out of the pale
of human justice or even dignity. Such terms are *Akkum*,
the notaricon of a compound expression meaning "worship-
ers of the stars," or, in general, idolaters. The worst the Talmudists have ever enacted against Gentiles was aimed against

these *Akkum*, or idolaters, first by following the Mosaic
severe injunctions against Canaanites.   More probably it
was directed against those Romans and Greeks who had
made upon them and their people such a war of extirpation
during the first three centuries of the current era, had
robbed them of their country, killed them by the millions
in war, slaughtered them in the Hippodrome and sold them
into slavery after the war was over.

A somewhat milder expression than *Akkum* is *Ammim*
and *ben Noach*, meaning simply a non-Israelite, of the
Gentile nation, or a son of Noach, the Patriarch.   The word
Goy finally means simply *gens*—nation, tribe or each individual of them.   Israel, too, is called *Goy*, sometimes, but
rarely, with the addition of "holy."   *Goy*, thus, is not the
equivalent of *barbaros*, as often believed by the ignorant.
(See I. M., 19, 6 ; V. M., 4, 8 ; and Isaiah, 26, 2.)

THE RABBIS CONCERNING GENTILES.

As a striking proof that the Rabbis had least of racial
prejudice, closely following Mosaism, and that they
abhorred idolatry for the sake of its crueltie-, absurdities,
licentiousness, its stupefying effects upon the masses, but
hated not the Gentiles simply as non-Jews, may serve the
following quotations.   Indeed, how could they?   Believers
in the doctrine of one creative Omnipotence and one parental
couple, they had to accept, as result, one right for native and
for stranger; hence there was very little room left for racial
bigotry—except when hidden under the cloak of idolatry·
Otherwise it was with Hindoos and Egyptians, Greeks and
Romans, etc., who believed in castes or different origins of
races and *gens*, descendants from different gods and divers
parents.   These progenitors were often at war with each
other.   Such polytheistic notions, applied to the different
sections of mankind, could not but make war the leading
idea of the State, and hence racial hate and contempt were

dominant features in ancient societies. There the stranger was a foreigner, the foreigner was an enemy; the enemy was not above the wild beast; war upon him, booty, enslavement, murder were deemed just and glorious. This was the necessary sequel of idolatry.

No doubt, as said above, there are in the Talmud many harsh expressions against the, then, Gentiles. These date from the times of the wars of extermination against the Ebrews, during the first three centuries of the present era, waged by Romans and Greeks. And who will think too hard of harsh words uttered in exchange of bloody deeds? . . . Nor must we misunderstand why the Rabbinical Law so intensely hated idolatry, no less than the Biblical one. We need only read of the superstition, the cruelty, the unnatural vices, the subversion of all morality, chastity, right and reason, connected with idolatry, to fully understand that antipathy. The following pages will afford us ample opportunity for illustrating the immense moral and intellectual superiority of Judæa over the religions of ancient paganism, the ethereal and sublime heights of Sinai and Carmel over Mounts Olympos and Ida, and hence the horror thereof in Judæa.

But as soon as both these elements, the horror of idolatry and the bitter sense of persecution, were out of sight, the Rabbinical law, as the biblical one, is remarkably tolerant. Thus we read (in Megillah 13): "Who denies idolatry is called a Jew." (¹) The following passages go to the same point. (Sanhedrin 96, b.):

"The righteous of all nations participate in eternal life." Sefra (to Sanhedrin, 59) says: "A great many biblical verses mention that the righteous are most pleasing to God; the '_righteous_,' simply, not the priests, the Levites or Israelites, for even the Gentiles are included therein." That means: "God cares for moral goodness, not for race,

---

(1)   ‏בל הכופר בע׳׳ז נקרא יהודי.‏

caste or condition."—This was Paul's reasoning to the
Gentiles; this his lever to move the world. He admitted
them into the pale of Monotheism on the sole ground of
the moral law, without insisting upon the ceremonial one,
as binding alone upon the Jew. (Baba. Bathra 10, *b*.) reads:
"Since the destruction of the Temple the sacrificial service
has been supplanted by benevolence, indiscriminately, for
Jew and Gentile."

In Sanhedrin 58, *b*., we read: "A heathen occupying with
the *Thorah* (Bible) is as good as the high priest."—(Cholin
13): The heathens nowadays are no longer idolaters; they
but follow thoughtlessly the customs of their fathers.[1]—
(Sanhedrin 38): The Bible teaches but one God and one
parental couple. Why? In order to obviate to any pride
of origin (as castes in Hindostan and Egypt), and that
nobody should think theft and murder of other races
allowable.—Rabbi Gamaliel II and Rabbi Akiba (of second
century, Palestine) subscribe to that equality in all legal
matters. (See Baba Kama, 35 and 113).—Tosephta Baba.
Kamá, 10, adds: "To rob a Gentile is worse than to rob a
fellow Jew, for there is additional desecration of God's
name,"[2]—(Cholin, 94.) Rabbi Samuel declares: "It is forbidden to steal people's good opinion; so it is, even of an
idolater."[3] Everywhere in Mishna, Talmud and Casuists there is no trace of unfair discrimination between Jew
and Gentile in all legal matters, closely following up the
Mosaic law in this regard; they stigmatize usury and
forbid it toward a Gentile as toward a Jew. It is, unfortunately, the Middle Age Church—interpreting wrongly
a Bible verse—that thought the Jew can take interest of a
Gentile, even when a countryman, and force him into the
pawnbroker's shop, thereby drawing upon him fresh ill-wil

---

(1) ‏מנהג אבותיהם בידיהם.‏

(2) ‏חמור גזל גוי מגזל ישראל. מפני חילול השם.‏

(3) ‏גונב דעת, אפילו של עכו״ם‏

from his neighbors, cursing that privilege. Rabbi Simlai, (third century) says, quoting the Psalm: "Who shall ascend the mount of the Lord? Who shall enter his sanctuary? He who walketh in righteousness . . . and gives not his money on usury." "*Not either to a heathen,*" (Makkoth, 24,) adds the teacher.—R. Hunnah (fourth century) quotes the known verse: "Who increases his wealth by usury hoards it for the benefit of the friends of the poor;" that means those who take usury of the Gentiles (Baba Mezia, 70.)— Usurers are stigmatized as apostates and atheists and are not admitted to the Rabbinical witness box (Sanhedrin, 3).— "Usurers are like murderers, they can never atone for their crimes," (Baba Bathra, 90.)—That will suffice to show that the Rabbis had no small horror of the pawnbroker's shop, and warned their flock often enough against it. Unfortunately, the Middle Age Church and State shut against them all avenues of an honest livelihood, leaving open but that one for them.—Jalkut, 250 *b.*, remarks that at the Jerusalem Temple, on the feast of *Tabernacles*, seventy bullocks were offered for the seventy nations (mankind) to pray for their welfare. The same, page 267, says: "Who robs a heathen will not spare a Jew either. There is but one law for Jew and Gentile."—(Gittin, 61.) It is our duty to feed the heathen poor, nurse their sick, bury their dead, save their property when in danger and keep up peace and good-will.—In Mainonides Talm. Thora, we read: "It is our duty to rise before an old Gentile as before a Jew (Gittin, 60), and to greet him, as a mark of respect (Aboda Sara, 6); to send presents to Gentiles on their festive days," etc.

LATER CASUISTS AND MORALISTS ON GENTILES.

Tana de be Elia (tenth century) chapter 9, begins: "I call heaven and earth to witness that all mankind, without any difference of creed or condition, free or slave, are to be judged only by their deeds, not creeds. "Whosoever holds converse with us is our *brother*, and it is unlawful to over-reach him, . . . and whosoever is guilty of fraud against him, desecrates the name of God."

In the twelfth century flourished R. Jehuda the pious. In his "Book of the Pious" he repeatedly enjoins: "Over-reach nobody, be peaceful, be honest in thy dealings and never take advantage of anybody, without any discrimina-tion, whether Jew or Gentile, or you desecrate the name of Israel and his law."

Maimonides, (Egypt, twelfth century), *Jad. on Kings*, 10, 12, says: "Any Gentile observing the moral law is entitled to our respect, to our benevolence, charities and all amenities, just as Israelites are."—R. Moses de Coucy (thirteenth cen-tury) in his work *Semag*, 143, enjoins: "Never overreach any one, Jew or Gentile, but be just and fair to everybody."

R. Isaac ben Shesheth, of *North Africa* (fifteenth cen-tury) declares in his "Responses, 119": "Christians are to be considered as (Guer Toshab) semi-proselytes to Judaism, hence are they entitled to all practical rights and privileges of Jews. The same is the opinion of R. Joseph Caro (in Baith Joseph, 266) (fifteenth century, Palestine.) The same says Moses ben Nachman (seventeenth century) in his book of the *Laws :* "We are bound to save the lives of Christians in any danger of fire, water, etc."

So Beer Hagola (seventeenth century to Choshen Mishpat, chapter 425): "All the harsh enactments of the Talmud concerning the Gentiles have reference only to ancient times of idolatry. The Gentiles of to-day keep the leading principles of religion, and hence do we owe them all good will and benevolence."

R. Isekiel Landau, of Prague (eighteenth century), in his "Responses," says: "I state expressly that in all legal affairs, concerning theft, fraud, robbery, murder, etc., there is no difference whatever between Jew and Gentile, and that

the Talmudical expression of *Goim* or *Akkum* (idolaters)
has no reference whatever to the present nations among
whom we dwell."

Dr. I. Hamburger, of Stettin, delivered an excellent
lecture on the above subject in 1880, to which we refer our
readers for any further information.

I close with the eighteenth century, the era of Moses
Mendelssohn, the era of pure and exalted humanitarianism,
represented by Mendelssohn and Lessing, the noble pair
that closed the sectarian dark ages and inaugurated the era
of fraternization of creeds and races—"*the true Renaissance*" of man.

REVIEW OF BIBLICAL TOLERATION.

What have we seen concerning the status of the stranger
in the biblical and post-biblical writings? The following:
The stranger in Judæa adopting the universal moral law,
though not yet the Mosaic creed, was entitled to all the
rights and privileges of the Judæan, and was termed a
brother. If a fugitive slave, he was to be protected and
not to be delivered over to his master. He was allowed to
compete, to work and earn wages and thrive. He could
acquire lands; nay, he could acquire as servants full-
blooded Israelites, for the legal term of six years, or until
the Jubilee. Read how justice was stronger than national
prejudice (Levit. 25, 47): "When the Gentile stranger will
thrive, and thy countryman, impoverished, be sold to that
stranger domiciled with thee, the sold Ebrew shall have
the privilege of redemption by one of his relatives; a fair
compensation shall take place according to the years of
service until the Jubilee. Should he not be redeemed, then
he shall go free on the Jubilee, he and his children." You
see, the lawgiver's heart, of course, yearns at the thought
of an indigenous Ebrew sold to a foreign Gentile, thriving
there where the native impoverishes. Does he cry at over-

reaching, usury, blood-sucking? No; right is right, and property is property. He can't go against facts. The native got poor and was sold to the wealthy foreigner, and he must stick to the bargain. The lawgiver calls upon the relatives to come and redeem their kinsman. But if they do not, then the Ebrew bondsman stays. Only at the Jubilee he goes free. " For mine are the children of Israel, my servants they are, redeemed from Egypt." (Levit. 25, 55.)

What a noble national pride, tempered by meek submission to the laws of equity and justice towards a Gentile and stranger! Reader, ponder over that.

The domiciled Gentile immigrant could intermarry when he fully adopted the Mosaic creed and nationality. If he would not, he was not debarred from any civic rights in the State. He was not dragooned into the Ebrew Church, nor whipped into the Ebrew marriage, nor excluded from privileged trades or employments or streets, nor put into a *ghetto*, nor had he to wear a *yellow patch* for discrimination. King David was the offspring of a poor Moabite woman. King Solomon wedded an Egyptian princess. Hundreds of thousands of Gentiles lived peaceably among the Jews as fellow-citizens under the Davidians, the Hasmoneans and the Herodians. Thus, three thousand years ago the Bible proclaimed the law of human fellowship— " Love thy stranger. Oppress not the stranger. Love him as thyself." The founders of Christianity, Jews, too, abrogated the race question, and declared all Gentiles embracing Monotheism as children of God, participating in divine grace, conform to Bible and Talmud.

Thus Mosaism does not simply teach religion in the abstract. No, it is practical and realistic; so that to worship God means justice and love to men, indiscriminately. One God means harmonious creation; means good-will and peace to all, one right and one duty for all. Right creed means right deed. Theology is not a dead letter. No, it is a principle of life, permeating, vivifying, quickening body and soul, the individual, the family hearth, the relation of classes and of masses, natives and aliens, State and society, all, effacing the word stranger, making all men one family, worshiping one Maker.

As to the later Rabbinical law, though sometimes giving back hard words for bloody blows, though erecting Chinese walls to screen its followers from assimilation, it nevertheless never lost sight of the fact of *one right for Jew and Gentile*, and never discriminated in matters of fact, in right, benevolence, charity, amenity, and politeness, asking the same respect for the rights and virtues of all, Christian, Parsee or Mohammedan, with whom it came in contact.

BISMARCK'S BIASES.

Whilst writing these lines, I felt startled in just now reading, in the daily papers, the following cable news of to-day, April 29th, 1893. It reads as if it were dated from 1693. At an interview, Prince Bismarck said :

"I was never a friend to the Jews, owing to my education. I was in 1847 the adversary of Jewish emancipation, which I subsequently favored in 1869, because the late Baron Bleschroeder appreciated my national projects. The reappearance of anti-Semitism after an epoch of speculation is natural, because the deceived people confound capitalism with Judaism. . . .

"In 1880 the anti-capitalist movement could have been moderated only by the safety-valve of anti-Jewism. The Ahlwardt era will result in politics with no important or lasting consequences.

"Prince Bismarck added that the adoption of legal means against the Jews would be useless, and expressed the opinion that the cross-breeding of the Ebrew and Gentile races would gradually bring about a settlement of the vexatious question."

Thus in 1893, in cultured Germany, in the country of Mendelssohn, Boerne, Heine, Baron Hirsch, etc.! Prince Bismarck, the assumed architect of Germanic unity, was just interviewed on *anti-Semitism*, or the feasibility whether a class of people living in Germany just as long as the Teutonic nations do, shall be worsted, because they worship God after the fashion of their fathers; because they claim to live according to that very same Mosaic law we just now speak of; that law that over three thousand years ago proclaimed to the world the brotherhood of the entire humankind; that taught: "Thou shalt love thy neighbor as thyself," "Love the stranger as thyself." Yea, some of its votaries even taught "Love thine enemy as thyself." Anti-Semitism is agitating against half a million of that biblical people. And what is Bismarck saying in the interview? He is very philosophical, very composed, whilst some of his neighbors are about firing the roofs of other neighbors. Drinking his bock-beer and smoking his long pipe, he delivers himself with the ambiguity of an ancient oracle. Not for a moment does he allude to justice and fairness and decency deeply involved therein. Not even to State—wisdom and utility. He begins: "I was never a friend of the Jews, owing to my education." That is frank, indeed! But why, Prince, don't you correct your educational prejudices at your age of seventy-eight? It is never too late.—"In 1847 I was an adversary of Jewish emancipation."—Why were you so, Sir? Again prejudice, in a statesman!—"Which Jewish emancipation I subsequently favored, because of Baron Bleschroeder." Ah, so! Baron Bleschroeder's money did it! Why not rather on account of the gold mines in the Bible?—the justice and the wisdom as in the Old and the New Testament, both teaching: "Love thy neighbor as thyself," as a leading doctrine? Why not

rather in imitation of America or of civilized Europe?
Prince, you claim to be a religionist, a Christian!—"The
people confound capitalism with Judæaism." Are you not,
perhaps, Prince Bismarck, the cause of that confusion?
You sided with freeing the Jews for Bleschroeder's sake.
Did you not thereby set the fatal example of confounding
religion with capitalism? Why not rather, for the sake of
Moses, Isaiah, Hillel, Jesus, Paul, Washington or Monte-
fiore? "In 1880 the anti-capital movement could be moderated only by the safety-valve of anti-Jewism." That
frankness is astonishing! After freeing the Jews in 1869
on account of Bleschroeder's capital, they had to be sacrificed in 1880 to save the capitalists! You offered them up
as a scape-goat to Mammon. Remember the adage, Prince:
"*One mistake brings another.*" Are nations to be handled
as figures on the chess-board? Prince, you sacrificed the
"knight" to save the "queen." Had Bismarck helped
emancipating the Jews because it is just and wise, there
would never have come the occasion for arousing anti-
Semitism as a safety-valve for the capitalists. "One mistake brings another." Here are the fruits of a Machiavelian
policy. "Honesty alone is a safe policy," in the long-run of
history.—"The Ahlwardt era will have no important
result." I hope not. But in the meantime it disgraces the
century; it dishonors civilization; it renders unhappy its
victims; it fills with dismay all honest men of enlightened
Germany; entire civilized society feels unsafe at such an
equivocal policy used in such high quarters.

"Love thy neighbor as thyself," is the only safe social
basis. As to Ahlwardt, Bismarck must not forget, either, that
"Ahlwardt's era" is but a phase in Bismarck's era. History
will hold the latter responsible for the former. Prince
Bismarck alone is dangerous. Here I remember the prayer:
"God save me from my friends; as to my enemies, I'll take
care of myself."—"The adoption of legal means against the

Jews would be useless." No, Prince, it would be dangerous, hurtful and shameful! Consider: to-day, Jews; to-morrow, Catholics; Socialists, Liberals, Democrats, etc., next. Where will you stop? "War of all against all?"—"The cross-breeding of Hebrew and Gentile would gradually settle that vexatious question." Prince Bismarck is amiable when he wants to be. But we must not forget the words of Lessing's (Nathan the Wise's) *Judge*, in the known allegory of "The Three Rings," answering that question, viz: "By kindness, justice and urbanity let each party prove the virtue of the true *Ring*, the virtue of rendering lovable and estimable." To whip a man into the nuptial room is neither good policy nor good match-making. Don't you remember what Shake-speare has the Jew say on such an interesting occasion: "Sir Antonio, you called me dog, cut-throat, and spat upon my gabardine. Shall I give you now my moneys?" You send the Jew to the social Ghetto, abet on him anti-Semitism, kick him, oust him, and withal, he shall marry you? Begin with being just and amiable, and then sympathy will follow. "The vexatious question" between Jew and Gentile, Prince, will be settled without any dragooning to the dominant creed nor whipping into the nuptial room. It will be set-tled amicably when politics will not be governed by Mach-iavelism, but by "Thou shalt love thy neighbor as thyself." When people will worship God in sincerity, then they will love man without discrimination. When the Jew will be a sincere Jew and the Christian a sincere Christian, then a cordial understanding will be reached. For the time being, the doctrines of "Love thy neighbor," "Love the stranger; do not overreach nor oppress him," taught three thousand years ago, is yet an ideal. For the present, Prince Bismarck has invented Pan-Germanism with two millions of soldiers. He is an admirer of the Czar, with Pan-Slavism and three millions of soldiers. He was a friend of Napoleon III, the pretended inventor of Pan-Latinism, with so and so many millions of soldiers. For the time being, the Russians make war upon the Germans, the English, Turks, Poles, etc., and these reciprocate duly; whilst Prussia is distrusted by Germany and hated by France, Austria, Denmark, Hanover, etc.

In Russia we see ostracised millions of Baltic Germans. Thousands of disinherited, starving families are ejected in Ireland. There are Christians worsted, and there Jews, and there Mohammedans. The Jews, counting many millions in Russia, once citizens in Poland, formerly masters of the great Chazar Kingdom on the Volga, later swallowed up by Moscow, are treated like wild beasts, as out of the pale of humanity. They are dragged away in the night, in mid-winter, pillaged, ravished, famished, and forced into the Polish pale to starve, or driven into exile to far-off continents as pariahs and vagabonds. Contemplate the fate of the Poles, the greatest nation of the North yet one century ago, now broken, gagged and distributed as the price for perfidy and remorseless dynastic ambition—a national assassination in the face of this nineteenth century! Behold gallant, unhappy Ireland! What a heroic fight for now three hundred years! A small minority, disinherited, impoverished, ruined by selfish, one-sided legislation and by industrial jealousy. She loses not courage; she goes on fighting for her inalienable rights. Judæa and Poland submit in despair. Ireland fights on, and will surely conquer. More lucky or more plucky! Yet Russians, Germans, French, English, Turks, etc., etc., worship the Bible, which is repeating a thousand times, *"Thou shalt love the stranger as thyself."* After three thousand years the world has yet to learn that doctrine. They swear by the Bible, they are idolatrous of it, but they do not practice it. Ancient and modern society stand yet upon egoism. True love and justice without bias, without any back-thought of self, family, race and sect, have yet to be learned. All the above-mentioned *"pans"* and *"vexatious questions"* are but ill-disguised screens for brute egoism. The Bible alone, with one God and one mankind, rises to the high plane of universal right, corresponding to universal duty. This, mankind has yet to learn. Will they ever?

The march of history seems to move exceedingly slow. Started three thousand and two thousand years ago, mankind has just invented the needle-gun, dynamite and pan-Latin—Slav—and Germanism. Some of our Americans would like to follow suit with " Pan-Americanism." The contemplative beholder is nigh despairing of human progress. But let us not despair. Let us rather hopefully labor and toil for human advance. History's march is slow, yet mankind moves onwards. Plato and Aristotle yet jeered at the *"barbarians"* as just fit for spoil and the yoke. We, two thousand years later, have at least the courage to remember: "Love the stranger as thyself;" and let us hope the thoughtful reader sympathizes with us.

PART III.

EQUAL DISTRIBUTION OF NATIONAL WEALTH.

In the foregoing pages we have made some researches concerning the Mosaic Civil Code as set forth in Laws and Judgments (II. M. 21.) We have seen that code embodies four cardinal principles in reference to the relation of the inhabitants to the State. The absolute liberty of the citizen is the first feature thereof. The absolute equality before the law is the next one. The economical ratio, the equal distribution of wealth, is the third. Solidarity, or community of interest, is the last.

We have already treated of the liberty and the equality of the Judæan State. Now we shall discuss the third feature, intimately connected with the first two.

Let us take, for an example, England, the classical country of individual liberty and political equality. Is there equality a real fact? Are not there equal duties, rights and chances a mockery? a cruel wrong? a dead letter? Compare the rights and duties, claims and enjoyments, of the eldest son of a lord and those of a son of the working-man. Of what avail is even voting to the poor son of Albion, except to sell his vote? Now, this is the result of the inequality of wealth. Lord A and Marquis de B have respectively the yearly rent of £100,000 and of £60,000. Baroness C enjoys one of half a million pounds. There are a few hundreds of such great fortunes in England. On the other hand, there are in London alone a hundred thousand paupers, living on alms, and several hundred thousands of proletarians, living from hand to mouth, neither of them knowing what the morrow would bring them; whilst forty thousand lewd women infest the streets in dead night, and thousands of men are addicted to crime, from lack of any other means of sustaining life.

Now, behold the arduous struggle for existence! "Where you see a palace, look and you will find a hundred wretched huts," says J. J. Rousseau. "*Le droit du peuple c'est le pain,*" St. Just pointedly said. If liberty and equality were realities and not mere words, then every young man and woman starting into life ought to have the same chances to succeed. Have we all the same chances? By no means. Your father is rich, and he gave you an education; mine was poor, and my education is neglected. You have been raised in comfort, and hence your bodily health; another one in misery and sickness. You have powerful and wealthy relatives, who back you in your competition; his relatives are poor and helpless themselves, and cannot afford him any patronage. Is liberty and equality here of much avail? Think of a battle—one soldier is armed, the other is not. Two persons have to swim across a dangerous stream—one is prepared from childhood for the occasion, the other is stiff and heavy. Are the chances equal? Two persons run a match of five miles. The one has wings at his feet, the other chains dangling down his. Who will win? What value has liberty and equality in such an arena of existence? Hence, liberty and equality will never be complete without their necessary complement—equal distribution of wealth among the members of the community.

SALISBURY, CHAMBERLAIN, HUXLEY.

Some years ago Lord Salisbury, the English Conservative leader, made a sensational motion, *à la* Beaconsfield, in an effort to take out the wind from the sails of the liberals. He proposed that the State should build cheap dwellings for the poor. Professor Huxley, equal to the emergency, demonstrated the futility of the idea. He said, "not poor-rates and poor-houses and poor-rents, but manhood—suffrage and education, would remedy the evil of pauperism." Mr. Chamberlain, on another similar occasion, remarked: "that the rich must pay a ransom to the poor." The fact is, we have to frame such laws, as to give each person the same chances in the arena of existence. This done, and in the course of time, we shall bring about—not by communism and spoliation, but by the natural logic of things—we shall slowly succeed in bringing about a desirable sameness of wealth. Now this great problem, termed the *Social Question*, and recognized as of first political importance, the Mosaic lawgiver has well known, and tried to solve over three thousand years ago, by several great and far-reaching economic institutions, standing forth in bold relief through his entire system, as bold as those of Lycurgus, but which, for reasons easy to explain, have been mostly overlooked by commentators. These institutions were well calculated to settle the social question of *his time* and circumstances, and may contain some solution for our times too. They went straight towards bringing about equality of fortunes among the citizens. This solution of the social problem the lawgiver endeavored to reach, first, by starting with a just distribution of the national wealth ; next, by securing one day out of seven as a respite for the hard working masses of which we shall speak later; then by a set of laws providing for the maintenance of that average economic equality, by providing against land grabbing and *accaparation*, by equal chances of acquiring, accumulating and keeping wealth. All that he did without resorting to the unnatural methods of old legislators, or to the dangerous methods of modern crude communism ; upholding property as a fundamental and sacred, social principle.

JUBILEE AND SEPTENNATE.

We have said that in order to make liberty and equality a reality, it is urgently necessary to insure a proximately equal distribution of the nation's wealth. For in spite of individual, personal equality and liberty, a too great difference of wealth will soon destroy the former and bring about a discrepancy in the rights and duties of citizens. Sooner or later the rich will buy out or squeeze off the vote of the poor. Legislative science has not yet found any efficient remedy against this greatest of social evils. This evil is nearly as great in America as in England, or Russia, Turkey and China.

Socialism and communism try their hands on that problem, recognized in our times as the *Great Social Question*, more important than all others, political, religious and national combined. The movement began with St. Simon, Owen and Fourier, etc. Karl Marx, Engels and Lasalle are the socialistic apostles. These latter ones deprecate apparently any violent expropriation, yet desire for the Social Democracy the direction of all, capital and labor, parcelling out to each citizen his work and his emoluments. As yet the system is not settled, and offers no definite base for action.

That panacea against the great human misery, that safety-valve against exorbitant wealth on one hand and abject pauperism and proletariat on the other, with their long train of misfortune, discontent and crime,—that panacea was suggested by the hoary genius of Mosaism, and enacted by its legislation over three thousand years ago. It is the Institution of the Jubilee with its subdivision, the *Year of Release*, both basing on the *Sabbath*. In II. M. 23, 10, the lawgiver alludes to that great Sabbatic Institution. Whilst in III. M. 25, the entire chapter is consecrated to it, with a grand emphasis of speech and space, fully conscious of its paramount importance.

It reads : "When you will arrive into the land I, God, am giving to you, then the soil shall have a rest (Sabbath) to God. Thereupon during six years thou shalt sow and reap and gather in thy field harvests and vineyard crops. And in the seventh year the soil shall have a Sabbath— rest. There shall be no sowing and no reaping ; whilst the spontaneous growth shall belong to thy slaves, thy hire- lings, strangers, and cattle for their food. Thereupon thou shalt count seven weeks of years, seven times seven years, making forty-nine years. Then shalt thou have the solemn trumpet sound through the entire land on the tenth day of the seventh month, on the day of Atonement. And ye shall consecrate the fiftieth year, and proclaim freedom to all her inhabitants. It shall be unto you a *Jubilee*. And ye shall return every one to one's own inherited lot, and to one's own family. A Jubilee-festival shall be the fiftieth year unto you. No sowing nor reaping shall take place on it. It shall be a consecrated *Jubilee*-year. All selling and buying of the soil shall be in accordance with the computa- tion of that *Jubilee*-cycle. Do not overreach one another. And ye shall perform these ordinances, and you will dwell safely in the land. . . . So that the land shall not be sold for ever. For Mine is the land ; you are but My immi- grants and tenants. Therefore shall you grant the boon of redemption to the soil. Should anyone sell his allot- ment, his kinsman shall redeem it. And if he can not redeem it, the sale remains good till the Jubilee, when the acre must return to its original owner."

Many more details follow thereupon. This is the grand Mosaic institution of the *Jubilee*, one of the boldest eco- nomical suggestions ever uttered by a lawgiver. It ordained that : Every fiftieth year everything shall be restored to its original condition. The entire status of all property and all social relations underwent a renovation. Man and land and houses, dislocated and rent asunder heretofore, reassumed their pristine status to each other. When Joshua had conquered Canaan, he divided it out into tribal districts, and these again into family lots. The entire Israelitish people were divided into twelve tribes, and the Levites formed extra a thirteenth one. The tribes of *Reuben*, *Menasse* and half of *Gad* were assigned to the territory beyond the Jordan, to conquered *Gilead*. Nine and one-half tribes were placed this side of the Jordan, in Canaan proper, each group having a territory or canton, which was again sub-divided into districts, boroughs and lots, and wherein were placed the tribes, *gens*, families and all male individuals, nuclei of future families. The *Levites* had their hamlets scattered among all the tribes, forming the connecting link of all and uniting them into one integral nation. Thus every and each adult Ebrew had a lot of ground assigned to himself and his future posterity for ever and ever. That ground he superintended, tilled, husbanded and enjoyed its produce, but not beyond that. It was disgraceful to alienate it. It was considered a sacred heirloom, rather to improve than to disintegrate. Remember the touching and tragic story of *King Achab* usurping Naboth's family vineyard (II. Kings, 21). Only in desperate cases was it sold until the *Jubilee*. This simply means that the owner gave away its crops, till the Jubilee, for a consideration.

Thus, the *best part of the modern socialistic idea was at the bottom of the Mosaic State.* The State owned the land. *Jahveh*, the king, or his representative, the State, was the only and absolute proprietor. He was the real master of the soil, then, the only national wealth, and he remained so forever. The citizens were simply the tenants thereof; they had to work it and lived upon its produce; they could not alienate it. Thus the family-lot remained intact for posterity. No one of the Biblical Society was born poor, nor was any one born over-rich; no one could acquire his neighbor's property by any amount of power, wealth or stratagem.

Queen Jesabel had to hire assassins to grab a vineyard. The agglomeration of the soil, the modern large property-holdings were impossible there. Originally and since the very occupation of Canaan, the approximate equality in property among the Israelites having been thus established, the care of the lawgiver was now to keep up that economic equality, which was the necessary base of civil liberty and political equality. This, Mosaism was endeavoring to realize by the *Jubilee* and *Release-Year* institutions. Every fiftieth year all sold property returned to its original owner. Hence, the two extremes, *proletariat* and grand property-holdings, could not grow up. The *Jubilee* formed every fifty years a new equalizing readjustment of wealth, on the original basis of apportionment *pro capita*. The Year of Release was a powerful auxiliary in that direction. The Ebrew slave was held but for six years. In the seventh he went out free. Hence, slavery and pauperism were, too, rendered impossible. Again, with the arrival of that seventh year, all debts were cancelled (V. M., 15, 1,) (Maimonides, *Yad*. Release and Jubilee, I and IX.) (See, too, Philo Septenar, 1173.) The debtor thus got rid of all his indebtedness and began work clear of all former obligations. These seventh-year and fiftieth-year institutions amounted to a total renovation of the social status, a real "*restitutio in integrum*." They were mighty bulwarks against Ebrew pauperism, slavery and proletariat on one hand, and on the other against the tyranny of great landlordism, of *accapparating* all the soil into a few hands and all the poor as their clients or serfs. Rome and Constantinople were ruined by that mode. An equal distribution of wealth was kept up, especially as the lawgiver did not encourage either conquests or extensive industries, the two other means of enrichment and deterioration. The only inheritance was the family lot. Thus, a fair average equality of wealth was rendered possible and actually maintained according to the Mosaic scheme, without resorting to violent means, as the *Gracchi*, etc., attempted in Rome.

SEPTENNATE AND INDEBTEDNESS.

Did the *Year of Release* actually release the debtor definitely and fully? Or, rather, was the *Seventh Year* but a suspense of debts, a year of *grace*, a patient waiting, the debtor having to pay thereafter? Commentators and economists are divided thereupon. Some take the *Release Year,* "*Shemitta,*" and its root, "*Shamot,*" to express but a stay of debts, meaning that during that year no debtor could be prosecuted, analogous to the modern *Sunday* privilege, leaving on Monday the debt perfectly valid. They find the idea absurd that a practical lawgiver ever could have imagined the extinction of all debts at each seventh year. That would destroy all business and all confidence and all industry (See Michaelis).[1] Carefully surveying all the passages bearing on that, pondering over them in connection with the contemporaneous circumstances of ancient Canaan, keeping in mind the leading aims of the Mosaic law, I think that the traditional conception of the Release-Year to really mean a *total and absolute extinction of all pecuniary debts*, is the correct one.

We must, namely, judge an ancient author by his standard, not by ours. We, now, give to industry and initiative, to the desire of enrichment and enterprise all possible impetus, freedom and encouragement. This is our, modern, way of understanding freedom and happiness. If well applied or not, that is another question. The Mosaic lawgiver had another ideal before his eyes. His ideal was not a rich, luxurious, competitive, conquering, encroaching nation, filling the world with its arms, its glory, its luxury, its edifices and its monuments, as the Assyrians or the Athenians tried or realized. No, his model was rather nearer

[1] Gesetzgebung Mosis *ad locum*.

that of *Lycurgus*, than that of Raamses, Herod, or *Louis XIV*, each surnamed *The Great*; with that difference, that he aimed not simply at strength and endurance as the Spartan lawgiver, but at moral greatness, at perfection and holiness (II. M. 19, 6.) Therefore, he discouraged conquests and war, great and luxurious industries and enriching commerce. He aimed really at a "KINGDOM OF PRIESTS and *holy nation*," humble and meek and pacific; fulfilling the law, kind to each other, keeping their own and not encroaching upon other nations, remaining obscure, modest, poor; but sound, hale, pure, and thus, really happy. This political and ethical ideal is at the base of the Pentateuch. The later prophets constantly point to it and lead the nation back to it; with all the fire of their enthusiasm, and with the warm heart of patriots they oppose the vain and glittering schemes of *Jeroboam* and *Ahab*. With the rising of the great empires, Assyria, Media, Babylonia, Persia, etc., that ideal appears to have been totally lost sight of. The Great kings of those countries aimed at universal empires, and conquests, huge armies, centralization, splendid monumental structures, immortalizing their fame, and eternizing their dynasties and their names. The Mosaic ideal of a people's happiness and endurance, can therefore not be much younger than three thousand years. Later, that ideal was supplanted by sterner, coarser realities. Later conquerors and politicians realized that *"hammer or anvil"* is the lot of nations, and that in order NOT to be subjugated, a people must subjugate others. This is no doubt a sad sort of political wisdom, but it is one in a certain state of society, especially a young, inexperienced one, as were those of the biblical times, comparatively. This is one of the many reasons, why the bulk of the Pentateuch must belong to a higher antiquity than often accepted by certain critics. The practical, good sense of the Mosaic legislator can not be questioned. Yet by the time of Isaiah and Jeremiah,

600 and 800 B. Ch., that ideal was already superseded. Hence must that Mosaic state-polity, of modest law-abiding peace and justice-loving national life, without war, commerce, great industries, wealth and luxuries,—that must be of a more hoary antiquity.

STATE POLITY AND ECONOMY OF THE BIBLE.

Thus the biblical laws enjoined: Do not sell your inherited family-acre. Do not enslave your persons. In distress, hire out for six years' labor. Do not lend money or goods on interest or profit. A loan was to be half and half a charity. You need no marble houses nor coach and livery. Therefore, give of your superfluity to your poorer neighbor lacking bread, and God will bless you for it: Every seventh day take a rest for thee, thy servant, stranger and cattle. Every seventh year keep an agrarian Sabbath for man, beast and the soil, too, all needing it. Every seventh year the Ebrew slave goes out free, or the rogue shall be bored in the ear. Every septennate the bondage of debts shall be cancelled, debts being the worst slavery. Half the poor in ancient States fell into slavery from non-payment of their debts, as chattels of creditors. Ancient, powerful Rome, mistress of the world, was many times on the brink of revolution and collapse, yea, of total ruination, from that cause.

DEBTORS IN ROME AND JUDÆA.

The great civil commotions in the times of the Gracchi, Sylla and Marius, Cæsar and Pompeius, etc., were largely brought about by the mutiny of the debtors against their cruel creditors. In his second oration against Catiline, Cicero alludes to that important fact again and again, as one of the principal sources of Rome's social embarrassments. "Do you expect war? Will your possessions be spared in the general devastation? Or do you wish the abolition of debts?—*an tabulas novas?* *Errant qui istas a Catilina expectant.* They who expect it from Catiline are in error."— Catiline, and later, Cæsar, were popular, holding out the hope of debt-abolition. "The very first class (of Catiline's supporters) are great nobles deeply in debt, and not wishing to pay them," says Cicero. "*Unus genus est eorum qui magno in aere alieno,* . . . *quarum dissolvi nullo modo possunt.*" (Oratio II. in Catilinam, 100.)—Moses discouraged the accumulation of debts by interest or speculation, checking that tremendous avidity for *accapparating* and grasping, the leading features and the curse of old and of modern nations. In a society constituted after the pattern of the Bible, one would entertain no fear of communism, anarchy and dynamite. Indeed, the Mosaic polity contains probably everything rational and safe in socialism, expunging all its crudities. Look close to these verses (V. M. 15, 1): "At the end of six years let there be a release (*Shemitta*), namely: Every creditor shall release his debtor from his indebtedness, and not press his neighbor and brother, for it is a release to the Eternal. The foreigner (in his own country) thou mayest press for payment, but he living with thee, thy brother, take off thy hand from him, that there shall be no pauper among you, and God will bless thee, He who gave thee an inheritance in possession. When, nevertheless, there will be a poor one in thy city, do not harden thy heart, nor close thy hand against thy brother, the poor one. Should thy wicked heart think, the release-year is near, and thou wouldst give him nothing; that would be mean. Indeed, open thy hand to thy poor brother, and God will bless thee in all thy doings." That sounds by all means, if not as a peremptory command, at least as a strong recommendation to abandon and annul all debts in the seventh year. The passage following is to the same point (V. M. 15, 12): "An Ebrew, being sold to thee, shall work six years; in the seventh he shall be free. And when leaving thee, let him have a portion, according to the wealth God blessed thee with. For a slave thou hast been in Egypt, and God has redeemed thee." I think, therefore, to be nearer the truth in siding with the Rabbinical interpretation, that the year of release meant a complete cancellation and abandonment of all pecuniary debts. It was, namely, a sub-division and auxiliary of the Jubilee. Every seventh year debts were extinguished and slaves set free. Every fifty years there was a total renovation and restoration of the entire Judæan society and a return to its pristine condition. Let us not forget the difference of times and circumstances.

PRESENT AND ANCIENT ECONOMICS.

In our present era of fierce competition, selfish individual efforts and unbridled acquisition, such a law would be tantamount to communism and confiscation of property. All commerce and trade would come to a stand-still, and society would celebrate an involuntary and uninterrupted holiday; work would be stopped and starvation might follow. Not so in ancient Ebrew Canaan, the scene of that legislation. Imagine Sparta, clinging yet to the letter and spirit of the Lycurgian laws, and before its days of corruption by conquest, would enact such statutes of Release and Jubilee, there would not result the least social disturbance. Just so it was in Judæa, with a tolerable equality of property and political status, with little wealth, industry and commerce, a modest nation given to agriculture and a simple mode of life; that could have no other effect than to uphold the original scheme of the legislator. This aim was the founding of a State and of a people for absolute freedom and full equality, frugal and sober, strong enough to repel invasion, too weak to encroach upon the neighbors, having little intercourse with other nations, the lawgiver deprecating amalgamation, having placed his God-idea and purity of morals as the corner-stone of his State, so much in contrast with the neighboring tribes, worshiping *Baal, Moloch* and *Astaroth.* The method of Moses is more congenial to our modern taste than that of Lycurgus. The latter sacrificed everything, even property, morals, nature and family, to secure the existence of the State. Moses secured the State, while yet upholding all these; remaining true to nature; the family was dear and sacred to him; so was property, so filial piety, chastity, ethics and all the instincts of nature. Nevertheless did he keep in bounds fierce avarice, competition, plutocracy and pauperism, building up human holiness upon the "*holy God*" principle.

THE NUMBER SEVEN.

Why did the legislator take the number seven as his norm? To the supernatural import thereof I have nothing to add; that is well known. It is the seven-days creation doctrine. Critically considered, it appears to recall the ancient view of the solar system of the universe, with its seven heavenly bodies; hence, the sacredness of the number seven. Seven in Ebrew "*Shebha*," is the root of *Shebiah*, meaning swearing, taking an oath; as in English, *seven and swear*, or affirming by the seven heavenly bodies. Thus, there are six days of creation, and the seventh is a "Sabbath," consecrated. The seventh month is the holiday month. By seven were computed the cycles of time, Release Year and Jubilee. At the completion of that cycle, the return of slaves and of their property to their original status was proclaimed. The ten days before the atonement day were given free to the slaves, who then appeared in wreaths, as the equals of their masters, recalling the natural state of man. [1] Later, by the Rabbis, these ten days were turned to moral account—liberation from sin—called "Ten Days of Repentance." Seven days yearly are biblical holidays. The seventh year again is the

[1] Maimonides, *Yad*, Releases and Jubilee.

holy rest, without any agrarian work, as tilling, sowing and reaping, for the soil, too, needs a rest. Its spontaneous produce belongs to every one, thus again remembering the original state of natural society, when the soil belonged to every one. After seven times seven years, the fiftieth year is the grand *Jubilee*, where everything and every man returned to their original condition, without any artificial dislocation of man and matter.

Is Septennate a Fact?

Were those institutions, the Sabbatical year and the Jubilee, really facts, laws realized in practical life, or simple theories, ideas, desirable suggestions? Here we must discriminate. During the whole course of the first period of Ebrew history, from Moses to Ezra and Nehemiah, it appears they were much neglected, if not totally ignored; as, indeed, most of the Mosaic legislation was; as even the leading doctrine of Monotheism was, the prophetic school alone entertaining the sacred hearth of nationality and pure worship. The mass of the people, with the princes at their head, were given to the surrounding idolatries. During that long period, the Jubilee and Release year were at the utmost, ideals and pious wishes, not general facts. So we find Jeremiah remonstrating with the nobles against their detaining Ebrew slaves. His denunciations (34, 8) of king and princes are bold, vehement and sweeping. So do we read of the poor woman, complaining to the prophet about her creditors, having taken away her children in payment of debts,—utterly contrary to the biblical law. Isaiah (61, 1) and Ezekiel (46, 17, etc.), to all appearances, allude to it as a philanthropic ideal. Another solid hint that that vast and far-reaching institution was but a pious wish, do we already find in III. M. 26; in that severe and gloomy chapter, delineating the infidelity of Israel and its grave national consequences.

EVIDENCE THEREOF.

There the sacred orator denounces in a severe, scathing, long passage the grievous sin of having neglected the institution in question (ibid 26, 33): "I shall scatter you among the barbarians, unsheathing my sword after you and destroying your cities. Then will the land make good its Sabbaths (time of rest or Release-years). As long as you stay among your enemies, the land will make good its Sabbath-rest—a bitter irony!—since it did not rest during your dwelling thereon."—According to Isaiah V, 8, and Michah II, 2, the poor man's family-lot often was remorselessly appropriated by the strong.—II. Chronicles 36, 21, alludes to III. M. 26, 34, apparently. Wonderful, he ascribes it to Jeremiah and in nearly the identical words. May be that Jeremiah, too, contained that allusion to our passage, which in our version, now, is omitted. It reads verbatim : " The remnants of the sword he exiled into Babylon to fulfill the word of God to Jeremiah : Until the land will make good its Sabbaths during all the days of its being deserted, it will rest to complete *seventy* years." Of course the bold critic would conclude from that utterance of Chronicles that III. M. 26, 31 to 36, has been written by Jeremiah. I believe that assumption not to be necessary.

With *Ezra and Nehemiah,* the restorers of the Mosaic polity, the Jubilee and Sabbath year were, it appears, reinstated. In a solemn convention of the Ebrew Estates, (Nehemiah 10, 1, etc.), they wrote and signed a solemn compact to abide by the Law of God, they and their families, and affirmed upon oath to walk after that doctrine as taught by Moses, etc., not to inter-marry with the Heathen Gentiles nor to buy anything on the Sabbath and holy days, and *to forego (work) on the seventh year and remit all indebtedness, etc., etc.* Thus we see here that in the *sacred pact* of the national convention under Nehemiah, the law concerning the Release-year, in its two leading features, viz.: no tilling of soil and cancelling of debts was solemnly instituted and declared valid. In I. Maccabeans, VI. 49, we read expressly : " And they, (the Judæans), left the city, (Baith Zur), for they had no provisions to stand any longer the siege. Because there was the *year of rest* in the land." And Ibidem, verse 53 : " They, (the Jews), had no provisions in their vessels, since it was the *seventh year*, and those who had fled to Judæa from the Heathens, had consumed all their provisions."

This can mean nothing else but the Mosaic Year of Release. Further, do we read in Josephus (Antiquib. XIII, 8, 1): "As the siege was drawn out into length by this means, that year on which the Jews use to rest, came on, for the Jews observe this rest every seventh year, as they do every seventh day;" and Ibidem XIV, 10, 6, we read : " Caius Cæsar, imperator, for the second time, hath ordained that all the country of the Jews, excepting *Joppa*, do pay a tribute yearly for the city of Jerusalem, excepting the seventh year, which they call the Sabbatic Year, because thereon they neither gather the fruits of their trees nor do they sow their lands."—The same Josephus mentions it in many other places—ibid. 16, 12, 15, and Jewish Wars, 1, 2, 4.— So Tacitus' History, 5, 4 : " The seventh day they give to rest, the seventh year to laziness." [1] That this Sabbatic institution was a practical one, is proven too by the fact that the Rabbis elaborated that system with all their wonted minuteness and exactness in Mishna, Talmud and Casuists. (See Talmud, Bably., Schebiith and Maimonides, " Release and Jubilee," chapter X, 3.)

According to tradition, there were seventeen plus eight Jubilee cycles celebrated, since the Ebrew occupation of

---

(1) Septimo die otium placuisse ferunt: quia is finem laborum tulerit; dein blandiente inertia septimum quoque annum ignaviæ datum.

Tacitus knew little of the facts and less of the spirit of Mosaism, destined to reign even in Rome herself.

Palestine until Ezra and the *diaspora*. I, therefore, do not in the least doubt that these institutions were intended as actual facts and positive laws, commanded, and, at least during the II temple, really practiced. But I think they never were realized in their full sense and entire essence. I think rather, as with many other Mosaic ordinances, they were buried under the mass of Rabbinical traditions, the law was kept in letter, but changed materially in spirit, whenever the original spirit no longer was believed to be the "spirit of the times;" a method followed by Mishna and Talmud, as also in later times. A proof thereof is the Rabbinical arrangement of *Pros-bouly* or Reservation. [1] (Maim. Yad. on Release and Jubilee IX, 16.) Namely, as the Mosaic code required the relinquishment of all debts every seventh year, and as towards the latter part of the II Ebrew Commonwealth the Judæans, especially those living in foreign countries, had adopted largely mercantile pursuits, the release of indebtedness proved to be simply ruinous. Now there is a maxim in Jewish jurisprudence, that a law is intended to be useful and beneficial, [2] not detrimental, as long as it is to remain in force; and that when it becomes obnoxious to the majority [3] it must be abolished.

ABOLITION OF SEPTENNATE.

Even so did Hillel and the leading authorities act in that instance. They abrogated it, because "Judæa was no longer independent." They formulated a legal deed by which the debt and the right of collecting it at any time, except the Release-year, was reserved to the creditor, and then the Septennate was reduced simply to a postponement of payment, as it is even now interpreted by many jurists, as Michaelis and others.

---

(1) פרוזבול.

(2) „וחי בהם". ולא שימות בהם.

(3) רוב הציבור אינן יכולין לעמוד בו.

The interesting passage thereon is in Talmud Bably. *Shebiith*, 10: "The *Pros-bouly* act saves the debt from cancellation. This is one of the arrangements of Hillel the Elder, seeing the people's hesitation in lending money." (¹) By a similar *legal fiction* the later Rabbis allowed to take interest on money, contrary to the express Mosaic law, by a deed declaring the creditor a partner of the debtor, with a right to share in the profits of the business for which he is lending the money, at the same time intimating that he is relinquishing that profit for a percentage on the capital. Even so, no doubt, did the Rabbinical sages deal with all the features of that far-reaching institution, originally intended for a small agricultural, isolated people in hoary times and primitive surroundings, but altogether out of harmony with the Ebrew development fifteen centuries afterwards.

SEPTENNATE NEVER TRIED.

We can, therefore, not say that this institution ever had a fair trial, nor do I believe that we can actually have an estimate of its bearings in real life. I presume that this far-reaching institution, of the utmost import to the economical, political and social development of a people, though formally kept up in puny Judæa during its second historical period, is yet, in truth and reality, a *terra incognita*. We cannot judge of its grand results, what it might be . when fully in practice, for a long period of time, on a large scale, realized in essence and in spirit, and supervised by statesmen and wise economists. I think it worth while for philosophers and philanthropists to take it into the most earnest consideration. It strikes my mind that it can not be accidental that so many of the leading scientists and systematizers of modern social democracy are of Ebrew

---

(1) פרוזבול אינו משמט, והוא אחד מן הדברים שהתקין הילל הזקן כשראה שנמנעין העם מלהלוות זה את זה.

origin. I mean, in the first place, Karl Marx. So, too, are next Lasalle, Singer, Bamberger, Dr. Max Hirsh, etc. Even others, as St. Simon and Prudhon, the French social initiators, have drawn their sympathies and ideas from that same fountain, the Mosaic aspirations, to base the State, not simply upon personal liberty and political equality, but *going* deeper, upon a comparative sameness of *property*, an equal distribution of wealth, a system compounded of property and community, of individualism and socialism, of supremacy of the citizen and that of the State, a communism combined with full individual initiative, so unlike modern communism, and as unlike that of Lycurgus and Sparta. As so many other great thoughts, so social democracy, too, may be but a recent revival of a biblical idea. I think economists have only to dig in that antique gold mine, and they will find there more genuine treasures than in all the finds of Babylon and Greece.

Septennate and Modern Charity.

Mutilated and curtailed as the Jubilee and Release-year have been realized, their influence upon the character of modern nations is, nevertheless, potent and vast. Their political and social benefactions have been greatly frustrated by legal fictions, downright misunderstanding and misapplication. An equality of wealth they have not brought about, because they were never fairly tried. Nevertheless, they have realized practical, grand results of a moral nature. That sensibility, sympathy and fellow-feeling in the modern man's temperament are undoubtedly their effects. Those biblical charity-laws of which I shall treat soon, are their logical outcome. That Israelites are proverbially *charitable,* (¹) that organized sympathy exists among modern nations in Europe and America, that charity is a leading feature in the New Testament and in the

---

(1)   ‏בישנים, רחמנים, גומלי חסדים‎.

Koran, all this re-echoes the great heart of the author of the Septennate system. The modern all-pervading idea that active goodness and philanthropy are the very marrow and essence of religion, standing out in relief before and above dogma and race and class-interest, filling the heart of enlightened Christian, Jew and Heathen, that idea is hewn from the great quarry of the Mosaic, humanitarian legislation. The New Testament is brimful of it; it starts with a communistic society; it declares the Kingdom of Heaven especially belonging to the poor; it asks of the rich "to give away all, if he desires to enter that kingdom." The Koran did not remain far behind in that respect, holding to the identical supreme idea of love to man. As the Sabbath, the means of educating, elevating and sanctifying man, originated in the Bible, expanded in the vast Christian world and then in the vaster Mahommedan one, encompassing now the civilized portion of mankind; even so may its perfect development, the institution of the seven-years'-cycle, become the panacea against our great social evils, the solution of the "social question," the remedy against proletarianism, pauperism and plutocracy.

EXEMPTION LAWS AND FRAUD.

That Institution has, besides the above-mentioned politico-social purposes, also a legislative one. It is the bankruptcy and exemption law of ancient times. Nearly every modern statute book has enacted some provisions against totally depriving a man of all means of subsistence in case of misfortune. Some leave a certain allowance in goods for himself and his family; some, his homestead; some, his furniture and clothing; some, his life-insurance; some, the dower brought in by his wife, etc., etc. Now behold the abuse of such exemption laws. Here is a merchant, living extravagantly, out-doing and out-shining all his neighbors.

To cover up such display, he must *over-speculate and under-sell.* To hide that, he falsifies his books.—Even his clerks are kept in the dark.—Even his books are made to hide the truth.   He never was a friend of honest double-entry book-keeping.   He had his own crooked ways of keeping accounts. As the Holy of Holies of old, his personal stock-account was shrouded in darkness, his bookkeeper never approached it without trembling.   A crisis comes on, failure sets in, and there is a woeful deficit.—But his lady is so charming; he was so hospitable; she gave such fine dinner-parties and musical soirees.   *"Society,"* the courts, the creditors themselves, sympathize with him and her.   They can't endure the thought that such people should leave the brown stone house and the diamonds.   The exemption laws are twisted and tortured in their favor, and a compromise of twenty-five cents on the dollar is effected.

Here, again, is a modest man, living humbly, keeping a small store, with a large family behind him.   He is crushed by competition; he has but few customers; his goods are depreciated by going out of fashion, and he suspends payment.—Little sympathy is there for him.   The sheriff sells his humble stock under the hammer, at thirty cents on the dollar.   His creditors lose and are furious; nobody has a good word for the fellow; and he and his family are forever ruined and forever bankrupt.   Now, where is here justice? Is not justice here a mockery!   The extravagant and fashionable are exempted.   The modest, the honest, the thrifty, ruined by reckless, soulless competition—they are sent to the poor-house.

CODE NAPOLEON.

When the famous Code Napoleon was prepared, at the dawn of this century, by the French Council of State, such exemption laws were proposed in favor of the wife of the bankrupt.   With his usual good common sense, Napoleon I.

argued the case as just set forth, viz: "That display and diamonds are mostly at the bottom of failures, and that the sin must be laid at the door of the sinner proper, without distinction of sex."—The Bible is eminently just in its exemption laws.—No man shall be born to absolute poverty. Everyone is possessed of his family lot. In marrying he has some speck of ground to rely upon as a last resort. He enjoys its fruit. He cannot alienate it. It is the leaning staff of his widow and his children. It cannot be wrested from him by debt. It is inalienable. In our times people marry on air, pay the last hundred dollars for a bridal present, begin business on air and moonshine, and rely on exemption laws and "stolen sympathies." Could we not learn here, too, from the wisdom of the ancient lawgiver?—A hundred times he warns against wronging widows and orphans. He forbids to take a pawn of a widow,—to take away the "SIMLA" or shawl used in time of night. God is the special protector of the widows and orphans. A portion of the crop is theirs. But she is not exempt from the law of responsibility. Again, we must not forget that the status of woman now, and once, is immensely different. Anciently, she was sold into marriage; she had little or no choice of her lord. He was entitled to have several marital establishments. Hence, often could he ruin the family without her concurrence, even against her will. Now it is the wife who is mostly the mistress of the house, who arranges her household and its expenses, who has her full share of its enjoyments. She can coerce, restrain or destroy. Hence, she must be responsible. "Nobility obliges."

Resume on Jubilee and Septennate.

The biblical passages on the above institutions are: II. M. 23, 10—III. M. 25—V. M. 15, and many, many more. The import of the institution is a restoration of man and soil to their natural and original conditions. Originally, both were free. Social and economic alterations changed that status, and both were enslaved. The lawgiver estab- lished the seventh year cycle for the freedom of persons and of soil, and the Jubilee as a total restoration of society to the original state, a *restitutio in integrum*. It is realizing thus the ideas of "Mine are Israel, devoted to Jahveh's service, by Him redeemed from Egypt," and "Mine is the land; ye shall not sell it for ever.—Ye are but my tenants." —Now these are, closely seen, the views of modern democ- racy, those, especially, pervading modern socialism. Man and soil are absolutely free, the property of the entire society, not of king or class. Mosaism thus has happily compromised between property and community, individ- ualism and communism, consecrating the first, yet con- stantly remembering the latter: "Ye were slaves in Egypt." That means, poor ye were and oppressed. Hence, learn to live and let live; be no oppressors in your turn, no plutocracy, no landlordism and no proletarianism.

The remission of debts in the seventh year is absolute, a relinquishing and total cancellation thereof. It is not simply a suspension during the Sabbatic year, as believed by *Keil* and Michaelis. Such is the sense of the Septua- ginta (Deut. 15, 1.) (1) The same is the opinion of Philo (M. II., 277.) The same, originally in the Talmud (Shebiith 10, 1), declaring without any discussion or doubt that (2) "the seventh year cancels and releases from all indebted- ness, with or without a legal deed." The Rabbis go to the very extreme, declaring that "even the hireling's wages are forfeited when left as a loan to the employer." Later, exceptions began to crop up. No doubt this took place

---

(1). Διὰ ἑπτὰ ἐτῶν ποιήσεις ἄφεσιν, καὶ οὕτω τὸ πρόσταγμα τῆς ἀφέσεως. ἄφεσις πᾶν χρέος ἴδιον, ὃ ὀφείλει σοι ὁ πλησίον, καὶ τὸν ἀδελφόν σου οὐκ ἀπαιτήσεις. ἐπικέκληται γὰρ ἄφεσις κυρίω τῷ θεῷ σου.

שביעית מישמטת את המלוה, בישטר וישלא בישטר. (2)

when the Ebrew nation left its primitive agricultural state
and became more largely industrial and commercial. So,
debts on pawn were not forfeited; and above all by the
legal exemption of the "*Prusbul.*" (¹)

Thus we read in "Shebiith" Mishna (10, 2 to 8,) the
following : There is non-cancellation of debts secured by
pawn, and for him who registers his asset-notes at the courts.
Nor does the *Prusbul* admit of cancellation. This is one of
the enactments of Hillel the Elder (first cent. B. C.) Seeing that the people abstained from lending each other (on
account of the Release-year), he contrived the above *Prusbul* (or act of postponement of payment). The act read
thus : " I herewith declare to you, Judges N. N., that on all
my active debts and assets, I reserve the right of collecting
and receiving payment for, whenever I please "—" which
act judges or witnesses signed."—The *Mishna* continues—
ibidem :—" When the debtor offers, during the Release-year,
to pay his debt, then the creditor should offer to relinquish
it, and when the debtor insists to pay, the creditor can
accept. *Which act is meritorious.*" (²) Allusions to the
Jubilee and Release Institutions we find enough : In
Isaiah 37, 30, and Jeremiah 7, 12; Ezekiel 46, 17, calls it
the year of liberty ! (³) a new term, then. The word Jubilee
is derived from the Ebrew יבל, meaning to stream or to
violently flow; from the strong sounding of the cornet, proclaiming on the tenth day of the seventh month the entrance
of the Liberty-year. According to various allusions in the
Bible, the family-lot was fairly kept up and retained in the
respective families and tribes. According to *Sibra* (Behar.
2, 3,) the first interruption in that institution occurred when
the two and a-half tribes residing beyond the Jordan were
driven into exile. Later, again, after the *ten tribes* of the

---

(1) Pros-bouly, פרוזבול

(2 רוח חכמים נוחה הימינו.

(3) יבת הדרור.

kingdom of Israel were conquered and exiled by King Salmanassar, of Assyria. It was reintroduced by King Josia, of Judæa; again suspended after the destruction of that kingdom, and again introduced by Nehemiah (10, 32). During the II Temple and empire, that institution is frequently mentioned by Jewish and Gentile writers, in Josephus, Tacitus, etc., as a live institution and described as above.

After the destruction of the second Jewish empire, it was again revived and kept up, but hardly understood. Thus, it became a great drawback. Rabbi Jehudah, (II century P. C.), the prince had the idea of abolishing it entirely as no longer opportune, but he was foiled in this, his intention, by his other more conservative colleagues. (Jerushalmi Taanith, 66 a.) Slowly it decayed, and when, later, the Romans insisted upon their tribute even during that year, it was suffered to fall into desuetude. (See Hamburger's Real Encyclop. on this subject.)

Where we find in our forest ramblings a mighty tree with a sound, round, vast stem and lofty, thick, powerful branches, stretching into all directions around and above, towering to the ethereal sky, yielding exquisite shade to brute and man, and a refreshing pool or well murmuring at its feet, we are vividly reminded of the mighty roots entwined deeply in the earth, giving support and strength and sap to that tree. Even so when we contemplate that far-reaching Jubilee and Release-Year Institution, we ask, where is the deep root of that vast tree? How powerful must it not be to give support to such a growth? This root is the Sabbath, of which we shall speak later in the following pages, having first to survey a great question intimately connected with the above theme.

BIBLE AND COMMUNISM.

A rough, crude attempt at settling the all-absorbing social question, is communism. It is a remedy suggested by hunger, folly and despair, developed into some sort of system by inebriated science, taking brute force as a measure of right, a remedy against the two extremes, grasping accumulation on one hand and excessive poverty on the other hand. That crude, first outline of communism attempts at making the State the only one proprietor of all and everything, and all the citizens one great herd of passive subjects and obedient workers, unfree tools in the hands of the leaders. It is a trial to make man a machine, to rob him of all his rights to individuality and to property. He shall not own his own will, his person, taste and inclination, aspiration and effort. He shall not own his own house, his wife, his child; he shall labor as an ox, a machine, for the State. The State shall be the sole employer, the only boarding house, furnishing him with meagre, Spartan meals, scanty raiment and lodging, without any regard for his taste, his merit, his work. That system deprives man of all inclination, of every incentive to effort, labor and distinction; it robs him of all personality, all moral freedom, all noble emulation; it opens the crib for all, happiness to none; it satisfies the beast, not the man. To all appearances, that kind of communism is the first rude trial of socialism, its later, higher evolution. That communism cures the patient by decapitation. The veteran Frenchman, St. Juste, sardonically said: "The right of the people is bread." The communistic politicians took him at his literal word. They offer the people bread—at the expense of all human happiness; they save the animal by sacrificing man. But man wants something more than bread; he wants education, culture, sympathy—a happy, developed self. Communism forgot that.

Not so Mosaism. It suggests to solve the question as old as man is, in a more rational way—by the Jubilee Cycle. It secures the bread of the poor, but also his freedom, his individuality, his culture—Sabbath—his family, his happiness. Mosaism allows us to acquire as much as our skill

and industry permit. "Conquer matter," utilize forces
and chances (Genes. I. 28), have the advantages of your
talents and your thrift. But be moderate, reasonable, merciful. Crush not your neighbor; take not advantage of his
weakness or simplicity. Remember, live and let live; his
person is sacred; his field, his home, his wife and children,
are sacred. His patrimony must never be estranged from
him and his family. When poor, you are bound to help
him to a competency, not by alms, not by making him a
pauper, but by encouraging him, backing him, helping him
to an independence, for he is your brother. What a vast
difference between that genuine benevolence and the one
usually in practice; the hypocritical, painted benevolence,
the real bitter competition, the venomous jealousy or
revenge, offering a neighbor some showy assistance, in order
to gain the appearance of charitableness, and at the very
same moment making all efforts to crush him and his
manly independence, to lower his public standing and
stamping him a pauper. . . . The biblical way alone
solves the social question.

Whilst our present economical system is crushing competition and "ring" policy; whilst communism is robbing us
of all our individuality, making us machines, the Pentateuch takes a middle course, yet teaches, "Live and let
live. Work and acquire, and let room for others, too.
Enjoy and let enjoy; emulation, yet sympathy, too; egoism
tempered with altruism. Love thy neighbor, love the
stranger as thyself." Hence, let not be all accumulation
on one side and all destitution on the other. Human effort
has free scope; yet remorseless, soulless competition is
stigmatized and checked. In that manner is individual
liberty and social equality built up there, upon the solid
rock of economical equality; upon fair and impartial distribution of the national wealth among all the members of
the commonwealth. The Release-year is partial restora-

tion, the Jubilee is total restoration of the freedom of man and soil, yet fully in accord with the principle of property. That Septennate is a social, peaceful revolution, a fair readjustment, a *restauratio in integrum,* without violent commotion or bloodshed. It is the gravitation force of the social pendulum ever vibrating off, to the right and the left, towards plutocracy or proletariat.

MATTHEW ARNOLD.

According to that late English critic, we have not in our United States any ideal civilization, not much of distinction, nor much of the beautiful. But we have a good deal of political and social advancement. American legislators, he says, "see straight and go straight on all political and social questions." This is something to atone for and to render us hopeful concerning the ideal sides of our civilization. Let our American lawgivers and economists ponder over the institutions just discussed. Having realized so much in the domain of liberty and equality, something should be done now for their necessary complement—a fairer distribution of the national wealth; or competition will run mad and may ruin democracy. Think of it! Messrs. Gould are complaining of over-taxation!

BIBLE AND SOCIALISM.

We have seen that the first rough outline of communism does not contain much for the edification of the humanist or the economist. That is a trial to help up the brute, to fill his crib, not to rescue man and woman with all their nobler aspirations. Otherwise, it stands with the later and more recent development of communism. Otherwise, it is with its present evolution, *socialism* as formulated by Rodbertus, Engels, and especially by the scientific expounder of that doctrine, I mean Karl Marx; as introduced into practical politics by the German Social Democracy, headed by

Lasalle and by the English *International*, inaugurated, too, by Karl Marx. Rejecting the communism as attempted in olden and in modern times by men of the calibre of Catiline, or by adventurers of the temper of John of Leyden, and in our own times by such as Babeuf or Spies, etc.—rejecting such attempts at violence and incendiarism, as contrary to common sense and contrary to the Bible, we cannot refuse our respect and full consideration to its latest evolution, denominated Socialism, or Social Democracy; without being hasty, even there, in giving our indiscriminate assent to all its propositions.

Wonderful! There we shall find out its many points of contact and many other points of striking contrast with the Mosaic scheme. Nay, we shall recognize even a strong affinity between the two systems, a kind of derivation, as between parent and offspring, as one developed from the other, no doubt with great variations in essentials and accidentals. Let us begin with the practical part of that system, as embodied in the program of the followers of Karl Marx and of Lasalle—fused in Gotha, Germany; the program promulgated in May, 1875. We shall have later enough of opportunity to dilate on the theory and abstruse principles of the State according to Marx and of society according to Moses. But for the moment let us begin to look at the practical features of the socialistic system in parallel with the Pentateucal one. The above-named Gotha program proclaims the following:

PROGRAM OF SOCIALISM.

" I. Labor is the source of all wealth and of all culture. To society and all its members, belongs the entire product of labor; by equal right; to each according to his reasonable wants; all being bound to work. In the existing society the tools of labor belong to the capitalists; hence, the subjugation of the working classes; this is the source of their wretchedness and servitude. Their emancipation therefore demands the transfer of such instruments of labor into the common property of society. Further, it demands society's control of all labor, the product of that labor to be for the common good and use, for just distribution among all.

" II. The socialistic workingman's party aims at a free State and a free society; at destroying the *iron law of wages* and removing exploitation and inequality. That party acknowledges the international character of the labor movement and desires the realization of the universal brotherhood of men. . . . In order to solve the social question, the party demands the establishment of socialistic productive associations, with State help, under democratic control by the laboring people, for industry and agriculture, slowly developing all labor. . . . They demand universal suffrage, universal military duty, no standing armies, direct legislation by the people, no exceptional laws, one single progressive income tax, etc., etc."

Now, we must not forget that this programme of the German Socialistic party of 1875 is a practical exposition of its aspirations, a good deal tempered with prudence, aiming at the *now* feasible and possible, under the *regime* of Bismarck and successors, etc., and the *Kaiser*, by no means merciful towards socialism. That programme is the lion's paw in a fur glove of prudence and caution. In order to know the real tenor of the doctrine, not even according to the versions of *Bakunin* and *Babeuf*, the revolutionary anarchists, but after the scientific, humane and prudent Karl Marx, Engels, etc., let us study the latter system in its general outline at least.

KARL MARX'S DOCTRINE.

Karl Marx, in his great work, "The Capital," a wonderful scientific work, the fruit of forty years' experience and of a lifetime devoted to ardent study, philanthropic aspirations and practical initiative in the workshop and in behalf of the proletarians,—this work, "Capital," the Bible of socialism, teaches essentially the following doctrine:

Labor is the source of all value. All objects of human usefulness derive their mercantile value from the labor bestowed on them. Air and sunlight, for instance, are most useful, but since they require no human work, since nature yields them spontaneously in great abundance, they have no marketable value. But in order to create a pair of shoes, do we not need also materials and tools? No doubt, but they, too, are the result of labor. Hence is labor the creator of the article in its present form, as shoes, and in its former form, as leather, skin or animal ;—the first elements come from the soil, and the soil is nature's, and belongs to all alike. The present use-value of the shoes, is therefore the labor bestowed on them. *"Labor, as the source of all value,"* is a kind of acknowledged head-principle of the leading political economists before Marx. He only developed it to a grand system of economics, the doctrine of socialism.

Now, that all-absorbing and all-creating labor is performed by the workingman ; hence all the value extant, all useful things, all real wealth, is the product of his toil, and by right is his—the just reward of his work! Now, what do we see in actual society, as it is, before our eyes? The laborer, the producer of all value, gets but a pittance thereof, hardly enough to sustain himself and his family, viz., the present and the future workers and drudges, whilst the surplus of value goes to the—Capitalist, under the pretense of rent for his lands, his machines, his tools and his outlays.— But lands are nature's; the capitalist did not create lands ; and the machines, tools and outlays have been, too, created by the workingman's labor, and are, therefore, his, and their produce ought to be his; all real value and wealth being the fruit of work, they must go to the worker, not to the capitalist, the drone. But what happens actually? After the pittance-wage for the work has been paid, the *"surplus value"* goes to the capitalist, and accumulates his capital. Capital is thus the accumulation of *unpaid labor*. The laborer got only a fraction for his sweat, his waste of life and his enslavement. The surplus goes to the capitalist, who has been living in idleness and luxuriance. Thus is established the startling doctrine that capital is robbery. But has not the capitalist powerfully contributed to the creation of the goods by his lands, his machines, his tools, his superintendence, his outlays? No! These claims are fictitious. The land is owned by nature.—"He that first enclosed a field and declared 'this is mine,' was the first robber" (J. J. Rousseau). Machines and tools are the product of work. The capitalist never did any work; his claims are thus contrived; he cheaply came to lands, tools, machines, etc., by conquest and robbery, or inheritance, a doubtful title, too, or by accumulating the surplus of unpaid labor—that is, by over-reaching the laborer, who had to give his work for a song. There was no free contract. He was compelled by the fierce competition of his fellow-proletarians to undersell his labor; he was handcuffed by the *"iron law of wages."* Indeed, when there is but one morsel of bread and five hungry mouths, there is no free competition, but actual slavery. Says Odysseus tersely, Odyss., VII, 216: "There is not such another formidable thing and more doggish than a hungry stomach, forcibly compelling us to think of him."[1] Our workingman, the real and only creator of wealth, being poor, was not free to wait and abide his time; hunger compelling him, he was no free party in his contract with the cunning and wealthy capitalist. The so-called free laborer is actually a slave, and

(1). οὐ γάρ τι στυγερῇ ἐπὶ γαστέρι κύντερον ἄλλο
ἔπλετο, ἥ τ' ἐκέλευσεν ἕο μνήσασθαι ἀνάγκῃ.

the employer is his tyrant, who puts him to such a stress as to work for half value and leave the other half to the master himself. The doctrine, universally accepted, that all wealth derives from work, flagrantly contradicts the principle of the "*iron law of wages*," this being but the tyranny of soulless competition, the workingman being really compelled to his bargain.—Hence, is there flagrant over-reaching; the capitalist is accumulating the *surplus value of unpaid labor*, and he is simply a robber, a usurer, a "Harpagon."

CRITICISM OF MARX'S SYSTEM.

So far Karl Marx's reasonings. But they are not wholly correct. Admitted that some capitalists may have come to part of their capital by foul means, or at least doubtful means, as conquest, fraud, violence, etc., that does not imply that all capitalists have acquired all capital by foul means. Admitted that conquests, over-reaching, pandering to princes, etc., are impure sources of acquisition, reason and fairness can but respect capital when it is the outcome of one's own honest savings and industry, or that of our father's life-long accumulations; and the rent of that economized capital is as justly ours as the capital itself. And if with that we buy lands or machines or tools, which are indispensably necessary for work, we are too, no doubt, entitled to their rent.

Thus all the great learning and ingenuity of Marx to prove the doubtful sources of some ownership, cannot shake the firm base of property in general; cannot prove that all ownership is robbery, that all is the result of taking advantage of the distressed laborer, crushed by the iron law of offer and demand. Still, there is some truth in all his reasonings. They prove that great landlordism, etc., may be tainted with a foul origin; that *often* profits go the wrong way; that employers, being stout-hearted, few and rich, whilst the

workers are many and poor, these labor under great disad-
vantages; that there is no freedom of contract between
such unequal parties; that competition may be carried to a
dangerous excess, or rather, that there is, on such terms, no
real, free competition, but a taking advantage and over-
reaching, coarse and mean, and that the law ought to look
to it. . . .

Let us take as an instance the landownership in our own,
young American society. No doubt, the first title to the
lands by the first conquerors is a precarious one. The American land belonged either to the Indians or to any human
being settling on and fertilizing it. Originally, the Bible
states correctly: "Mine is the land; ye are but My tenants."
Each shall have his lot and keep it. But does that prove
that the owner of the house I live in is a robber? That he
is not entitled to his rent? By no means. The land, originally seized upon, robbed or surreptitiously got for a toy, a
string of beads or for a barrel of whisky, a pistol or a pouch
of powder, has since passed through a hundred hands; the
last hand has paid the full price thereof, and asks now his
rent. Is he not entitled to it? Of course he is. The same,
when Charles V or Philip II of Spain got their *galleons*
of gold from Mexico and Peru by putting its owners, the
"*savages*," on burning coals, or by "teaching them true
religion." That gold dollar had a sad origin. But for that
same dollar you, honest reader, have been working a day or
an hour. Is that dollar not honestly yours? Can I say
that property is robbery? That would be absurd.

HERBERT SPENCER ON PROPERTY.

In his "Sociology," Vol. I, p. 292, and more especially in
"Sociology," Vol. II, pp. 536 to 541, Herbert Spencer makes
a profound study of the property question. With his usual
mastery of facts and sagacity of reasoning, he shows that
"the desire to appropriate and keep that which has once

8

been appropriated lies deeply not in human nature only, but in animal nature, too, being indeed a condition to survival. The consciousness thereof tends to establish the custom of leaving each in possession of what he has obtained by labor, and this claim is soon admitted by primitive men. . . . We see the claim to exclusive property understood by a dog fighting in defence of his master's clothing, left in charge of him. . . . So savages are boldly insisting upon their own weapons, canoes, huts, women, children, etc."

Herbert Spencer admits that the property title to the soil is not so clear as that to movables created by private labor. He says, then, §539: "At first land appears to be common property; how did possession of it become individualized? Force in one form or another is the sole adequate cause to make the members of a society yield up their just claims to the area they inhabit . . . to an external or internal aggressor, (conquest or usurpation)." He ominously concludes: "While private possession of things produced by labor will grow even more sacred than now, the inhabited area which cannot be produced by labor will not be privately possessed. . . As personal slavery was slowly abolished, so may be that of the land, and again become the property of all." Let us return to the original question, having given Spencer's opinion in parenthesis and having seen that the theory that "Property is Robbery" is untenable.

DISHONEST AND HONEST COMPETITION.

But now comes another side of the question, entirely overlooked, it seems, by socialists, viz: the important intellectual part of business, lodged in the chief. Now comes mental work, risks, force of initiative, commercial enterprise, capacity, solidarity, breadth of combination, etc. All these belong not to the workingmen in the factory, but to the careworn, thoughtful proprietor, partner or business manager in the rear office box, in the stately front cabinet or parlor, the *sanctum* of the head of the vast combination. Can any reasonable man say that the clerks and porters and office boys run the establishment, and that the leader, standing on the watchtower with frowning mien and anxious look, scanning the newspapers and telegrams and telephones, calculating the chances of the crops in America, the wars in Europe and the uprisings in Asia, weighing mentally, and balancing whether it is opportune to sell or buy, to wait or act, to take hold or let go,—can any one say that that brain, which gave the impulse to every motion, upon which everything is staked—that that busy *mental worker* is a drone, an idler, living upon the "surplus value of unpaid labor" of the workingmen? By no means. Hence, the first axiom of the system, viz: that labor is the source of all value; that value is produced by the labor of the mechanical worker alone, and without the chief and proprietor's initiative; that, therefore, rent for land, tools and machines, and the interest of the capital and the risks underlying the business and the profit of the leaders, are contrived and fictitious, and hence a robbery—that doctrine needs a strong qualification. It is practically untenable.

As matters have come down from hoary times, have crystallized and become organized thought of civilized men, the idea of property is firmly rooted in the human mind,—it is an instinct,—and the claim that it is but robbery is simply a paradox.

LAISSEZ ALLER.

What, then, has mankind gained by the studies of the modern economists, especially by those of Marx, Engels and Rodbertus? A good deal! The conviction that the old policy of *"laissez faire"* and *"laissez aller"*— *"Let go"*—is incorrect; that unequal as the struggle for

existence is between classes and masses, free competition
does not take place between privileged and ostracised, rich
and poor, educated and uneducated, etc.; that free competition is a misnomer, and that the State must step in, into
the unequal contest, and equalize chances. Now the extrem-
ists want us to throw out competition and give everyone
his share according to his needs, not his deeds; that, too, is
utopian, and will make society starve. The moderate view
is, let competition stand, but make it equal, free and with
the same chances for all. Then nobody will crush out his
neighbor, nobody being so much superior to his competitor·
Each will have work and bread, whilst the industrious, the
gifted, the thrifty, will and shall have more than bread, for
to that they are entitled. And society, too, will gain by
superior work. In such a way we shall have noble emulation, not beastly competition, and that alone will prove
sufficient, I think, to settle the social question.

I thus believe Marx's scientific analysis has shown, not
that "property is robbery," nor that competition is unjust,—
that is not warranted; that is jumping at conclusions.
What he has shown is: that some property is doubtful, that
the relation between employer and employe is not a free
one; hence, the contract between them is not free either;
that wage-labor is but a masked slavery, that there is no
free competition in reality; there is but a taking advantage of destitution; that society ought to step between and
protect the weaker party. Further, that we ought by education, State help, unions, etc., help the masses to RESTORE
FREE COMPETITION, when the social question will be solved;
at least until something better has been evolved. What
really Karl Marx has shown is: that the great property
holdings are not all allright; that much accumulation was
going on by *unfree* competition, by real over-reaching;
that the humbler party of the labor contractors are handcuffed and compelled to undersell their work. Human

society, therefore, is in duty bound to interfere in order to avoid moral and economic bankruptcy and social collapse. It must restore the equal chances in the battle for existence. It must make competition free and open. These are the legitimate results of Marx's labors, and they are vast and serious enough to help solve the social question.

This solution might be tried in the following several ways: To declare at once all property the property of all— that would not do! It would not be just nor prudent. The present property-holders will fight, and will probably come out victorious.—To proscribe all competition will be nearly as difficult; for by what measure else shall we decide upon merit and the value of things? The rational socialists do not propose revolution, confiscation, immediate assumption by the State of all capital and all production. They believe socialism to be the slow growth of the time, the necessary and gradual outcome of our public difficulties. They claim the present private competitive system is anarchic and nigh bankruptcy, and socialism bound to be the savior of society. Hence, let us go slowly and by degrees. What, then, would be the middle course and the connecting link between now and the future? Might we not try first by having this social drawback remedied, viz., competition being now handcuffed and lamed by privilege, *let it* (competition) *be free, fair and honest;* remove all obstacles; set free the combatants in the arena, and let us see whether that alone would not do. Indeed, as far as I see, there is rather no competition, and that is our real drawback; there is but sham competition allowed. The *commoner* cannot compete against the noble, the civilian cannot against the military, the foreign-born not against the native. The clericals have intrenched their rights against free competition. The learned profession have reserved their privileges against free competition. Such is the effort by every trade and profession to erect artificial intrenchments and privileges against free choice.—Wherever a vacancy occurs and candidates compete, look behind and you will find the backdoor open for some privileged aspirant. Not merit, but patronage, family, race, denomination, etc.; prevail. Publicly is *free competition advertised*, privately is *privilege practiced*. Ten to one is that the case. The people elect the best flatterer to office. The board of trustees, of directors, of managers, etc., appoint, not the superior candidate, but the best-sustained one—him with the largest backing. Why, then, overlook that? There is really, in most cases, no competition. The social contest goes on really by mere force, not merit; that is most glaringly. unjust and palpably wrong, and easily to be remedied. Let us begin *there* our reformation. Society is going by force; let us begin going by merit, real and honest. Let us begin with the introduction of real and honest competition. Any chance in life shall be given to the most competent one—to him who can offer the best work in return. Let us sincerely abolish brute force, covered by rotten privilege and patronage. Among the different candidates, let he or she be selected who can do the best work; let him or her profit by their own industry, or skill, or talent, and society will be the winner. Then let us see whether that alone will not do to solve the social problem. As far as I see, social wrong is going on, not for crushing competition, but for competition crushed out and privilege and favoritism put in instead. Let us, therefore, give a fair trial to fair competition. Next may come another social phase. We have been going by force and privilege. Let us now try right, viz., competition, fair and just. *Later we may come to love in place of right.*

This proposition of real competition has at least the merit of a wise and honest experiment. Society has been really going on by the principle of favoritism, patronage and privilege, under the false pretenses of free competition.

The masses, crushed by feudal privilege, mistook it for competition; thus duped, they think that to be at the bottom of
our social Pandora-box: "Down with competition; it is
cruel and crushing!" shout the woe-stricken in their dilemma: "It is giving all advantage to the stronger." No doubt,
free competition is not ideal. It does give the premium
to the stronger, the wiser, the more persevering.—But at
least it is just, if not ideal.—Let us give it a fair trial.—Let us
begin going by free competition. Let us give to the greater
merit, the greater premium.—Anyhow, society will gain
by it, it will realize better work; whilst by patronage
society is undoubtedly the loser—and none the gainer, but
inferiority.—Should time show that free competition will
not remedy the social question, we can then resort to the
No-competition-policy, and give each according to needs, not
merits. In one word: The hue and cry that free competition is at the bottom of our social evils, is anyhow prema-
ture, unproven and perhaps contrived, for it is a fact,
palpable to every close observer, that society goes as yet
by privilege and stratagem, not by honest and free competition, hence the present social evils cannot be put at its
door.—Now consider: privilege and patronage are decidedly
wrong and foolish. Competition, indeed, is hard and sharp,
but it is just. Socialism aims at the ideal of non-compe-
tition, at giving according to needs—not merits. Would it
not be wiser not to jump to the ideal, but begin with the
just and the real, before we take refuge in the ideal?

Now this tempered competition, to give everyone his
reward according to his real merit—not favoritism or privilege—is represented in the Biblical State. "One law for
native and stranger." "Discriminate not in justice,"—
"favor not the poor, nor the rich." "Have not two stones
and two measures." "Justice is God's; tamper not with
it," etc. Could not statesmen learn therefrom?

KARL MARX—CONTINUED.

Karl Marx believes to have proven, after reviewing the history of wealth and property, that lands, instruments and capital belong to all and have been usurped by a few. Therefore are these few not entitled to them, nor to their rent. He shows that political history began in hoary times with slavery; that thereupon, after the migration of the Teutonic nations and the collapse of the Roman Empire, came serfdom and feudalism ; that with the reformation, the confiscation of church-property, the discovery of America, of gunpowder and the printing press, the collapse of feudalism, the utilization of steam, the inventions of machines, etc., and after the American and French Revolutions—serfdom gave way and made room for wage-labor. He shows that this is but a masked slavery, that the proletarians are severed from the means of human comforts and human culture, that society is on the way to anarchy and bankruptcy, and that a new social phase is ready to dawn, which is to right this long wronged fourth estate, the masses; in place of the present, private, competitive capital and wage-labor is coming the era of collective capital and associated labor, for the good of all. The profit is to belong to all society, to all its members and workers, which profit shall be divided out according to some "equitable principle."

What is that equitable principle? Shall there be some discrimination made among the different crafts? Between the degrees of capacity? Between excellent, good and indifferent work? Who shall be the arbiter? Who shall formulate that equitable principle? Who shall administer the distribution of profits? Shall there be rulers in the future society or not? These different questions are diversely answered by the several doctrinaires of the system. Indeed, these questions are hard to answer; yea, they are absolutely impossible to answer, for they are relative.

They depend upon factors we know not, and which alone will determine the mode of solution.

BAKUNIN'S FALLACIES.

Bakunin, the Russian Anarchist, wants no rulers whatever, for rulers will soon be tyrants. They will rule to keep forever the people as slaves for exploitation, for the advantage of the leaders. He wants only such laws and restraints as are self-evident and dictated by nature, and will be obeyed without coercion.

A great idealist is he, that terrible Anarchist Bakunin! His ideals will need a long while before they be real. It may need *æons* of years before man will obey the laws of nature without coercion. All good laws now extant, from the decalogue downwards, are mostly, if not all, rational, natural and self-evident to the impartial and honest reasoner. Yet they need coercion to make them be obeyed. "Pray for the government," says an oriental proverb; "If not for that, men would swallow each other alive." (¹)

Again, if we shall have laws, king, Senate or Parliament must make them, and that means again monarchy or aristocracy or oligarchy; that means rulers, and we have thus come back to the position where we started from. Again, *Saint Simon and Owen* had an idea of utilizing the existing governments, the patriarchal, the sacerdotal or the monarchical, for the realization of their designs. Bakunin's ideas appear thus utopian. Men need government.

KARL MARX'S OPTIMISM.

Karl Marx, the most scientific and sober-minded of the socialistic galaxy, is at the same time the most noble idealist, and, I am afraid, the greatest dreamer, too. He expects a real millenium from social democracy. Having himself spent a noble life in toil and sacrifice, in abnegation

and poverty for the good of the masses, he believes in a
whole crop of such unselfishness and altruism. His nobility
of idealism strikingly proves him to be a son of the
prophets—a self-sacrificing Messiah of our own times. How
does he solve the problem? The social democracy will
need laws and lawgivers and leaders, and these will be the
best, the noblest, the most refined, just as the Mosaic "elders"
and the Platonic "sages." They will be picked out by the
people, not for flattery, but for real merit; and this office,
this opportunity of *doing good, will be their reward.* The
best of the people will feel rewarded by working for the
good of the people.—That the people will, perchance, chose
the worst demagogues, those flattering and corrupting them,
Marx has never realized! The best men and women, he
thinks, will be rewarded by being called to govern. That
was Plato's dream, too, and Moses' belief, too; yet Socrates
had to drink the hemlock and *Korah* had almost supplanted
Moses. We moderns have made experience enough, carefully studying history, that the people will select those
that corrupt and exploit them, if left to their own feelings;
and if influenced, their choice will not be quite so bad, but
surely not the best. How, then, get out of that dilemma?
Perhaps by indirect selection; choice by deputy.—Anyhow,
it is not so easy to tell.

The Socialistic Ideal.

Karl Marx believes that the leaders of the democracy
will soon be their political rulers—the noblest and most
unselfish of mankind. They will make the laws and administer them to the satisfaction of all parties concerned.—
Yes, the leaders of the present democracy may be so. But
let that system triumph, and you will have a crowd of
demagogues and camp-followers yelling with the crowd
and getting their own nominations and sinecures.

Curious to remark, that, with so much enthusiasm, so much faith in the good instincts of the masses and the nobility of their leaders, Marx is a materialist of the most despairing kind—no God, and yet an ideal man! You see, he has a Hegelian head and a prophet's heart; there is no God, but there is the Messiah! "The kingdom of heaven will dawn upon earth," though there is no heaven. . . .

He believes that democracy is now coming to the front. Democracy, he claims, has now the helm of government. It is changing monarchical, aristocratic and plutocratic rule into the rule of the masses. These democratic rulers, indeed, are now but proletarians, carpet-baggers; but once they are well established in power and have changed politics, they will soon change economics, too. By what means? Violence and confiscation, as advised by Bakunin and tried by Babeuf? Marx answers: "By the slow process of evolution," viz: Society will find out that it must change its system from slave and wage-labor to collective socialistic labor and equal distribution of profits; that it must do justice to the laboring masses, now pariahs and dynamiters, or perish. That he proves in this manner: The present system of wage-labor is but one century old, and already it has drawn the State into the straits of plutocracy and pauperism. Infinite vice, idleness and luxuriousness on one side, and on the other, wretched poverty, lack of education, coarse crime and vice, and dangerous dissatisfaction.

MARX'S DENUNCIATIONS.

Again that system ruins not only rich and poor, but even work itself. For competition is commanding cheap labor and cheap goods, at the price of beauty, taste and strength. Next it ruins the moral sense of all, each thinking only of himself, all society being rivals and enemies. Already it shows signs of threatening danger; the Damocles sword is hanging over the heads of society, with its wars of nations, classes and masses, races and countries, its anarchy, confusion and insecurity for all, even the strongest and wealthiest. Again he shows that the small agriculturist, tradesman and laborer, once fairly happy with their lot, have been crushed out by the capitalist. Soon, the capitalist has been so by the great capitalist, and this one in his turn is so by the great companies, which will be absorbed by the State, at last. Again, our gigantic, modern improvements in agriculture and industry, with huge factories, machines, steam, etc., require things to be done all on a grand scale. The former individual worker can now no longer successfully compete. Small producers and individual workers, as of old, become less and less possible. All is now centralized, all done on a grand scale, or crushed out by the huge combinations. Even these huge companies are often crippled by rivalry. They over-produce and over-stock the market and starve each other by over-production, and by underselling. As a man dies by over-feeding, so they by creating too much wealth, by *plethora*. To save themselves, they, at last, are compelled to agree upon some equitable plan, good for all, by *union*. Just that is what Socialism drives at. Slowly it will supplant individual labor and individual capital, with their soulless envy and competition, with fraud and anxiety, etc., by *collective labor* and *collective capital*. Slowly it will include the entire State, with all its individuals, thus avoiding both bad work and competition, making each do the best for all, and yielding him or her a fair share in the profits. This is the noble ideal of Socialism.

DEMOCRACY, INVENTIONS AND SOCIALISM.

Mankind thus expects its regeneration, its emancipation, the solution of the great social question by a combination of the great social factors, viz: Democracy, Inventions and Socialism. By Voltaire's and Rousseau's doctrines of fraternity and equality for all on one hand, and on the other by England's industrial inventions, combined with lands, tools and capital belonging to the State, the State controlling all labor, and dividing its profits equitably among all, with no difference of creed, race, sex or country; all nations to be sister-nations; all men brothers—what a noble idealism? What a breadth of thought, embracing the globe and mankind in one mighty bond of justice and love to all! Marx is a son of the prophets. His ideal heart and his vast brain show it.

PARALLELS AND CONTRASTS IN BIBLE AND SOCIALISM.

We started with the proposition that the Bible has nothing to do with communism, or that cruder form of socialism, as tried by anarchists in bygone times, from Catiline to Babeuf and the Chicago Haymarket tragedy. But the Bible has a great deal to do with its higher and nobler evolution, now termed Social Democracy. Nay, I may say that many of the noblest aspirations of the latter, grew out, perhaps unconsciously, of the prophetic ideal about State and Society.

Social democracy, in its above-mentioned Gotha manifesto of 1875, aspires to a commonwealth "where everything belongs to the community and all its members; land, tools, capital and labor, by equal right, all bound to work, and all to share, according to their reasonable wants." This programme is entirely biblical. Mosaism declares: "Mine are the children of Israel; they cannot be enslaved." "Thy brother, hired out for six years, thou shalt not crush under hard labor." (¹)—"Mine is the soil; ye are but its tenants. Ye shall not sell it for ever."—On the Jubilee the family-lot and the family-house shall be restored to the original owner.—"Thou shalt take no interest on money nor profit upon any goods of thy brother."—"Ye shall not press nor

(1) בכרך.

over-reach each other."—But the Mosaic system has the advantage over socialism in giving to each definitely his portion, for himself and his posterity. Thus, it makes him interested in the improvement of his acre, he providing by it for himself and his descendants. It is not utopian in its propositions. It proceeds slowly from experience to experience. It proceeds with less startling innovations, and, hence, it is much surer of practical success. The entangling socialistic scheme of having everything turned over to the State, and then the State to become the treasurer of all the wealth, the superintendent of all the work, the sole *enterpreneur* and employer, the sole distributor of labor and emolument to the communal members, renders the system hazardous and hard of execution, problematic and utopian, perhaps never to be realized.

Social democracy demands the surrender of all lands and of most of movable property to the State. It asks the surrender, too, of the citizen's individual work, talent, inclination, taste, etc., to the good judgment of the State. How shall that be realized? since every one, possessing anything, inherited or acquired, naturally clings to it. By confiscation? That is doubtful justice or wisdom, and will bring on discontent and social war. How else, then? By slow compromise? But the urgent necessity of satisfying the starving, threatening masses! That is a long road to travel by and very precarious. To begin with tearing down the well-tried house and build up, perhaps, a castle in the air! What do we know how that exceedingly complicated system would work? Compromise will need five centuries; but the masses won't wait.—The Bible contrived something plainer, quicker, safer, less drawing upon the imagination, viz: The equal distribution of the chief capital of those times, *land;* leaving all other things, as effort, taste, inclination, acquisition, competition, etc., a private matter, all tempered with sympathy. It enjoined the descent of land, peremptorily, to posterity, prohibiting rigorously all land speculation and grabbing, thus erecting a dam and bulwark against plutocracy and pauperism, landlordism and serfdom. Of the two schemes, I think the biblical one the less hazardous and more realistic, pretty well calculated for primitive conditions and modest claims, where every one was content to live "under his vine and his fig tree."

Socialistic democracy desires a State without a despot, ruling classes and serving masses, no proletarians, no paupers, no inequality, no exploitation and no exceptional laws· It acknowledges a brotherhood of peoples and of men, the equality of the sexes and races. All that is biblical; it is Mosaic and New Testamentary. The Bible began with nothing. Later, even when it admitted a ruler, he was to be a "*brother*," not a despot, without seraglio, exorbitant wealth and a standing army.

Social democracy labors with might and main to eliminate the "*iron law of wages*." Such a "law" was not in the biblical state, nor was there any remedy necessary against it, for every one had his own house and acre. There were few, if any, baronial planters, grand industrials, etc., and no opportunity to leave one's own workshop and crowd into factories, with bad air, immorality and slavery; each worked on his own farm, adding occasionally one or two "hand laborers." Very few had work and wages wherewith to buy off their neighbor's liberty or morality. Boaz, cultivating a large farm, and Nabal, master of many flocks, were the rare exceptions, and their "hands" were slaves, no doubt.

Socialistic democracy demands State help for grand socialistic industries, slowly to form one unique State-industry, with all the citizens crowding into its workshops. This is depriving each citizen of his individual inclination, judgment, initiative and stimulant for effort. This policy

is very problematic. We may form in that way good tools,
but the tools may prove poor individuals. We may establish in that manner good workshops, but create a poor
community.

That may cost mankind half of its men of genius and
talent. The great aim of society is to build up solid and
noble citizens.—Industry must be subordinate to it. The
Bible needed no such contrivance. It left every man to
his native initiative, yet preventing competition from
becoming mischievous. It rather allowed emulation, not
competition.

Social Democracy demands universal suffrage, direct legislation, no exceptional laws, no privileges, and no discrimination of race, creed, sex or class. It insists on one simple,
progressive income tax; no standing armies, but military
duty for all. All that is literally Mosaic. According to
the Bible, the people consented to each and all the laws.
That is expressly propounded by Moses and emphasized by
Joshua; there was ONE law for classes and masses, one for
native and stranger; no legal discrimination against whom-
soever. The categories, "priests," ("*Cohanim,*") " Levites "
and "Israelites" had an ecclesiastical bearing, not a civil
or lay one. They intermarried, interchanged professions
and trades; had no castes, no privileges and no restrictions. Many a public teacher, many a Synhedrist or Sena-
tor, was by trade a shoemaker or carpenter, a smith, a
weaver, a physician. There was impartial and free justice
in Judæa; no standing armies and no pretorian guards; no
dynasties by "divine descent," no noble "blue blood," and
no extravagant display of loyalty to, nor adoration of, king
or highpriest. There was but one tax from the produce of
the soil and the flocks; a direct income tax, levied without
harshness, rather voluntarily prompted by mere conscience.

Socialistic Democracy declares for international solidarity
of the peoples and for the brotherhood of mankind. Hence

comes their personal freedom and social equality. Hence their right to share in all the boons and the wealth of nature. This principle, the grandest and noblest idea of Socialism, hails directly from the Bible. Hindooism, Egypt, Greece and Rome knew it not; the Bible did. It lacks, unfortunately, in Socialism a firm basis and all substantiation, though the entire system hinges upon it; for the Socialistic leaders are materialists, and materialism yields no standing room for solidarity and brotherhood; Monotheism does. That all men are free and equal and entitled to happiness, culture and bread—how will you prove it from the standpoint of materialism? Is there freedom in nature? Are children born equal? Does not the stronger and the more cunning rule in nature? You build upon the ideal goodness of man, his sympathy, his altruism, —are these to be found in brute nature?

The materialists repudiate the God-ideal and deny the divine Providence which made right slowly supersede might, commanded virtue supernaturally, or ordained it primordially, in the deep essence of things, having fitted our instincts and our interests for virtue and goodness. These ideas they rule out, and yet they hope for them and postulate them as their corner-stone! No, these ideas and aspirations are pieces of mosaic, taken over from Mosaism, blocks of stone, hewn from the biblical quarries, the Old and the New Testament, the two breasts whereat you Socialists first sucked in your humanity; they remained, unconsciously, at the bottom of your hearts, to serve now as the needed foundation of your system, otherwise, hanging in the air. You see, materialism is no base for the old nor the new system. You can build up no humanity without idealism, and idealism is the offspring of the God-belief.

A profane wit once remarked: "The Mosaic religion is a religious mosaic." That is good enough for a witticism, not for truth. The unprejudiced student can not but admire

9

the adamantine solidity of that legislation. Created by a man or a school, during a lifetime or centuries, we cannot help admitting that there is one set of principles running through its many,.varied books, from Pentateuch to Chronicles, from beginning to end, making it one grand, harmonious whole, all answering the legislator's purpose, viz: the establishing of "*a kingdom of priests and a holy nation.*" The entire work is growing out of one piece as an antique monolith, or as the "golden chandelier in the Temple." Look how the Bible is solidly consistent, without being less rational for that. It starts the world and the State with its God-idea: "In the beginning God created Heaven and earth." (Genesis I, 1.)—"I am the Eternal who liberated thee from Egypt." (Exodus 20, 1.)—Thus is He the very corner-stone of the entire social structure. He delivered his people from oppression, gave it freedom, a country, lands and laws, freely accepted by it. He is a "Holy One."— " He is not to be bribed or intimidated " by "king or priest." —" He is the holy Being," hence shall his people be holy (III. M. 19, 1.)—This very same chapter gives the definition of its grand opening verse, viz: "*To be holy,*" means to be moral, just and educated, chaste, forgiving, sober, merciful and charitable.—All the biblical peoples, with all mankind, spring from one parent couple; hence are they brothers! All equal and all free; hence shall the weak, the women, the children, the poor stranger, etc., be treated with mercy and forbearance.—Property is sacred, chastity is holy, hence the sacredness of marriage and parenthood; hence " Honor thy father and thy mother."—" Love thy neighbor as thyself."—" Love the stranger as thyself."—Hence the New Testament. " Love thy enemy as thyself; if he insults thee, pardon him; if he strikes thee, disarm him by meekness; if he robs thee, rather give him more."—A trifle, perhaps, too lofty for man as he is. Yet it is a noble ideal of goodness and meekness, yea, even of prudence. It is

good and worthy of a man who dies for what he thinks to
be right.

Now whilst social democracy is aspiring to an ideality
even greater than that of the Old and the New Testament,
postulating unselfishness and self-sacrifice, not as an exception, but as the rule, as the daily habit and nature of each
and every man, it, nevertheless, rules out God and worship,
providence, marriage and family! Yet these latter ones
are perfectly compatible with reason, and at the same time
give the human state a firmer base than socialism has ever
contrived. Materialism is a poor background for a State
based on morality and ideality. I am afraid materialism
rather suits despotism and coercive duty, controlled by a
tyrant.

MARX, SON OF THE PROPHETS.

As in Spinoza's system we recognize its best elements to
have come from early educational impressions, from
Bible, prophets, mystics and philosophers, whilst its sad
aspects were derived from strange sources: even so in the
system of Karl Marx we perceive how his best political
material, his broad humanity, his noble social solidarity,
his deep, thrilling sympathy with human woes, his great
anxiety and bold initiative to remedy them, were imbibed
with his mother's milk, drawn at the breast of Moses and
the prophets; whilst the weaker points of his system, the
denying of any and every religious ideal, of any Providence
working deep in the bowels of nature, his abandoning all
divine piety and family piety, all worship and all churches
as exploded theories and effete institutions, yet asking, at
the same time, all the noble virtues cultivated through
them,—disclose spiritualism and materialism, inconsistently
yoked together.—Having learned from Hegel self-deifica-
tion, he needs no higher ideal. His brain is his Sinai.
Yet, Prometheus-like, he feels the vulture of doubt gnaw-

ing at his vitals. He feels the urgent need of a base for his system, and accepts man's goodness from sheer despair. That reminds us of Heine's satirical remark: "Kant had first destroyed the God-ideal with his demonstrations in the 'Theoretical Reason.' But he thought '*Lampe* must have an ideal,' and he restored it in his 'Practical Reason.'" Even so Karl Marx: "My followers must have faith in human goodness, and I postulate it without any further proof." He claims to believe in evolution, and this is utterly incompatible with materialism. Evolution really means: Things are so primordially arranged that the wise and the just will and must slowly succeed. Whether he believes it, or only claims to do so, is hard to tell. The Bible believes in Providence, and bases consistently its society upon it. It can claim virtue and self-sacrifice of man,—because there is a "holy God."—And why not? *When there is evolution, must there not be Providence?* When there is primordially ordained an eternal fitness of things, must there not be a Providence having shaped things that way? . . .

SOCIALISM AND BIBLE.

We have seen that a higher evolution of Communism is Socialism; here the points of contact with the biblical system are numerous, and the contrasts are striking.

The Marx-Lasalle Socialism begins with declaring for the necessity of society acquiring all lands, instruments and capital. But how will they realize that, since these lands, instruments and capital are at present private property? By open confiscation? That is Communism! Marx and Lasalle as yet deprecate that; Bakunin's anarchy and downright spoliation having been repudiated by them. If so, how, then, make private lands and capital public?—The next difficulty is, perhaps, even greater; supposing all belong to the Socialistic Democracy, the future evolution of society; supposing that miracle is performed, what next?

The social leaders will inaugurate associated and collective industries for the general benefit, giving to each a share of the profits, according to his or her capacity and their reasonable wants.—But who shall be the judge thereof? Again, who shall determine the nature and the amount of the work, and the share of profits or the "reasonableness of every one's wants?" Who will be judge and ruler, and who will meekly accept the role of the drudge, with the poor wage of such? Arbiters? Will there not be heard the old hue and cry at partiality? Will the drudges abide by it? Do we expect the arbiters to be angels and never be partial? But supposing even they would be angels, and treat every worker "according to his true deserts," his talents, diligence and self-sacrifice; "Who will then escape a whipping?"—to speak with Shakespeare —"If the greater merit will have a larger share, and the humbler talents a smaller one, what have we gained by Socialism?" We shall again have the old competition, crushing competition, which was expected to be eliminated in the future Socialistic Democracy! Or should we follow out the hints of some other socialistic idealists and assume the utopia that all workers should be treated alike, all fed, housed, dressed, etc., alike, as in old Sparta—and that we should reward merit only by a civic wreath, only by an honorable recognition of public services, by enrollment into a democratic "legion of honor?"—How many such self-sacrificing men and women, for the sake of philanthropy, can we reasonably expect? Will not the vast majority of usual commonplace people prefer doing as little as possible, and declare to be "ladies and gentlemen," having many wants, but little inclination for hard work? No doubt there are a few select persons who are happy in doing good deeds for society's sake, with few needs to sustain life; but the vast majority of mortals are just the contrary. If not stimulated by hunger and want, if not fired on by personal advantages and substantial emoluments, they will do as little as possible, and society will soon starve. The socialistic scheme is expecting, therefore, a second miracle, viz., that all people should become ideals, and do the most and best work for philanthropy's sake.— May it not be utopian?

And the biblical scheme! Three thousand years ago, in the hoary past, that Mosaic scheme seems to have been more practical. The first miracle, it needed not. The lawgiver had a *tabula-rasa* society to deal with, whose members were nearly equally circumstanced. Their instruments of labor were as yet in his own hands, God being King. He divided the lands fairly among the citizens, and provided for the perpetual maintenance of the family-lot. He thus could hope to have put a barrier against *accapparating* the soil by a few. Each cultivating and enjoying his crops, the difficulty of distribution was avoided. Nor was there allowed internal profitable commerce, or external enriching wars, to disturb that balance of wealth among the social members. Moses kept, therefore, the original economic relations of the wealth of his community pretty well stationary. Add to that his demanding personal liberty and social equality; add his grand, ennobling, weekly Sabbath institution; his frequent Release-years, with their extinction of debts; his other numerous benevolent statutes, tending to keep up the feeling of solidarity and brotherhood among the nation; add his entire system, identifying State, religion and people, permeating and fusing each with the other, without any fear of abuse; adding all that, we might be warranted to come to the conclusion that his political economy system had many chances of success, at least during the first period of Ebrew history, if ever fairly put on trial. For the circumstances then extant (three thousand years ago) it was vastly superior to our socialistic scheme. All capital and instruments of labor, land inclu-

sive, were in his grasp. Hence, this difficulty did not exist
for him. But the second one—how to fairly distribute the
profits of labor among the workers—he likewise avoided by
giving each a lot to cultivate and enjoy its fruit. Everyone
had, therefore, his share in his own hands, needing thus no
arbitrators and avoiding jealousy and discontent. The
family-lot was inalienable; it remained for ever and ever
to the descendants of the original owner, or rather tenant.
Hence, it operated against proletarianism. No one ever
was born absolutely poor. It evaded landlordism by giving
no food for land-grabbing, absolute acquisition of new acres
being simply impossible. The no-commerce and no-war
policy, stopping all avenues of suddenly acquiring or losing
wealth, insured the average economic equality, and, hence,
the liberty and equality of all was never undermined.

THE SEPTENNATE.

The biblical system no doubt has many advantages. It
combines the old and the new State-ideas. The individual
has all free play, yet grasping and soulless competition is
checked. Work and emulation are stimulated by self-
interest and emolument; yet there is room left for every
one's efforts, even for the humbler talents. There is freedom of thrift and acquisition, yet these are kept in bounds
by the fact of the soil being stationary and inalienable, and
no internal commerce or depredatory wars being allowed.
The unity of the family, of the nation and of worship is
kept up.—Society rested upon idealism; superior to materialism, to a shifting family, a vague internationalism,
without any base and *raison d'être*, those three pillars
of the Socialistic Society. Imagine! No religion, no fixed
family, no national feeling, and yet the claim of the fraternity
of mankind. Yet to ask of one to work and toil without
any personal reward—for goodness sake, for philanthropy,
for the love of humanity! Materialism and self-sacrifice

to humanity? We should therefore incline to think Karl Marx's system more utopian than the Mosaic one.

SEPTENNATE NEVER TRIED YET.

Yet many drawbacks are in the way of suggesting the Mosaic social democracy for our times and our circumstances. For would present mankind ever consent to the Judæan simplicity, poverty, uniformity? Could we ever think of breaking our soil into as many lots as male citizens? Could we then utilize our present machines and instruments of labor, railways and steam engines, by making each laborer work for his own account? Or shall we give up our fine industries, our noble arts, our grand commerce, and come back to the simplicity of Judæa? Evidently that would be retrogression. Besides, the simple fact that the biblical, political economy never was tried, may be a fair presumption that even in antiquity it was not feasible. There were among the Talmudists solid thinkers, men not inferior to our modern economists and socialistic leaders, full of philanthropy and sympathy for the proletariat. When, two thousand years ago, the Herodian policy, or the school of Hillel, abolished, stone after stone, all of the biblical economic structure, that may suggest the fair presumption that the system seemed not realizable, and that conditions had altered greatly, at least under the rule of the Herodians, the slaves of the Cæsars. Nevertheless, present political economists may ponder over the biblical way of solving the social problem, for, anyhow, there may be yet many elements left, if not the entire structure, fit for adaptation to our evolving society of the present time. Great lawgivers have suggestions in store even for late posterity.

SABBATH AND THE SOCIAL QUESTION.

We have largely spoken of the Jubilee and the Release-year-laws, and we have hinted at their root being the *Biblical Sabbath.* We now come to that weighty theme, one of the most important traits of Mosaism, slowly developing through the Gospels and Islam into an institution of the grandest dimensions. Well, that Sabbath forms the basis of the Jubilee and the Release-year.

What is the Sabbath? A symbol, a sacrament, a ceremony, religious rite, and no more? Let us take time and elucidate the question; it may prove of great interest to the thoughtful.

For thousands of years the Ebrew people are celebrating that day; for nearly fifteen centuries the vast, Christian world does the same; and for six hundred years the Mohammedan world has adopted it, too. Nay, even Rationalists and non-Sectarians recognize its necessity. The German Social democrats at Gotha, in 1875, mentioned, too, in their program that Rest-day as necessary for the welfare of the workingman. The Sabbath is one of the great traits and characteristics of the Sinai-law; both the Decalogues enjoin it with great solemnity. It is repeated a hundred times in Pentateuch, Prophets, etc. It is termed ([1]) the "sign of the Covenant," the "eternal Covenant," between God and his people; the distinguishing trait of Monotheism and Mosaism, the flag and badge of that ancient legislation (II. M. 31, 13-15.) ([2]) Humanely considered, what is the object of that institution? At what does it aim? We said it is the *symbol of Mosaism.* Well, there was another symbol for *Abraham,* ([3]) and still another for *Noah.* ([4]) Is, then, the weekly rest-day of no greater practical importance than these two last mentioned? Is it nothing more

---

(4) קשת.   (3) מילה.   (2) ברית עולם.   (1) אות ברית.

than a sign and a means to bring home to the votary of
Jahveh some certain idea of consequence? What is that
idea? The Sabbath-commandment is most frequently
repeated in the Pentateuch. *After* the doctrine of the
unity and immateriality of God, the strict observance of
the Rest-day is most frequently and forcibly enjoined in
Sacred Writ, especially in both the Decalogues. And all
that pomp and display means but a *mere sign, a symbol*, a
sacrament? Is that probable? And if not, what else is the
real object of that weekly institution?

THE BIBLE ON THE SABBATH.

In order to be enabled to fairly answer this important
question, let us read the more conspicuous biblical passages
concerning it. (Gen. II., 1-3). "Thus the heavens, the earth
and all their hosts were finished, etc.; and on the seventh
day God had accomplished the work to be done; and He
rested on the seventh day and sanctified it."

Shall we now understand that the Sabbath institution is
contemporaneous with the creation? Is it, so to say, the
day of divine rest and the inauguration of the world?
Modern science cannot be satisfied herewith. Even the
Ebrew Agada does not take it literally. See *Jalkut* thereto.—
Next let us read (*Exodus* 20, 8-11): "Remember the
Sabbath day to sanctify it. Six days shalt thou labor, and
the seventh day is a rest to thy God . . . for in six
days He had made heaven and earth and rested on the
seventh. Therefore he blessed the Sabbath day and sanctified it."

Here in the grandest passage of S. Script., the Decalogue,
the covenant between God and His people, the constitution
of mankind, the corner-stone of human civilization; here,
immediately after the sublime declaration of the divine
unity, we read the commandment concerning the Rest-day,
in the most solemn and most emphatic manner. And this

apparently refers to the above tradition of the cosmogony :
"For in six days God created heaven and earth and rested
on the seventh ; therefore, He blessed and sanctified it."
(Gen. II., 2).—Which the Agada correctly takes as a preamble to the Sabbath.

Let us read a third passage on the subject (Deut. V. 12-16) :
"Observe the Sabbath day and sanctify it, as God has
bidden thee, etc., etc., that thy male and female-servants
may rest like thyself. And remember that thou hast been
a slave in Egypt, etc., therefore, God bade thee to have a
Rest-day."—Here, in the second Decalogue, we find in the
same place, with the same solemnity and with even more
circumstantiality, the commandments bearing on our subject forcibly repeated. Yet remark : as the aim and reason
therefor, we find no longer the cosmogonical divine rest
after the six days creation, but the practical, human object :
"that thy male and female servants may rest like thyself,"
especially remembering the Egyptian slavery. Here we
see that the aim is not mystic and supernatural, but entirely
practical, palpable, humanitarian, moral, yea, social and
political.—Plainer yet it reads in II. M. 23, 12 : "That thy
beast, thy slave and thy stranger may rest and recreate
themselves."

These passages bearing upon our question, will be our
guides in trying to ascertain the scope of the legislation in
this weekly institution. The first quotation (Gen. II, 2,)
bases the Sabbath rest-day upon the divine rest after the
six creation days. Exactly the same version is given in the
second quotation (Exod. 20, 11.)—The third (Deut. V, 15,)
brings in two new factors of an entirely natural and human
character, viz: the rest, the re-creation of the dependent
enslaved masses, and the commemoration of the exodus
from Egypt. Finally, the fourth passage (in Exod. 23, 12,)
is the plainest, setting forth the aim and sense of the lawgiver in the simplest terms, without a shadow of supernatural-

ism, viz: The re-creation of the hard-working people, and the sympathy even with the toiling beast. The supernatural and the historical motives are passed by; the physiological, the political, or the philanthropical one is set forth with all desirable plainness and simplicity. It is this aspect of the Sabbath institution which interests us here, in our study of the sociological bearings of the Bible and its legislation. Let us closely examine these texts and endeavor to get at the political idea of the legislator. Beginning with the first: "God had finished his work and he rested on the seventh day, and he blessed that day and sanctified it." (I. M. 2, 2.)—Speaking here of the Bible from the legislative standpoint, we are not called upon to treat of these words in their literal sense and as matters of fact. That is the domain of theology. The historian has another range of thought, having seen that even the Agada takes them as but a poetical substantiation of the Sabbath, instituted at a later time.

The second Decalogue gives, moreover, as the aim of the Sabbath-day, the remembrance of the event of the exodus from Egypt. Is this to be taken literally? Is the Rest-day a commemoration of Ebrew national independence, .a kind of weekly Passover? Who can be in earnest with this acceptation? Who ever brought the Sabbath in historical connection with Egypt? Do we not, so to say, intuitively feel that our verses in Genesis, Exodus and Deuteronomy must be understood in their deeper sense?

TALMUD AND PHILOSOPHERS ON THE SABBATH.

Rabbinical, as well as modern, thinkers contrived many other explanations, perfectly well worth looking at. Some said: The Sabbath is an institution in memory of the world's creation; that the world was created and had a beginning; by God, alone uncreated, alone without beginning, free-willed and self-conscious.

Thus, these Rabbinical philosophers think Sabbath to be a kind of demonstration in favor of the transcendental, spiritual, Mosaic God, in contra-distinction from the Pantheistic conception of Deity, identical with or inherent in the world. We feel how little interest such abstract questions, such abstruse speculations, offer to the mass of the people. Is it possible, then, that the great lawgiver should create an institution of such magnitude, for all eternity, and such practical bearings, with an abstract, philosophical object in view? With no other aim, indeed, than to favor one philosophical system and protest against another one? Where do we find Moses so anxious about abstract ideas and opinions which never had any practical influence upon the people? There is another theory in store on our subject, viz: Some modern philanthropists believe Sabbath to be a kind of sanctification of labor, a protest against the contempt of work, so prevalent in antiquity. But how should an injunction for rest, absolute abstention from work, have for its aim the rehabilitation of labor? To honor labor by commanding rest? I have to call attention to one circumstance more. I mentioned before how often, how circumstantially and emphatically the Rest-day is repeated. The lawgiver spares no means of impressing it upon the physiognomy of his system. He designates it as his special sign. He punishes its transgression with death. He places it in the Decalogue, the great essence of the Pentateuch. Now, look at the commandments contained in that Decalogue. Each and all of them are plain, practical, real, urgently necessary for the salvation of every civilized people and every rational being. There is in it nothing mystical, nothing supernatural, hardly even dogmatical. For the declaration of the divine unity itself is so rational, so self-evident, that it is rather a principle of reason and sentiment than of creed. Why, then, should the Sabbath alone make an exception—Sabbath alone, out of all the *Ten Words*,

be of a mystical or symbolical nature? Whilst the entire
Decalogue is its own object and aim, the Rest-day alone
should be but the means for some end, should be but a sign
or sacrament. Is that probable?

Let us mention yet the following commentators and
thinkers on the subject: Philo (Decalog., 758) finds in the
Sabbath the teachings: " Ever to imitate the divine Creator.
As He worked for six days and rested on the seventh, so, too,
must we do." That doctrine of work and rest is perfectly
congenial to human nature, not to the divine one.—Even Ezra
finds in it a hint that: "Six days we shall devote to the needs
of the body, and work, and the seventh to spiritual culture."—
Maimon. (More, Neb. III., 343) is even more positive and
plain-spoken: " It is a day set apart for the rest, recreation
and happiness of men."—Albo (in Ikk. III., 26) takes it as
"a symbol of the creation by God, of the exodus, or freedom
of Israel and of Revelation."—With the ideas of a sanctified
Sabbath and of freedom, modern commentators and thinkers
penetrate deeper into the profound meaning of the institution, viz: It is a day set apart by divine Providence for
the bodily, mental, moral and spiritual welfare of man; a
day devoted to bodily rest and cheer, to moral improvement, mental culture and spiritual elevation; it is a soaring
up to a higher existence, a liberation from the earthly
drudgery and cares to spiritual freedom. Dr. Hamburger
summarizes thus: " It is the symbol of man's likeness to
the Deity in freedom and holiness. As God is the ever-
active Creator, yet ever-free Master of the universe, never
absorbed by his work,—even so should man neither be the
slave of nature nor its contemner, but work in full freedom
for his own development, and neither flee the world, as does
the Hindoo, nor be absorbed by it, as the ancient Greek."—
This interpretation is interesting for a metaphysician—not for
Moses. It is ingenious and pretty, but it is too metaphysical
for a practical institution.—Others take Sabbath for an

expiatory sacrifice, (Ewald)—or to stem human greed, (Knobel)—or as a corrective against moral defects deriving from worldly activity, (Keil)—or as bearing most usefully upon health, morality, family, etc., (Proudhon)—Midrash Tanchuma (Kithisa) declares: "The Sabbath alone is of as much weight as the entire Thora."—Michilta to III. M. 20, takes it as the symbol of the divine creation.—Talmud, Cholin 2, states: "Who desecrates the Sabbath is just as bad as he who denies the entire law."—Treatise (Talmud) *Sabbath* is entirely consecrated to that subject. The work prohibited on it is divided by the Rabbis into thirty-nine chief kinds, and many more subordinate ones, denominated "Aboth and Toldoth."—Art is mostly allowed, yet later again it was prohibited. In the ancient Temple-service the necessary work was allowed on that day. So was lighting fires there.—To avoid danger, work is allowed. So it was during the Maccabean wars. "The Sabbath is given unto you, not you to the Sabbath," is a Rabbinical saying, later quoted in the New Testament.—In the Jewish wars against Rome, there was discriminated between offensive and defensive warfare, the latter alone being allowed. The "*Chassidim*" sect rather died than worked thereon.—In Joshua, Judges and Samuel, there is no mentioning of the Sabbath. In Isaiah, Jeremiah and Ezekiel, there is. From the second Jewish Empire to the present days, it was a leading feature in the Synagogue and Ebrew home life.—According to Josephus (Contra Apion II., 39), many Greeks, Romans and Barbarians imitated the Sabbath-rest. Seneca complains that this was the case (Seneca III., 427).

NUMBER SEVEN.

The sacred number of the Bible is seven; be it because the ancient computation was the four phases of the lunar month, or the seven days of creation, including the divine rest; or on account of the sun, moon and five visible

stars. Whatever the reason may be, *seven* underlies all
sacred enumeration. The seventh day is the rest-day, consecrated to God. The seventh month, *Tishre*, is the sacred
holiday-epoch. There are seven holidays in the year.
Passover and Tabernacles have seven days each. In seven
weeks is harvest time and Pentecost. The seventh year is
Release-year, and seven such Septennates make a Jubilee.
The festive sacrifices were seven. Seven branches were in
the chandelier; such were the sprinklings and the purifica-
tion days in the Temple; such are yet the wedding week and
the mourning week, each of seven days, etc., etc. Seven
became slowly a solemn affirmation; to take an oath is in
Ebrew expressed by a word meaning: "make seven." As
the Greeks swore by three: Orcus, Styx and Hades; or by
Zeus, Apollo and Athenê, so the old Semites by seven; the
Christians by Trinity or cross, and the later Judæans by one
(God). The claim that the biblical Sabbath is but a rem-
nant from the hoary Saturn or luna-cult, is futile. In
neither was it a day for sanctification, rest, freedom or elevation. In the Saturn worship it was accounted an unlucky
day. It was the first of the week, not the last. It may be
older than the Sinai-epoch, but it is the Bible that made it
what it is: a day of liberation for man and beast, of leisure,
recreation and elevation for all, as we shall see hereafter.

Survey of Sabbath in History.

In order to find the key to that labyrinth of opinions,
sayings and theories, old or new, let us refer to positive
history; let us look soberly, impartially, and closely to the
institution itself. When we examine the numerous Sab-
bath-verses, especially the *Manna* passage, Exodus 16, 26,
we find there, plainly stated, that the Sabbath was known
to the Ebrews before the Sinai proclamation; known, if not
fully observed. Now, more than three thousand years after
Sinai, the Sabbath, instead of being disused and forgotten,

like so many other obsolete customs and rites, or instead of being limited to the practice of the people of Israel alone, that institution has become a universal feature of the civilized world. Three hundred millions of Christians celebrate that day, in their way, and in connection with their creed. Four hundred millions of Mohammedans do the same in connection with theirs. The first do it, *indeed*, *on Sunday;* the latter on *Friday.* Yet the *time does not change* the intrinsic nature of the fact. The two daughters of Judaism did not think it necessary to everywhere bear the features of their mother. As everywhere else, so here, things went on by compromise; the Gentile world accepted the kernel and changed the garb. To spare old time prejudices, forms were changed to *disguise* features, and hide the origin; whilst the essence of the Sabbatic Institution was retained. *Christianity is Biblical spirit* in a Hindoo-Germanic body with an Egypto-Greek drapery. Mahommedanism is biblical, spirit and body, shrouded in oriental colors and brandishing an Arabian scimetar. With the spirit, the principal institutions of our Christian brothers and our Mahommedan cousins are of biblical origin. And thus the Sunday of the first and the Friday of the latter, each is simply the Mosaic Sabbath. Again, when the French Revolution of 1793, in its paroxysm, abolished Catholicism and Christianity, with all positive religion, and introduced that of *"Reason"* under the attractive form of a noted Parisian beauty, even those deicides and regicides could not kill the Sabbath; they kept up a decadical one, as the ancient Egyptians, each tenth day was devoted to rest. Even the Social Democrats in 1875, at Gotha, declared for the Sabbath-rest, though they are religiously indifferent. So, too, all our most modern iconoclasts, thundering against any and all Sunday restrictions, are but aiming at the abolition of Church privileges and ecclesiastical interference; but they, too, acknowledge the absolute necessity of a spe-

10

cial day for rest and culture; the *Mosaic* Sabbath is not questioned by them, since it is a human need: "For six days shalt thou labor and do all thy work, and the seventh day consecrate to rest, freedom, thinking and moral elevation,"— religious, scientific and humanitarian; a day consecrated to everything divine in human nature; until slowly man's entire life will be one great divine service; until duty, virtue and happiness will become synonymous.

Now let us look to that manna passage (Exod. 16, 26); it is fully worth our while. That chapter states that at the Wilderness of Sin, one station before Mount Sinai, on the fifteenth day of the second month after the Exodus, the people were murmuring, dissatisfied with their food. Then the *manna* was given them, to collect daily, fresh, *except on the seventh day*. It continues: "To-day is Sabbath to Jahveh; ye shall not be out; six days shall ye collect the manna and the seventh day is Sabbath. Behold, God gave you the Sabbath; do not stir from your places." This took place *before* the Sinai legislation. The logical congruity is easy to guess. The Egyptian Ebrews did know the Sabbath, but did not much observe it. Moses, after the Exodus, and especially at Sinai, gave it aim and purpose and all the solemnity of revelation, raising it to an "*Oth brith*," a sign of the covenant. From the new Assyrian discoveries we learn that the moon's monthly four phases gave rise to the four monthly weeks, one day of which was some sort of a holiday, known to the Babylonians and Assyrians; not, indeed, as the Mosaic Sabbath, an epoch of rest and sanctification, of freedom and culture. That higher evolution the Bible, later civilization, later experiences and needs gave it. Originally it may have been merely a day of pleasure, a free, popular, weekly festival, consecrated to the moon or some other deity. It may well have been such a day with some or with all the Semitic races since hoary antiquity, connected with the star worship of ancient Chaldea—older

than Abraham and Sinai. Yet special and particular promi-
nence it received in history, as a solemn rest consecrated to
God, for body and for mind, for rich and poor, freeman and
slave, as the symbol of a great doctrine and people, only
and singly at the epoch of Sinai and the advent of the
Ebrew liberator. It may have footprints older than Semi-
ramis and Nineveh, but history only dates it from the
Decalogue and the Sinai epoch. I am strongly inclined to
that view, not only by the simple statement of Exodus 16,
verse 26, expressly declaring Sabbath as pre-Sinaic, but
also from analogy. From comparative religion we justly
assume that festivals do not suddenly spring up, but they
slowly develop from natural data, and then are authori-
tatively consecrated as men's ethical needs. The spring
and fall seasons, the different harvests, life's events, etc.,
offer opportunities for such festive days. The "human
heart craves to connect them with the Deity; men ever
yearning for God"—as said by Homer ([1]) and by the Psalmist.([2]) Now, when after long centuries of experience, we
have found out the practicability and refining influence of
such days, the Deity speaks and consecrates them, and the
truly popular and sympathetic lawgiver embodies them in
his code and makes them the pivot for new combinations,
the vehicle of new boons for his fellow men. Thus it is
with all festivals; thus with the Sabbath, too, having a retro-
spect even anterior to Sinai and a prospect of near three
thousand five hundred years, with all the chances of a
boundless future, as we shall see in the following pages.

SABBATH, THE GRAND SOCIAL INSTITUTION.

In fact, we may say that now, more than three thousand
years after it had been confirmed and proclaimed from Mt.
Horeb, that institution has become universal; it is to be

---

(1). Πάντες δὲ θεῶν χατέουσ' ἄνθρωποι.—Odyssey, III, 48.

(2)   מן המצר קראת יה, ענני במרחב יה.—Ps. 118, 5.

found wherever man has emerged from his native savage-
ness. Wherever we find civilization, there we also meet
with a Rest-day. "Adam, the first civilized man of the
Bible, appeared on Friday, and at once the Sabbath became
a necessity." Are we not by all these circumstances and
concurring facts logically compelled to infer that our Sabbath is not simply a symbol, a sacrament, a sign, for some
idea or commemoration, but itself some moral or social
institution of the highest moment? That it carries with
itself some of the greatest interests of the State or of entire
mankind at large? The more we ponder, the more we are
positively compelled to come to the conclusion that our
weekly institution must be one of the great instruments for
bringing about, in the slow process of time, some great
moral or material boon of human happiness, though we can
not as yet exactly tell the nature of that boon.

After having recognized the great part of the Sabbath in
history, let us now try to find out the nature thereof, the
real, though secret cause of its importance, that we may
learn why it has become a universal feature of civilized
life. In order to be enabled to do that, let us suppose a
people perfectly unacquainted with that institution; a
people without any official rest-days, commanded by divine
authority or law of State. In the present times, and much
more so in antiquity, the great majority of men, called the
people, are and were hard-working, bodily—laboring. In
antiquity they were slaves; later, serfs. They were not
blacks, nor barbarians, nor vicious; no, they were for the most
part prisoners of war. The conquered lost their liberty.
And to the conquered were reckoned all who were bodily
weaker and had the misfortune to displease the stronger.
Plato, the famous Athenian philosopher, a descendant from
Theseus and Solon, was sold into slavery by Dionysius, the
tyrant of Syracuse, for a few free words uttered in the hearing of the latter. The slave's labor was hard and incessant,

done under the stern eye of the master. And there is no harder master now than want, than a hungry family, for the mass of the present people. Now, according to our supposition, this large class would work all the seven week-days and all the thirty days of the month and all the three hundred and sixty-five days of the year. One year after another will pass in that unceasing toil without a rest or holiday.—How long, may we imagine, could such a hard-working man or class of men bear up under such a *regime?* Ten years? Twenty years? Anyhow, hardly long enough for bringing up a new generation, for substituting the unhappy child to the unhappy, fainting parent. What signifies that? The great majority of the people, the labor-ing class, would soon die out and become extinct. In order, therefore, to insure the perpetuity, the material life, the propagation of the race, God gave to man the boon of the Sabbath, "that he may (as says Maimonides) pass at least the seventh part of his life in peace." On that day, at least, he can take some recreation, restore his powers, so as to be enabled to repair again to his work of the ensuing six days.

Thus, we find, as soon as men begin to congregate in larger bodies, in gens and tribes and compound societies, they must work; spontaneous nature being no longer suffi-cient. The barbarian has few needs and little exertion, but civilized man needs more, hence, overwork; and overwork will soon destroy him. Here steps in the law and regulates work: *"six days shalt thou labor and one day rest."* Our institution begins to reveal its import. It is the great reg-ulator of work; just as our generation agitates for an eight hours' day work. We likewise begin to understand the lofty conception thereof as contemporaneous with the crea-tion of Adam (Genesis II, 2). Adam, the noblest, the highest development of creation, the dawn of civilized human society,—Adam needed a rest-day after the weekly toil, and the seventh day was consecrated to that purpose for his benefit. Hence the quaint Talmudical saying: "The Sabbath is given to you, not you to the Sabbath."

The Sabbath is, therefore, as says its etymology, the grand day of rest, of abstaining from all menial labor. It is the recreation day for the masses, the hard-laboring human strata.

We begin now to grasp the meaning of our other texts: "That thy male and female servants may rest"—"that thy stranger may recuperate." It is the safeguard of the dependent masses of old and of modern times. It regulates work; it hand-cuffs the hard master from abusing his power. It restrains our inner, individual masters, greed and gain. As the parent restrains the child from harming itself, even so the lawgiver interferes in our own behalf, often against our own short-sighted volition.

THE SABBATH'S MANIFOLD SOCIAL BEARINGS.

Let us continue our hypothesis, viz: a people without public Rest-days. The majority of that people is continually and exclusively occupied with material labor. The poor, laboring man will be strictly kept under the yoke. Bodily work, and nothing but bodily work, will be his lot. The poor, the dependent, has no time for the mind. All spiritual occupation, all culture of the mental faculties, will be jealously withheld from him. For when educated, he may aspire to liberty! You remember the aristocracies, old or modern, were and are declaring that the poor shall have no education; it hurts them! Bismarck complained that it is the poor man's over-education that makes him a socialist. Now let us remember that the real distinction between man and brute is surely not in his food or clothing nor in generation or extinction. Our food is often less rational in its artificiality and complications than that of the common animal. Our clothing belongs to the *Spanish sheep, the Chinese silk worm, the Indian cotton tree.* We are "parading with other people's feathers."

We respire and sleep, digest, generate and die, just like the vulgarest of animals. Our true and real superiority over the brute consists, principally, in our spiritual faculties, greater brain and nerve power, greater intelligence; we are moral and conscientious beings; we try, at least, to practice right and justice whenever we can. We are rational beings; we aspire to truth, knowledge and reason; we investigate the laws of nature; we measure the heavenly orbits in their eternal march through unbounded space. We weigh the earth, search the ocean's abyss; chain the lightning and bid the elements: "Thus far and no further." We are affectionate beings, we love our families, our friends, our fellow-men, as far as it goes. Finally, we are religious beings. In the depth of feeling, in the height of thought, dawn the ideals of God, Providence and universal harmony, of soul, freedom, virtue, beauty, harmony, perfection, holiness, self-sacrifice, humanity, duty, immortality, etc. The domain of these spiritual faculties makes the essence of manhood and womanhood. Now suppose a people without Sabbaths and holidays—when will the great majority of that people, the laboring class, the ninty-nine out of each one hundred, arrive at that manhood? When will they become beings endowed with mental or spiritual culture? When will they aspire to truth and science, reflect on virtue and vice, right and wrong, the beautiful, the sublime and the mean? When sympathize with their friends; when give themselves up to the endearments of a child, a consort, a parent, a friend, a fellow-citizen? When reflect on the awful enigma of body and soul, world and God? Never! Never will they! Never can they have the leisure for it! Imperious wants absorb all their time with bodily work. The bread, the fuel, the house-rent, absorb all reflections. St. Juste pointedly said: "the people's rights, that is—

bread!" What, then, will be the necessary consequences of such a state of things? The great laboring masses will never arrive at manhood, at full maturity. Being used and abused as cattle, they will soon descend to the level of cattle. Providence, all-wise and all-benign, foreseeing this greatest of possible misfortunes, gave mankind the great remedy: On "the sixth day, evening, he created Adam and Eve," (1) and gave them the seventh day as the noblest of presents. There shall be no labor on the Sabbath. The workingman shall rest bodily, and spontaneously he will cultivate his mind. On the Sabbath at least the laborer shall be a man, intellectually, morally, affectionately and religiously.

And thus we perfectly understand the verses in Genesis II, 1. When heaven and earth and all their hosts of creatures were in their final developments and so far advanced as to bring forth Adam, viz: civilized man; when the cosmic conditions were so far matured as to admit of moral and rational beings, then God sanctified one day out of seven for the benefit of man, that man should rest from his toils, refresh his body and cultivate his mind, civilize and sanctify himself. Thus, the first Decalogue bases the Sabbath on that noble metaphor—that the seventh day rest is contemporaneous with creation, viz: with the advent, the creation of civilized man. Immediately man began to be rational, not a mere instinctive brute, the rest-day was instituted in his behalf.

DEMOCRACY AND ARISTOCRACY.

Thus, our institution is of the highest importance for the material and for the mental welfare of man and woman. But it is much more than that. Let us continue our hypothesis. In the beginning of the formation of societies and states, it is a necessary evil that citizens

---

(1) Medrashic.

should divide into an aristocratic minority and a plebeian majority. The few, the naturally stronger, wiser, better gifted or situated, think, govern and enjoy. The many, the less favored, obey, learn and labor. Now, by sheer perverseness, or rather, shortsightedness, the governing minorities have often taken a narrow egoism for their rule of conduct or policy. They try to govern and educate the masses in such a way as to keep them the longest in a state of subjection ; inventing some foolish theory of assumed superiority for their downright usurpation. You remember the divine claims of the Chinese and Japanese emperors. Alexander was the son of Jupiter Amon ; Cæsar the descendant of Æneas, grandson of Zeus.—Vespasian, dying, said satirically, "I feel I am becoming a god."—The Incas of Peru claimed to be descendant from the sun.—It is the story of the "children of the gods marrying the daughters of men," ironically mentioned by the biblical narrator (Genesis VI, 4.)

These usurpers tell us that God is the father of the strong, the rich, the crafty, and that the poor and uneducated are just made for the yoke. You know the vain arguments of political and social oppressors, the Nimrods of old and of present times ; banditti, in reality, claimed as demi-gods. To counterbalance and neutralize these dangerous tendencies, the legislator, the friend of the poor, the stranger, the widow and orphan, gave to mankind the Sabbath. It is a divine veto against the aristocratic usurpations of all ages. The almighty law declared : On this day I recognize neither master nor slave, neither rich nor poor. All of mortal Adam's children shall be equal before mine eyes. The body shall rest ; the spirit shall cultivate and develop itself. And when the plebeian, the pariah, has but one day in seven for recruiting his strength and cultivating his mind, he will slowly acquire his entire liberty and rise in the social scale, rise to full equality. The aristocratic minority will give way, and slowly there will be developed a great democracy of free, equal, thinking and enjoying citizens. Thus, Sabbath is of paramount importance in a physiological, a psychological and a politico-social point of view. Let us continue. It is yet more.

As a stone, dropping into water, forms a circle, this forms another, and this again another one, until the entire surface is covered with such rings, even so are in history the effects of the Sabbath institution. As the rising sun is first visible only on the mountain tops, slowly descending upon the plateaus, and finally shedding his light upon high and low places, upon mount and dale, even so the Sabbath.—We have seen its first three rings. Let us observe its unfoldings.

As in every nation of antiquity we find a small reigning minority and a large, laboring, plebeian majority, even so were all the different branches of the human family divided up into reigning and serving races or tribes. Scattered over the entire globe, so manifold in soil, configuration and clime, which so differently influence the development of beings, the different races and aptitudes of mankind were the necessary outcome, dividing them up into superior and inferior ones, stronger and weaker, more and less gifted ones. Thus, the Gibeonites were subject to the Ebrews; the Helots to the Spartans; the Pariahs to the Hindoos; the Provincials to the Romans. Nearly the same in modern times in Europe, Asia and Africa. A few races born and educated under more happy circumstances, favored by climate, food, natural strongholds, great men, etc., took the lead of our species, representing the progressive, the civilizing element thereof, and soon became dominant races; whilst the younger tribes took their stand around the former, serving and obeying and looking up to them as to their superiors and teachers. And that was quite natural. The aristocracy of the mind will never be abolished. The intelligent, the moral, the industrious will always rule the stupid, the vicious and the lazy ones. So with individuals and so with races and peoples. This was not only rational and just, but even advantageous, even to the serving party itself. In order to rule, we must begin to serve an apprenticeship.

DEMOCRACY AND OCHLOCRACY.

All wars and revolutions and conventions and new constitutions are of no avail as long as there is no premium for being educated, honest and thrifty. *The rulers must be the natural aristocrats,* the wiser and the more moral ones. Full and unmitigated democracy is ochlocracy. As long as the ignorant and the vicious rule, as long as such vote, elect and are elected to office, as long as we have no just criterion at the ballot-box, the source of modern government, *so* long our fate will not be bettered one whit.

We can change persons and parties, but we may always have a mob at the helm of government. Our rulers, appointed by the majority, will be no more intellectual or just than the majority. Wise and good are the minorities. Our rulers will always lack in honesty and capacity. The majorities, with the best will, will be blindfolded by the *gift of the gab* and flattery. They can not find out the worthy candidates, and will appoint—duped by vulgar time-servers and sophists—no superior legislators. Remember our "fiat money" and "free silverists." There is but one salvation for real political improvement, viz: a fusion of Democracy and aristocracy, each to be modified by the other—government must be for the people, but by the best and noblest of the people. Only the wise shall rule, the wise, not the stump-speakers. Our modern democracies are somewhat averse to that wholesome truth, but they will slowly learn that lesson. Athens and Sparta, Holland and Switzerland did, and so will America, too. The mode of our elections, the criteria of electors and elected must

be modified in such a manner, that only the educated, the
enlightened, the honest, the experienced, if possible men
of genius, not the artificial arisrocrats, but nature's true
noblemen, those really more wise and virtuous, should be
appointed by the people to the helm of government;
appointed by the people to govern for the people, through
the best of the people; not the stump-speakers.—Hence, a
blending of democracy and aristocracy in the interest of
all parties concerned. Remember, it is a fiction to say that
men are born with equal endowments. Every pedagogue
will tell us that one child is strong, intelligent and moderate; the other weak, stupid and ungovernable. Through
education we should try to remedy natural defects and
discrepancies. Nature begins with inequality; circumstances continue that. Education ought to try to reach
equality. All that enlightened democracy can do is through
education and equal chances to remedy the inequalities
of nature.—Here it is where historical, artificial aristocracy is wrong. It denies education, and inequality
remains. Democracy justly offers the same chances to
every citizen to become all that nature and education can
make of him, by removing all contrived notions of hereditary inferiority and all artificial barriers, allowing him to
develop himself to his utmost capacity and will-power,
and as much as possible to remedy natural defects. This
is the good part in democracy and in aristocracy, viz: *To
let every one have his chances.*—Artificial aristocracy is a
lie; the natural one is true. Equality taken literally, positively, viz: to give no premium to honesty and capacity,
what they call "*rotation in office*" is a fallacy, a stupidity
and a misfortune.—It is not true in nature nor in right.—
The gifted lose by it, and the incapable lose even more,
viz: "the necessary stimulus to vanquish their laziness and
improve." Capable, incapable, all society slowly lapses by
that into barbarism. As long as this pseudo equality is

acted upon, so long is democracy a failure, and European
artificial aristocracies and dynasties have yet a chance to
supplant it.   Let us hope the American democracy, by fully
recognizing the true nobility of mind,—not of race, and not
of birth,—will not give them that chance.

Natural and Artificial Aristocrats.

Now the natural aristocracy, however legitimate and
advantageous, when well understood, ought never to become
a caste ; genius not being hereditary.   The natural aristocracy should never become a historical one, but ought to
aspire towards democracy ; the elevation of all should be
the highest aspiration of the true nobleman of nature.—
Nature's nobleman is not jealous.—"Would all the people
were prophets," prays Moses, whilst his servant is envious
of some claimants to prophecy.(¹)—The older superior races
ought to educate the younger ones in such a way as to bring
them up to full manhood.   The superiority of the wiser
and better developed classes ought to be used to the advantage of the less favored ones, and not for selfish purposes.
The wise men rule only then legitimately, when they render
the foolish wiser.   Unfortunately, the natural, legitimate
aristocracies tend to change into historical, artificial ones,
and hence the antipathetic significance of the word *aristocrat*, no longer meaning the best, but the privileged one.
They try to perpetuate their dominion by privilege.   They
continue to rule, not by being themselves superior, but by
making others inferior, by retarding the education of the
less favored races, by keeping back human progress in
general, by retaining the Helot and the Pariah in perpetual
childhood ; they willfully impede and retard all progress,
that of their own race inclusive, and thus harm their own
race in harming others.   This is the history of castes in
India, China, Egypt, etc., and of classes in Europe.   Now

(1) IV. M., 11, 29.

if matters had gone on that way, without any check, the old state of things, the original inequality, would have continued, yea, increased, in all eternity. A few classes and tribes only would have acquired some civilization, freedom and happiness, while the great majority of the different races would continue unto this day in dependence and barbarism as Pariahs, Helots and Gibeonites.

Would, then, the object of humanity be attained? Would it not be rather frustrated? Is the Almighty the father only of the aristocrat, of the *Brahmin?* Is he not the author of all mankind, of all creatures, of all existence? Shall the State prefer one child to another? be the parent of one and the tyrant of the other? Society may give to the wise authority over the simple, in order to make the simple wiser, but not for nurturing the evil spirit of arrogance and dominion, of race and caste.

Sabbath's Vast Political Influence.

The biblical legislator, therefore, in his love and impartiality for all the community, put in his veto against the oppression of all times and of all forms. Full of the divine spirit, he bestowed upon mankind the gift of the *Sabbath.* *"Observe the Rest-day."* On that day there shall be no distinction between races, origins and castes; on that day the slave races shall be free; they shall *rest bodily* and recuperate; they shall cultivate themselves mentally, spiritually and develop their moral instincts; they shall acquire the notions of the noble and the good; of truth, justice and liberty. Thus acquiring through education power and volition, virtue and wisdom, they will soon find the means for their entire liberation.

The dominant races will gradually reconcile themselves to the idea of equality. They will slowly submit to a new order of things: the abolition of privilege, and there will gradually be established a universal republic of equal, civilized, happy, brother-peoples and sister-countries. Mankind will again be *one family* of brothers, with one father above, sprung from one parent-couple on earth. Education will make that Shem, Ham and Japheth will be again the equal and blessed children of the one patriarch, Noah, before the Babel's Tower of Egoism had divided them into different castes, races and classes.

Thus our Sabbath is powerfully promoting the great interests of our species in a *bodily, intellectual, social* and *humanitarian* point of view. Nay! Our institution extends its great boons even to the animal kingdom. For the brute, though not endowed with reason, is not without feeling; it is therefore entitled to its comforts. Its existence and well-being are necessary for the civilization of man. Hence the law must protect it. Even in order to insure its propagation the law must give it some rest. And this rest is extended to it, too, by the great Lawgiver through the same day.

Thus our institution is the noble benefactor of the dependent, the uneducated, the socially unfree, the conquered races and the brute. It extends its benign influence to the utmost boundaries of living creation, in a physical, educational, spiritual, social, humanitarian and universal sense. Now all these ideas are implied in the above-quoted texts. But they are explicitly set forth in the II Decalogue, in Deuter. 5, 14. "Observe the Sabbath day to keep it holy, as God has commanded thee. Six days shalt thou labor and do all thy work. But the seventh is a rest to the Eternal, thy God. On it thou shalt do no manner of work; thou, nor thy son and thy daughter, nor thy male servant and female servant, nor thy ox or ass, nor any of thy cattle, nor the stranger in thy gates—*that thy man- and maid-servants should rest like thyself*. For remember that a slave thou hast been in Egypt, but God brought thee out from there with a mighty arm, therefore He commanded thee to keep the Sabbath day."—Before analyzing these verses, let. us glance at our other texts. The first declares (Genesis II., 1): "God sanctified the seventh day, after the last creation," viz: Adam.—With the advent of civilized man, Adam, the Sabbath became necessary. The first Decalogue conveys the same idea. After the declaration of God's existence and spirituality looms up the Sabbath institution (II. M. 20,) as necessary for a civilized community, as the means of human spiritualization. The fourth text (II. M. 23, 12) corroborates plainly the sense of the aforegiven second Decalogue. It reads: "Six days shalt thou work, but the seventh day thou shalt rest, in order that thy ox and thy ass shall rest, and that there shall recreate themselves thy slave and thy stranger." Let us now analyze Deut. 5, 12: "Observe the Sabbath day to sanctify it."—That means, that day is set apart for the higher purposes of human life. He continues: "During six days shalt thou work."—The different needs of civilized life require toil. "But the seventh day is a rest to God"—hence total cessation from menial labor and the day to be consecrated to the divine, i. e., to the highest objects of human aspirations, the mental, moral and religious in our nature.—"Thou, thy son and thy daughter," ye all shall rise on it to higher planes of intellectuality, capacity and goodness. "And thy male and female servants," for their bodily, spiritual and social amelioration, too, for their gradual emancipation.—"And thy beasts of burden"—for their rest, comfort and preservation.—"And the stranger within thy gates,"—for the subjected races and pariahs in thy reach.—"That thy servants and dependents may rest and recuperate as thyself"—emphasizes the aim of the day.

SABBATH THE UNIVERSAL EMANCIPATION DAY.

Observe how the lawgiver is anxious that we should grasp the import of the Sabbath, as the opportunity for the

emancipation of the toiling masses. He knew human
nature! Lest the upper classes might cunningly mistake;
lest there should remain some doubt concerning the great
aim of our weekly institution; lest the employer, the
plutocrat and the historical aristocrat, should claim for
themselves, and alone, the divine privilege of that day;
lest they should pretend that they alone are the "*children
of the gods*," that they and their race sprang from the head
of Brahma, whilst the Pariah, the Helot, the peasant, the
wage-laborer came from his feet; lest the Baron should
exclude the poor son of toil even from the protection of
this grandest institution of freedom, the Mosaic lawgiver,
as a true son of toil and freedom himself, repeats with so
much emphasis, and lays so much stress on the subject by
summing up: "*That thy man-servant and thy maid-ser-
vant may rest as thyself.*" This is his principal scope, the
chief aim of the Sabbath day: the bodily recreation, the
spiritual culture, the gradual emancipation of the dependent
masses. The powerful ones, the free-born, the rich, can
have and do have leisure, ease and liberty enough! But
the great laboring class, the ninety-nine out of every one
hundred, they need all the solicitude, all the tender cares,
all the warm and strong protection of the sympathetic lawgiver. After God, he is their only friend! The rich can
have seven free days in the week; the poor shall have *one*
at least! Therefore, for them especially, is intended the
Sabbatic institution; they particularly were the objects
of the Biblical Rest-day.

SABBATH THE POOR MAN'S DAY.

And lest the haughty nobleman, the employer, in his
blind pride should forget the divine declaration of human
equality, of men being all "shaped in heaven's image,"
with feeling hearts, consciences and noble instincts, the
lawgiver recalls sternly to his mind (Deut. 5, 15): Well

11

mayst thou remember thy original slavery, that God
brought thee out from Egypt with a mighty arm—therefore
let the Sabbath boon be the boon of the poor, too. Therefore be not selfish, allow him his chance to recuperate and
use his opportunity. Remember, thou art not born a
master, not born in the purple, not born in a gold mine;
no, a "slave wast thou in Egypt," and the author of all
freedom and justice broke thy yoke and made thee free,—
hale, free and happy. Remember, therefore, that justice
has been done thee, O thou proud and wealthy one, do justice
to those poor and humble and dependent upon thee! For
the mighty arm of supreme justice is outstretched over him
and thee.

You remember, American reader, your ancestors' or your
own modern Egypt across the ocean. You are mindful of
your European Egypt of yesterday, or a century ago, of the
cruel intolerance and ostracism, the many great and small
tyrannies, the poverty, the disabilities yonder in Ireland,
England, Germany, or Russia, at the hands of hierarchs
or patricians. Here on the holy ground of Columbus's fair
land we all are celebrating our Sabbath, political and social,
under the ægis of the Constitution, declaring that every
human being is entitled to aspire to life, liberty and happiness. Here let us be mindful of the redeeming clause:
" Observe the Sabbath day *that thy dependent may rest as
thyself.*" Let us not begrudge the poor of that day. Let
the clerk, the hand-laborer, the shopgirl, the apprentice, the
housemaid not be robbed of it. Let us remember that its
special and express object is: the recreation of the dependent, laboring man and woman, his and her rest and spiritual
culture, his and her social elevation, his and her moral,
mental and economic redemption. When the bright sun of
the glorious Sabbath-day dawns upon the awakening eyes
of him and her, dependent upon you, American employers,
the first thought of each shall be: "To-day I also am a

free being, a rational, happy being! I can recreate my
body, cultivate my mind, rejoice at my home, convene
with my fellow-citizens, commune with my God! I feel I
am worthy of freedom and happiness!" Such let, employers,
your dependents feel on the Sabbath.

The diverse, far-reaching objects and aims of that day
are slowly but surely being attained. The goal is slowly
approaching. Observe the march of history for these three
thousand years from Sinai to Washington, from Moses to
Cleveland. Compare the gradual development of society.
Behold chains are bursting and tyrannies tumbling; slavery
is disappearing, mounts and oceans becoming highways of
brother peoples. Do you hear the revolutionary tocsin
roaring? These are the workings of our grand institution.—
They are announcing the emancipation-day of the masses,
the great Sabbath of mankind, the jubilee of right and
freedom, education and happiness for all.

SABBATH FROM THE POLITICAL STANDPOINT SOLELY.

We have tried to unfold the meaning of that institution,
without any theological postulate or any supernatural
assumption. We did not insist upon basing it on the
divine rest after the creation; nor did we decide whether
the creation was done in six days or in *æons* of years, or
is as yet going on. We did not make any sectarian assump-
tions whatever; being here concerned with sociology and
States' policy solely; with law and matters of fact, not
with theology and creed. We made *tabula rasa* with
all educated and acquired ideas on the subject. Thus
untrammeled, we began with the clear ground of a people
having no ordained official rest- and holidays. We examined how that would work upon the development of men,
and we saw that there would be no development whatever,
that mankind would dwarf and decay and slowly disap-
pear; that the first condition towards a gradual healthy

evolution and amelioration is just such a public rest-day
for all, and especially for the mass of the people; that the
physical preservation of the body and the development of
mentality, ethics, freedom and equality could never be
brought about, except with such a periodical rest-day as
the primordial condition.

SABBATH, RELEASE AND JUBILEE.

We have seen that the Sabbath is not simply a ceremony,
a sectarian symbol or a religious sacrament. No, it is an
institution of the grandest dimensions, of the most far-
reaching results, the condition of all human improvements·
Now this institution has slowly developed and unfolded and
grew into the mighty tree: the Year of Release and the Jubilee.
Utilizing some good material of older religious phases, the
legislator declared the seventh day of each week an epoch
for the higher purposes of human life, vindicating thus for
the masses, time and leisure for recreation and culture.
Proceeding by that sacred number, the seventh day of the
week became the Sabbath rest. Seven festive days were
consecrated during the year as seasons of holy memories
and rest. The seventh week after Passover closed with the
Pentecost and the commemoration of the law of Sinai, the
charter of popular rights and duties; the seventh month,
Tishre, became the sacred season of the great festivals, viz:
the day of Memorial, or of counting the civil year,—the
sublime day of Atonement, and the feast of Tabernacles,—
the modern Thanksgiving-day. Again, every seventh year
became the Release-year, for liberating every Ebrew slave
and remitting all indebtedness, the greatest curse in antique
times. Finally, the seventh Release-year culminated in the
Jubilee, the great national cycle, restoring persons, soil and
houses to their original condition; remedying all inequalities, all wrongs and all misfortunes; radically renovating
the entire State and Society, and replacing them as origi-

nally intended by the lawgiver, viz: every one being free, every one holding his family-lot, his house and his acre, free in the midst of his family; no one a dependent pauper; no one lording over his equals; a competence to each, plutocracy for none. Thus, better than Lycurgus, remedying social inequalities, allowing individualism, family, property and accumulation, yet tempering egoism by altruism, placing insuperable barriers against greed, avarice and soulless competition; compelling the cunning and the monopolist to leave some room for the less favored brother, keeping up a certain sameness of fortune and of power in the social ranks, and, by that means substantiating and perpetuating the original equality and liberty among the citizens.

The grandeur of that scheme explains the noble biblical verse (Genesis II, 2): "When creation had been accomplished, then God blessed the seventh day and sanctified it." Indeed, out of the root of the seventh week-day, consecrated as the rest and recreation for the laboring masses, and even the beast, slowly developed the festive calendar, the national union and its sacred memories, the Septennate and the Jubilee. Thus, Sabbath, Release and Jubilee constitute the three Hercules columns of the Mosaic State, in an economical, social, moral and political sense. The lawgiver built up the freedom, the equality and the economical happiness of his people upon these three grand pillars.

The Sabbath has since been adopted by the entire civilized world. May not the other two await a similar acceptance by advancing mankind? Would not an inalienable acre for every born human being be a feasible thing? Would not a periodical release from the bondage of debt be possible? Could not mad competition, with plutocracy and proletarianism, be put to the chain? Reader, think!

SABBATH AND THE SOCIAL PROBLEM.

In that manner tries the Bible to remedy the *social question*. This question is old as mankind. Formerly it was kept down by slavery and serfdom. The masses, now emancipated, clamor for their share, and hence looms up the social question. It is in the front rank in America, just as in Europe; it is growing more menacing day by day,—being now nearly all-absorbing; more important than even peace and war, freedom, law and government; the formidable question how to screen the weak from hunger and cold; how to house and shelter the masses from the heartless competition of the rich and the strong; how to inculcate the duty of "live and let live." It threatens existent nations with social war and dynamite—war bitterer than ambition or fanaticism ever were. "The right of the people is bread." (¹)

The biblical Sabbath-day has had its fair trial, and though spoiled in many ways by petty meddling in old and modern, yea, in present times, by Sabbath—and Sunday—laws, meddlings showing how little great ideas are grasped by the average expounders, lay and clerical, how often they are exploited by petty, cunning officials or ecclesiastics—though spoiled by abuse, yet the Sabbath could not be made inoperative. It yet succeeded, and did wonderful services in the development of mankind.

The seven yearly festive days have been, too, accepted by large portions thereof, and do effectively assist in bringing cheer, joy and noble reminiscences to human hearts and brains. The *Atonement-day* has not been yet sufficiently appreciated. The idea of assembling the people once yearly for reflection and improvement, for giving and for receiving pardon, is a grand one, as a simply ethical and humanitarian measure of advancement.

The church and the mosque have some sort of substitutes thereof, but rather in the shape of sacraments and fasts, not in its essence, viz., meditation and self-confession, improvement and reconciliation, with conscience and with fellow-

---

(1) St. Juste.

men. The racial jealousy is here the chief cause. From mere sectarian pride the world has neglected many grand biblical institutions; or, changing their robes, they altered their essence. The Atonement-day is a great idea, and lawgivers ought to bestow more thought upon it as a useful institution.

But above all have the last rings of that seven-fold cycle been neglected, viz: the Year of Release and the Jubilee? The fact is, these conceptions have never yet been fairly tried. They were ignored during the first period of Ebrew history. But even during the second one, only the letter of the institution was retained, not the spirit. The people got the straw, whilst the grain had been thrashed out, by the casuistry of the expounders or the despotism of the rulers. Indeed, Ezra and Nehemiah and Judas Maccabeus had heart and nerve enough for such a trial. But the later Hasmonean princes, and especially the latest Herodians, were not of that calibre. They had not the heart nor the head even to pay any attention to such far-reaching institutions; the less to realize them. Apparently they mistook them for usual ceremonies and observances. Later, Rome crushed out every attempt at individuality. *Tacitus* ridiculed them as a piece of national laziness (History V., 4.) For centuries, Rome herself stood upon the volcano of plutocracy and pauperism, and many a time she was shaken to her profoundest base. Mad ambition for the patricians: "Bread and play" for the proletarians—that was her State policy. To remedy the evil, herself, or to allow others to remedy theirs, that was out of the question. When the Roman world broke down, came the great invasions with the new political and social order, the Germanic peoples and feudalism, or landlordism, with vassalage, in place of former slavery,—a mitigation in degree, not in kind. Entire Society was enchained with one huge hierarchical bond; the very opposite of the Mosaic ideal. The Bible wants a State with equal and free citizens, with equal means and with solidarity. Feudalism developed a Society personified in and absorbed by the king and the baron, who absorbed all ; the people thus becoming their tools and instruments for personal ambition and perpetual wars.   In Switzerland, and later in Holland, the biblical idea gained some hold upon the State.   But it was the American and French revolutions that made the world turn its eyes again towards the Mosaic society. *Modern, American Democracy stands on Sinaic grounds.*   May be, philanthropists, economists and philosophers will yet find out that the biblical legislation contains some remedy for our all-absorbing social question.   May be that the teachers of Social Democracy may yet willingly sit down at the feet of the Legislator from Sinai and his successors.

It would be worth while to closely examine that grand, Mosaic trial at compromising between property and communism, between egoism and altruism : by the above-mentioned, vast, moral and economic enactments ; the full and entire Septennate system, the Sabbath-day, Sabbath-year and Sabbath-cycle of fifty years in their grand *ensemble*.   But let it be done without prejudice.   Formerly the Sinai laws were accepted as binding, upon all times and all circumstances, in all its details.   Now the opposite direction prevails.   Let all prejudice be dropped and an impartial examination be held : what elements thereof are available for our times ; and I think, the present State, with its all-absorbing social question, would profit by such an unbiased investigation.

PART IV.

THE BIBLICAL STATE AND SOLIDARITY.

Having spoken of the individual liberty, the personal equality and the equal distribution of wealth in the biblical State, we now arrive at the fourth cardinal principle of that legislation,—the solidarity of the members of the commonwealth. The rock underlying the entire social structure is mutual sympathy, the solid feeling of the community of interests among its social units. This feeling, natural between the rational parts of any composite body, as between husband and wife, between members of a family, slowly extending to the *gens*, the patriarchal group, the tribe and the people, the legislator strove to fan and kindle into full consciousness among the horde brought out from Egypt and established in Canaan. This is the feeling of *solidarity*, the conviction that the welfare of each is bound up with that of his fellow-citizens. Egoism is whispering that our interest is contrary to that of our neighbor's, that our advantage and his advantage are like the two buckets at the well : whenever the one is up the other is down. But altruism is the other instinct lying deeper even in our soul, with a "still, thin, yet divine voice," whispering : " No, mine and the neighbor's interests really and truly go together. I can not be happy without his being so too." Remark : Mosaism has here another tendency than the New Testament has. Mosaism endeavors to mitigate, curb and moderate selfishness by love to fellowship. But it makes no attempt at eliminating selfishness. For, indeed, human society could not subsist without love of self, either. Without the powerful stimulus of self, wife

and child, late offspring, future name, reward, glory, etc., etc.
we could never overcome the formidable obstacles in the
way of human advance, of work, toil, discovery and inven-
tion.   That prodigious amount of self-sacrifice and abnegation required by an Aristides, an Elijah, a Paul, a
Mendelssohn, to fulfill what they did, and under their
circumstances, must have had some backbone of self-grati-
fication too, besides ideality and self-sacrifice.   Moses,
therefore, endeavored to temper and fuse both self and
others, egoism and altruism, into one harmonious whole.
Upon both he created his social fabric.   Hence he said:
"*Love* thy neighbor and *love* the stranger as thyself."
"*Tolerate* thy enemy."—"Expostulate with him, but bear
him no grudge."   Never did he ask for: "*Love* thy
enemy," because a human State could not subsist wholly
upon self-sacrifice, could not stand without a strong alloy
of selfishness.

The New Testament starting from a monastic society, with
common property, a mystic "*philanstere*" of saints and
saintesses, all striving to realize the "kingdom of heaven
upon earth,"—such a community with such ideal aspirations
could make the trial at eliminating self and found its
system upon pure altruism.   Mosaism, less ideal, aiming at
establishing a human State with average human beings as
its units, with work and family as its corner-stone, had,
therefore, to keep alive the feeling of solidarity in order to
counterbalance egoism, by teaching not simply rigid justice
and equality, "*eye for eye*," but another deeper principle—
that of benevolence and kindliness, of reciprocity and sympathy to our species.   That remark disposes of the stale
criticism that Mosaism is but cold justice, the scales of
mine and thine, and that love and charity were waiting for
Voltaire to be revealed.   On examination we shall find
sympathy at the very bottom of the Mosaic system.

LEGAL PREJUDICE OR SOLIDARITY.

This principle of benevolence and solidarity to our species is surely one of the most prominent and most deeply rooted in the human breast. Let us hope for the honor of our species that it has never been entirely stifled. But how often has it been obscured, falsified or silenced by the prejudices of the blind masses, or even the passions of the leaders! The history of legislation, ancient and modern, sacred and profane, tells us how often prejudice of nationality, of tongue, country, caste, sect and condition,—vulgar, foolish and cruel prejudices, have been converted into laws and sanctioned by the authority of the State, nay, of religion. What a sacrilege! What a blasphemy against God, reason and justice to embody hatred and folly into a code of laws destined for the education and government of mankind! Mosaism is fairly free of such dark, bloody stains. Save its severities against the Canaanites and the Amalekites, severities, no doubt, urgently dictated by the given circumstances and conditions, except that Mosaism is free of those bigoted, narrow-minded, Draconic laws which fill half of the world's codes. Let us survey the verses of our section in question, and we shall soon feel convinced of the broad, humanitarian character of " *Mishpatim*," our chapters on "Laws and Ordinances" (II. M. 22, 20, etc.) There we read: "An immigrant thou shalt not overreach nor oppress, for immigrants ye were in Egypt."—"The widow and the orphan ye shall not wrong, for they will but cry unto Me, and I will listen unto them and shall retaliate upon you," etc.—"If thou lendest money, be not hard upon the debtor, nor take any interest of him."—"If thou takest as a pawn the dress of thy fellow, return it to him at sunset."—"Do not carry around false reports."—"Do not incline to the majority for evil, nor shalt thou favor the poor one in his contest."—"When thou meetest thy enemy's ox astray, return it to him."—"When thy enemy's beast succumbs under its burden, thou shalt relieve it."—"Nor shalt thou bend justice against the poor."—"Take no bribe, for bribery blinds the eyes of the 'wise."—"The growth of the seventh year leave to the poor."—"The seventh day keep as a rest for the poor, the animal," etc., etc.—What grand traits of broad sympathy, of fellow-feeling with fellow-creatures, man or beast!

THE BIBLE POOR-LAWS.

Let us see now the Mosaic poor-laws, arising from solidarity and reciprocity of interests. In the preceding pages we have taken England as an example for illustrating how little theoretical liberty and legal equality influence real, social equality. Let us now do the same regarding her pauper laws, for these are, most probably, the oldest extant, as is English liberty and equality. Already under the reign of Elizabeth, the British statutes provided in some measure for the destitute. Besides private, corporate and communal charities, the poor-rates of England in 1831 amounted to forty millions of dollars. England has, besides, many poor-establishments, as: work-houses and poor colonies, soup establishments, endowments of fuel, clothing, homes, poor-hospitals, etc., etc. Yet with all this fair expense of treasure and sympathy, Albion has probably the largest and most abject pauper class in the world; a million of English subjects are belonging to that class! There the indigent very rarely succeed in raising themselves from that abyss of economical and moral ruin. The English pauper has but one means of salvation, that is emigration. As long as he stays at home and gets his poor-rates and his poor-boons, he remains an outcast, a social leper; deprived of his civic rights, almost of his human rights. Why? Because of the terrible social inequality! Whilst society keeps him from starvation, it likewise hinders him in his efforts, it keeps him down in the bonds of pauperism. Such is England, the most enlightened and humane country of Europe.

Mosaism starts from another standpoint. All citizens are free, all equally noble born. "Ye shall be a kingdom of priests and a holy nation."—"Mine is Israel." "Mine is the land." All obey the same laws, all have equal rights and duties. Hence, equal interests and solidarity; no proletarians, no paupers! But shall the thrifty, the intelligent, the industrious, have no premium? Yes, he shall surely have one; the fruits of his virtues are his. No communism! Shall the vicious, the lazy and stupid one not feel his punishment? Undoubtedly! All the pangs of poverty, of dependence, of a biting conscience, shall stimulate him to improve. Pauperism is no privilege and no virtue, as in Brahmanism. The law declares: *"Favor not the poor in his contest."*—Shall he be crushed under his poverty; he and his innocent family? No! The Release-year rescues his personal liberty; it cancels his debts. Jubilee redeems his family-lot; Sabbath gives him a breathing spell. Shall he, in the meantime, starve or live on alms? No! There steps in solidarity: the thrifty, the intelligent, etc., profiting by the lazy and stupid, must leave them at least a pittance to keep them from starvation.

Thus the Bible levies upon the wealthy contributions for the poor; as Mr. Chamberlain said: "The rich must pay a ransom to the poor;" not because it is a sin to be rich, or a virtue to be poor. No, but because the rich, the cunning, the efficient, the thrifty profit by the ill luck of the poor and lazy. The first have not only their own, legitimate share; they have also the share of the luckless. Hence it is just, they should help those latter ones to a pittance; hence the *tithes* for the poor, the Levites, the unhappy, the impoverished and the vicious. This is a duty, not a charity. The grand principle is solidarity, aiming at [1] "Let there be no

.אפס כי לא יהיה בך אביון (1)

pauper class among you." Give each a chance to rise again and become independent.

POOR AND PAUPER.

We have seen that by the Sabbatic Year and the Jubilee Mosaism tries to remedy the greatest social evils, pauperism and plutocracy.—The English social conditions, viz: Lords of one-half million pounds yearly income, on one hand, and one hundred thousand paupers, with thirty thousand lewd women in London alone, on the other, are obviated in the biblical State. But as industry, capacity, frugality and good luck, etc., will always be great factors in the economy of a nation, just so will the above Sabbatic Institutions alone not suffice to equalize fortunes. A great discrepancy will always remain. At the utmost may we succeed in eradicating an hereditary pauper class, not in totally discarding proletarianism and poverty. Hence is the Mosaic double axiom perfectly conceivable, of V. M. 15, 4: "In order that there should be no pauper among you;" and further again, in V. M. 15, 11, affirming: "There will never fail some poor one in the land; therefore open thy hand to him." In both verses the original has the word "*Ebiyon*." But in the first one it means a pauper, in the last a poor one; as in all old languages, the same word means both. Indeed, the idea and the word pauper are of modern origin, our own social circumstances having created an hereditary pauper class; in antiquity it was unknown; rich and poor were always liable to change rolls and hands. But the Pentateuch, deprecating chronic pauperism, admits that there will ever be poor ones. Modern communism alone is claiming the utopia of an absolute equality of fortunes. In reality, luck, capacity, thrift, prudence, the number of children in the family, widows, orphans, exiles, idealists, weaklings, invalids, vicious, etc., will ever influence economic conditions. The Bible, wishing to extend the principle of solidarity throughout all the ranks of society, and endeavoring not simply to eradicate pauperism, but even to mitigate poverty and give the needy all possible chances of recuperating, except communism, has therefore instituted a long string of laws, to give the poor a competency. These laws are of a double nature, negative and positive. One set of laws forbids putting any hindrance in the way of the poor. The other set of laws commands active assistance for him. We shall begin with the first named, the negative ones.

NEGATIVE POOR-LAWS.

" An Ebrew servant goes out free in the seventh year." (II. M. 21, 2). The Roman slave, client, conquered, etc., never had any such boon. The Judæan's alienated family-lot was to be redeemed by his near kinsman. Latest the Jubilee set it free (III. M. 25, 25-28.) Thus he and his posterity always had something to fall back upon. Never was there a pauper born in the Biblical Society. The Judæan could never be crushed and buried under indebtedness, as in all ancient States it was the case; half of enslavements there had that for their origin. The Ebrew laws prescribed the cancellation of all debts in the seventh year—(V. M. 15, 2 and 9).

USURY, MONOPOLIES AND RINGS.

In ancient and in modern times the poor suffer especially under the burden of usury or interest, the original capital accumulating by it a hundredfold. The Ebrew law forbade all interest on money, and all profit on goods and eatables. (III. M. 25, 35.) Again, no monopoly was allowed.— In ancient and modern times the poor suffer terribly by the pushing up of prices of bread, meat, coal, etc., by the *rings cornering the market*, availing themselves of "unions" and combinations, profiting by monopolies and huge capitalism to enhance the prices of victuals, clothing and fuel, without any reasonable cause, just by cornering the poor buyer's market. The Bible proscribes not only money interest, but all kinds of usury or increase upon eatables and making profit on any kind of goods. (III. M. 25-36, and elsewhere.) Any kind of buying and selling with a view to profit is prohibited. All trade is thus forbidden, not only pawn-broking, as usury. Only with foreign countries such was allowed. The Gentile living in Judæa participated in that privilege. No interest or profit, on. money or goods, was allowed to be taken of him. " Be he Gentile-stranger or domiciled, take no interest or increase of him ; fear God.— Let thy brother live with thee." (III. M. 25, 35.)—The Ebrew, during his six years hiring out, could not be harshly treated. No hard slave-work, or any maltreatment was permitted. (III. M. 25, 39-44).—When killed he was duly avenged by the law. When his tooth was knocked out he went out free. (II. M. 21, 27).—His free wife and children were not at the mercy of a harsh or a lascivious master. (II. M. 21, 3, and III. M. 25, 41).—His daughter, when sold, was to be married to the master, or to his son, or go free (II. M. 21, 7, etc.), and her treatment was in all things humane. (II. M. 21, 9 and 10).—When the freed slave left he was to get a portion from the master's flock and corn and wine, according to means (V. M. 15, 14,) reminding the latter of his having been once poor himself. It was forbidden to enter the house of the poor debtor for pawning him, leaving the latter the choice of the pawn to be given, which pawn had to be returned to the owner every night. (V. M. 24, 10-14).—What exquisite delicacy! This was a kind of exemption law in favor of the poor; the lawgiver reckoning that the creditor will get tired of taking and returning the pawn, and give it up. A widow's garment was never allowed to be pawned, nor could the grinding-mill be taken away (V. M. 24, 6 and 17). The requisites of life were thus exempted from the grip of the creditor. The immigrant, the widow and orphan were to be protected at court. (Ibidem).—"Do not withhold the wages from the hireling, be he Ebrew or Gentile-stranger. Pay him on the same day, for he is waiting for it, and he may cry unto God and you will be held accountable." (V. M. 24, 14 and 15.)—What a broad sympathy, so humane, yet divine! Divine, because so broadly humane, including all races and classes and creeds.

MARRIAGE AND DIVORCE.

Look close to (V. M. 24, 1, etc.) What a nobility of sentiment! The lawgiver protects not only the rights of the weak, but their feelings and social standing, too. Read: ",When a man has married, and having found some blemish in his wife, he divorced her, whereupon she married another man and was divorced, or widowed of that other one, too, then her first husband shall not remarry her, since she has been the wife of another." There is here a fine feeling of the proper and the becoming. May be that it is a silent protest against the barbarous custom prevalent in Arabia (see Michaeli's Laws of Moses, Vol. II, page 138, London, 1814), according to which remarriage of a divorced wife could take place only after her marriage to and divorce from a second husband! The Mosaic lawgiver sacrifices here the chance of a home for the divorced woman to the gain of her self-respect. Let her not be treated as a milking cow, bought, sold and bought again.

MOSES AND MOHAMMED ON THE SAME TOPIC.

Let us dwell a while on this trait. It is interesting to follow up the thoughts of great legislators. In Arabia and in Judæa, as all over the ancient world, women were mostly bought by their husbands. The husbands, therefore, had the privilege of sending them off at a moment's notice; then they went free, losing their husbands and gaining their freedom, and thereby they lost nothing, having been originally unfree. Now both the Ebrew and the Arabian legislators were anxious to make woman gain and not lose in the transaction. They could not curtail the husband's rights to divorce her, since he had bought her. All they could do was to impede the divorcement and warn him not to be hasty in the usage of his barbarous privilege. In this sympathetic desire both the lawgivers participated. But they took different roads in attaining their object. Mohammed, by his adopting the mentioned current custom, meant to convey the following advice: "Fellow-Arabian, you are about sending away, in hot haste, your life-companion. Now, take counsel and ponder over it, for to-morrow you may repent it and wish to remarry her. But *Alahah* will punish you. You will not be allowed to remarry her, except after she has been the wife of another and then divorced from him."—Thus he was trying to sober the husband by arousing in him the feelings of jealousy; and that may often have deterred him from rash divorcement. But that was exceedingly indelicate, though perhaps often effective. Good enough for rough times! That was the custom long before the Koran in the Arabian world. Now, the biblical lawgiver could follow that usage, but he thought the remedy worse than the evil. It was repugnant to the ideal of "Ye shall be unto me a holy nation." There the priest could not marry a divorced woman; Mohammed did. The Mosaic community revolted against that proposition, and believed to reach the same object by the cleaner road, declaring: "Be not hasty in divorcing your wife, for if she marries another you can never marry her again, and thus you wrong yourself forever."—I believe there is here both more delicacy and more prudence than in the Arabian mode. Here is another law of great delicacy, viz:

The Levirate Marriage.

Among the Hindoos and Persians, anciently, and yet now among Mongols, Afghans, etc., there is a custom requiring that a man marries the wife of his deceased brother, in order to raise him a son and perpetuate his name. That custom prevailed, too, in the ancient Ebrew Commonwealth. Moreover, as there the lawgiver desired to retain each acre and cottage in the original family-group this constituted a second interest for retaining the widow in the family by having her marry a kinsman of the deceased. Hence the law (V. M. 25, 5): "When brothers dwell together, and one of them dies childless, but leaves a wife, then shall she not marry out of the family; but her husband's brother shall marry her, and the first-born son by that marriage shall bear the name of her first husband (and get his family-lot), that the latter one's name shall not be blotted out from among Israel." ([1]) But if her brother-in-law refuses to marry her, a ceremony shall take place before the courts to that effect, whereupon she is free to dispose of herself. Of course, the Rabbinical law amplifies and changes greatly these provisions. (Eben Ha-Eser, 156, and Ibamoth *ad locum*).

Here we find a custom of older date than Mosaism is, grown out of the agrarian and the marriage customs of hoary times, when the entire family had one lot and one wife, perhaps, which usage of Levirate-marriage the Bible allowed to stand, but modified, restrained, changed and slowly turned to such account as to bring out its good features, effacing its harsh ones, and, moreover, making it optional. Later, the Rabbis finally abolished it.

The whole is brought out in the Bible in such a way that we almost hear the heart of the feeling lawgiver throbbing at the thought of a man dying childless, and his poor widow wrangling with the selfish relatives, and about to be turned

(1) ולא ימחה שמו מישראל.

into the cold street, or to ascend the burning funeral pile, as in Hindostan. The law interfered, therefore, declaring: "The widow shall stay in the family, and an heir be raised to her deceased husband."—The conditions are foreign, old and rude, but the feeling and the sympathy is eternally fresh and humane.

NAOMI AND RUTH.

To sympathize with that custom in our far-away times and social conditions, we need but to read over the beautiful idyl of Ruth and Naomi—one of the noblest gems of Sacred Writ. A poor Ebrew family, during a famine, leave their country and their acre and move into a neighboring heathen land. The two sons marry there from among the Gentiles. Soon father and sons die and leave each a widow.—The old widow determines to return to her own country and farm. Tenderly she persuades one of her widowed daughters-in-law to stay in her own country, and this after many hot tears and kind words. But the other one, Ruth, persistingly declares never to leave her old mother-in-law, whom she would follow wherever she goes, whose country she will make hers, and whose God will be hers; she will follow her and work and toil for her, and glean in the fields and devote herself to her late husband's mother, the only relic and consolation of her past conjugal happiness. The two widows return to the Judæan village and acre. Many of the old neighbors remember Naomi. "Alas! I am no longer Naomi, the sweet one.—Call me 'Bitter,' for my lot is bitter, indeed, now!"—Ruth keeps her promise. She works and toils and gleans in the fields, and sacrifices her young beauty and her fine face for the nobility of a dutiful life, consecrated to tender reminiscences and to charity at home, entirely devoted to filial piety. Soon she is rewarded grandly and nobly, in the most touching and the most natural way. The richest man in the place, *Boaz*, perchance a distant relation of the family, having been witness of

Ruth's purity, her self-sacrifice and devotion, takes her as his spouse, by virtue of the above-mentioned custom of *Levirate marriage,* and one of the late descendants of the poor Gentile immigrant Ruth is King David, the "anointed of the Lord." You see here, as in many other passages, the Bible bears no prejudice to Gentiles, when good, pure and noble-hearted. It prohibited intermarriage with the Canaanites because of their barbarous and mean idolatry, of unchaste and cruel customs, doctrines and life—not on account of race or blood. Prince Bismarck recently acknowledged to have connived at anti-Semitism as a "safety-valve to save capitalism." That "anti-Semitic fury," a shame to an enlightened country and century, renders unhappy half a million of Germans, victims of that scourge, and totally ruins several millions of other human beings in the neighboring Russian countries—poor souls who never harmed Bismarck, nor even know the meaning of anti-Semitism. Whereupon he smiles, and declares: Jew and Gentile shall intermarry and reconcile—on the graves of the victims and the ruins of their homes. Ruth and Boaz, however, are a match consecrated by the Bible, cemented by devotion and sacrifice, not by "blood and iron."

Racial Intermarriage.

Here is another law of great moral beauty, of universal sympathy with the helpless and the weak. In V. Moses 21, 10, we read: "When thou goest to war and takest many prisoners, among whom thou seest a beautiful woman, thou canst take her—as thy wife." Whereat the law prescribes that from that moment she is no longer a prisoner, but "She is to be brought to his house; a month's time shall be given her for preparation; she shall wear no longer the prisoner's dress; she shall be allowed to mourn over her parents; then, after a month is lapsed, she becomes his *wife.*" Now, "Should he, thereafter, not like her, then he must let her go *wherever she pleases. Sell her* as a slave *he cannot,*

since he had been her husband."—Compare this with the
treatment of captive women elsewhere, even in our own
times in Russia, Turkey or Asia, and you will agree that
the biblical author had a great heart, including in his
sympathy all conditions, races and countries. You will see
that from there to the later recommendation in the New
Testament, "Love thy enemy," the transition is not too far.
Moses could not avoid war, from his purely human standpoint, but he mitigated its horrors. Of course, the Rabbis
turned that law rather in a sense to impede intermarriage,
pointing to the fact that disharmony, etc., will follow.
Of course, with their bitter experiences in view, they could
not think otherwise. Just as the Jew now thinks of Bismarck's proposition of intermarriage coming close after
inciting to anti-Semitism and ostracism.

PIETY FOR THE DEAD AMONG GREEKS AND ROMANS.

That sympathetic anxiety for perpetuating the name of
the dead, as seen above in the Pentateuch and the story of
Ruth and Boaz, is akin to the solicitude of the ancients "to
burn or bury the bodies of those slain in battle, to throw
up fresh turf upon their ashes, erect a hillock, even offer
sacrifices over their graves,"—so tenderly mentioned by all
the poets of Greece and Rome. A reminiscence thereof—
to-day yet, is the reading of solemn *Mass* in the Catholic
Church, the recitation of the *Kaddish* prayer in the synagogue, and the belief in Paradise, by both.

The idyl of Ruth is a beautiful instance of ancient pious
regard for the dead. Let us now look for some examples
from Greek and Roman poets.

Virgil, in the *Æneid*, tenth book, narrates as a noble
trait of Turnus, the Latin adversary of his Trojan hero,
that when he had vanquished and killed young Pallas, son
of King Evander, the friend of Æneas, he exclaims: "Arca-
dians, listen to and remember my words and bring them to
Evander. I send him back Pallas, such as he has deserved it,

that he may bestow on him the honors of the grave and all those funeral duties, which may console him,—indeed, he has dearly paid for the hospitality granted to the Trojans."[1] Æneas, thereupon arriving in the camp, is inconsolable over the death of young Pallas, the son of his friend, old King Evander. With his terrible sword he makes a fearful carnage among the enemy and takes eight warriors alive, to offer them in expiation to the manes of Pallas, who with his father are ever present to the mind of Æneas[2]. With especial callousness he massacres a vanquished enemy who is begging for his life,—shouting: "Here you have what the manes of Anchises, what Iulus ask, Pallas being dead."[3]

In the same book, X., Virgil narrates the death of ferocious King Mezentius and his son. The first, nigh succumbing under Æneas, is saved by his young son, who heroically dies in his stead. The ferocious sire is disconsolate and pathetic at that misfortune. He offers himself to the strokes of his antagonist with these tender words: "Bitter enemy, here, now, take my life, without committing a crime, for I wish not to be spared. Yet, if the vanquished may hope for some grace, I beg thee to allow some earth to cover my body, and, moreover, suffer that I rest in the same tomb with my son."[4]

The psychology of these verses is particularly fine, and among the moderns it recalls passages of Corneille and Victor Hugo. In the first three quotations, Æneas, the soft,

<hr>

(1) "Arcades, have, inquit, memores mea dicta referte Evandro: qualem meruit, Pallanta remitto. Quisquis honos tumuli, quidquid solamen humandi est, Largior: haud illi stabunt Ænein parvo Hospitia."—Virg. X, 491.

(2) "Proxima quæque metit gladio, latumque per agmen Ardens limitem agit ferro; te, Turne, superbum Cæde nova quærens. Pallas, Evander, in ipsis Omnia sunt oculis, mensæ quas advena primas Tunc adiit, dextræque datæ. Sulmone creatos Quatuor hic juvenes, totidem quos educat Ufens, Viventes rapit, inferias quos immolet umbris, Captivoque rogi perfundat sanguine flammas."—Virg. X, 513.

(3) "Belli commercia Turnus Sustulit ista prior jam tum, Pallante peremto. Hoc patris Anchisæ Manes, hoc sentit Iulus. Sic fatus galeam læva tenet, atque reflexa Cervice orantis capulo tenus applicat ensem." Virg. X, 534.

(4) "Hostis amare, quid increpitas, mortemque minaris? Nullum in cæde nefas; nec sic ad prælia veni, Nec tecum meus hæc pepigit mihi fœdera Lausus. Unum hoc, per, si qua est victis venia hostibus, oro, Corpus humo patiare tegi, . . . Et me consortem nati concede sepulcro."—Virg. X, 900.

the pious and the humane, is so cruel and ferocious, so strikingly contrary to his nature, because of the death of Pallas, who, he thinks, deserves all the victims now falling by his own sword. Even "prisoners' blood shall flow over the flames of his funeral pile." (Æneas, X., 520). Whilst the last passage of Mezentius is striking by the contrary trait; he is hated by his own kin; chased away by his subjects, followed only by his son, who sacrifices himself to save the hard-hearted father. He, usually so selfish, savage and brutal, is here, in this instance, all tenderness, love and pathos. Though out of the reach of the enemy, he yet returns to the battle-field, not to conquer, but to die, asking of his victor as a last and only favor, to be honorably buried, and at the side of his devoted son. That is of grand pathos, and true to nature. The ferocious Mezentius, in presence of his dead son, dead in his defence, dead for him whom everyone else hated and who hated everyone else, is suddenly turned into a humane, loving being; he is overcome for the first time in his life, by a tender feeling, piety for his dead child. For once he feels what it is to love, to admire and to have been loved—and this supreme moment is—his last one!—In Corneille and in Victor Hugo we find often happy imitations of the great Virgil.

THE SUBLIME AMONG THE CLASSICS AND THE MODERNS.

In " *Polyeucte* "(1) and in " *Horace*,"(2) Corneille attains

---

(1) Polyeucte V. 3.
> Je vous l'ai deja dit, et vous le dis encore,
> Vivez avec Sévère, ou mourez avec moi.
> Je ne méprise point vos pleurs, ni votre foi;
> Mais, de quoi que pour vous notre amour m'entretienne,
> Je ne vous connais plus, si vous n'êtes chretienne.

(2) Horace III, 6.
> *Horace :* Nous venez-vous, Julie, apprendre la victoire ?
> *Julie :* Mais plutot du combat les funestes effets.
> *Horace :* Rome n'est point sujette, ou mon fils est sans vie:
> Je connais mieux mon sang, il sait mieux son devoir.
> *Julie :* Que vouliez-vous qu'il fit contre trois ?
> *Horace :* Qu'il mourût, . . .
> N'eut-il que d'un moment reculé sa defaite, . . .
> Il eut avec honneur laissé mes cheveux gris,
> Et c'était de sa vie un assez digne prix.

at such sublime effects. In "Le roi s' amuse," "Lucretia Borgia," and in "Notre Dame," Victor Hugo reaches that climax. That sublimest of effects, that deepest thrill of our noblest passions the poet appears to reach in uniting into one and the same instance *the terrible and the tender.* Such is Æneas dealing his fearful death-blows around, yet aiming but at appeasing the shadow of young Pallas, inanimate, and of soothing his father, disconsolate; or Mezentius receiving his last stroke, asking of his victor the favor of a burial at the side of his only beloved son.— Here are the terrible and the tender united; at once excruciating pain and sweet gratification, horror and delight. Here is the sublime. That brings our noblest soul-strings into vibration. This is the highest of the poetic art. This but the greatest masters, Virgil, Shakspeare, Schiller, Corneille, Victor Hugo, etc., know how to reach. It is the *sanctum sanctorum* of poetry.

Another reminiscence strikes me, just parallel to this, coming from the far-off past: When a young man, I recollect to have found in a Roumanian poet, of blessed memory, my friend, *Dimitriu Bolintineanu,* such beautiful passages, uniting the tender and the terrible to a high pitch. I have not the book at hand to quote; be his name here remembered with gratitude.

Victor Hugo reached that pitch in depicting a grand, profligate duchess; having poisoned at a banquet her enemies, and fiendishly rejoicing over it, she discovers that her only, long lost and sincerely beloved son is among her poisoned enemies.—Her despair and remorse are exceedingly pathetic.—In another drama the same poet hits a great moment in the scene, when a father opening the sack presumingly containing the murdered ravisher of his dear child, full of hellish, yet natural glee, finds there instead— his poor dead child herself, dead to save the life of her ravisher!—The most pathetic, I think, is in a historic novel by the same poet. There we meet a beggarwoman, long mourning over her child—stolen in infancy by gypsies—who gets hold of, and delivers in revenge, to the executioner, an innocent gypsy girl, which girl, whilst dying, is found to be her own long-lost child.—Shakespeare has often reached that climax of the sublime; the tender, there, being often subordinate to the terrible. That is well known. But let us return to our subject proper.

FUNERAL PIETY IN HOMER.

Homer reports many cases of pious regard for the dead, their own, or their relations' keen desire for their obtaining a becoming burial; with accompanying funeral-rites, offerings, sacrifices, libations, incense, precious oil, flowers, tears and lamentations, with their habitual arms, favorite horses, oftentimes even with some favorite attendants. It was such passages in ancient authors which suggested to Herbert Spencer his hypothesis about the sacrificial service, etc., which, according to him, originated in by-gone prehistoric times in the naive and pious offerings of food to dead ancestors. Later they were raised to the gods, divine worship was paid them by posterity, and such offerings were continued to divinized heroes and remote tribal patriarchs. Such rites and such feelings we find often reported in Homer. Odysseus, for instance, is ordered to make a journey to the realms of Hades, the kingdom of the nether deities and the ghosts, to offer them sacrifices and consult them about the ways how to appease the superior gods, and reach home after his long wanderings since the siege of Troy. He says: "There Perimedes and Eurylochos held the victims, whilst I drew the sword from my side and dug a pit of the largeness of an ell, and filled it with a libation to all the dead; first with a honey-mixture, then with sweet wine, at last with water, and thereat I threw in some white barleymeal. Then I prayed and vowed

to all the unsteady-heads of the dead, that when I had
returned to Ithaca, a young cow, the best one, should be
sacrificed to them in the palace, and to fill the fire-altar
with costly gifts, and for *Teiresias* alone I shall offer a
black sheep. Having prayed to them, I took the sheep and
cut their throats over the pit, and the black blood flowed
therein. Thereupon came crowding all the souls of the
departed, coming from Erebus: virgins, youths, much-tried
old men, tender, mourning girls, war-slaughtered men with
stained armor. These came around the pit, in large numbers,
from all directions, and with great noise. Pale fear took
hold of me." (¹)

Biblical and Classical Funeral Rites.

Here I wish to call attention to the fact that, whilst the
Bible remembers the dead with a feeling of resignation and
quiet tenderness, and whilst, with the Romans, we find on such

(1).   'Ενθ' ἱερήϊα μὲν Περιμήδες Εὐρύλοχός τε
ἔσχον· ἐγὼ δ' ἄορ ὀξὺ ἐρυσσάμενος παρὰ μηροῦ
βόθρον ὄρυξ' ὅσσον τε πυγούσιον ἔνθα καὶ ἔνθα,
ἀμφ' αὐτῷ δὲ χοὴν χεόμην πᾶσιν νεκύεσσιν.
πρῶτα μελικρήτῳ, μετέπειτα δὲ ἡδέϊ οἴνῳ,
τὸ τρίτον αὖθ' ὕδατι· ἐπὶ δ' ἄλφιτα λευκὰ πάλυνον.
* πολλὰ δὲ γουνούμην νεκύων ἀμενηνὰ κάρηνα,
ἐλθὼν εἰς Ἰθάκην στεῖραν βοῦν, ἥτις ἀρίστη,
ῥέξειν ἐν μεγάροισι πυρήν τ' ἐμπλήσεμεν ἐσθλῶν,
Τειρεσίῃ δ' ἀπάνευθεν ὄϊν ἱερευσέμεν οἴῳ
παμμέλαν', ὃς μήλοισι μεταπρέπει ἡμετέροισιν.
τοὺς δ' ἐπεὶ εὐχωλῇσι λιτῇσί τε, ἔθνεα νεκρῶν,
ἐλλισάμην, τὰ δὲ μῆλα λαβὼν ἀπεδειροτόμησα
ἐς βόθρον, ῥέε δ' αἷμα κελαινεφές· αἱ δ' ἀγέροντο
ψυχαὶ ὑπὲξ Ἐρέβευς νεκύων κατατεθνηώτων.
[νύμφαι τ' ἠΐθεοί τε πολύτλητοί τε γέροντες
παρθενικαί τ' ἀταλαὶ νεοπενθέα θυμὸν ἔχουσαι
πολλοὶ δ' οὐτάμενοι χαλκήρεσιν ἐγχείῃσιν,
ἄνδρες ἀρηΐφατοι βεβροτωμένα τεύχε' ἔχοντες·
οἳ πολλοὶ περὶ βόθρον ἐφοίτων ἄλλοθεν ἄλλος
θεσπεσίῃ ἰαχῇ· ἐμὲ δὲ χλωρὸν δέος ᾕρει.]—Odyss. XI, 23-43.

occasions the terrible and the tender mingled together, we
see in Homer to these two elements a third one added, viz.,
that of *the funny*. Or do we find it funny because we do
not believe in it? Reading that poet, we imagine to see
him chuckle between the lines. A kind of tragic-comical
narrative seems to be Odysseus' descent into Hades and his
talk, etc., with the ghosts. But is it so? Is it not possible
that in those remote times that was all real earnest?
Indeed, could the ancient bard have intended to make his
leading hero ridiculous? That is hardly probable. More
plausible is that it was meant in earnest, and that the old
Greeks did believe in it. And that would constitute a dark
spot in Greek civilization, indeed. The deep hatred the
Bible entertains for these rites and practices, the sarcasm
the prophets constantly launched against them, seem to
show that the heathen world was very puerile in many
respects. Indeed, what a *hocus-pocus!* These funeral sacrifices may be, as alluded to before, the rudimentary origin
of the later pagan, widespread sacrificial services so much
insisted upon by priests and so little thought of by the
biblical prophetic school; so much so that Samuel already
thundered down poor, anxious King Saul with: "Behold!
to obey is preferable to slaughter offerings (I. Samuel
15, 22); to hearken, better than fat rams."(¹) The Homeric
prophet, Teiresias, is not so outspoken as Samuel. At the
invocation of Odysseus he makes, duly, his appearance.
Stalking with a golden sceptre in his hand, he eagerly asks
for the proffered blood, saying: "Step back from the pit
and take off thy sharp sword that I may drink of the blood
and tell thee the truth."(²) Of course, he tells him the

---

(1) הנה שמע מזבח טוב להקשיב מחלב אילים.

(2). 'Ηλθε δ' ἐπι ψυχὴ Οηβαίου Τειρεσίαο,
χρύσεον σκῆπτρον ἔχων, ἐμὲ δ' ἔγνω καὶ προσέειπεν . . . .
ἀλλ' ἀποχάζεο βόθρου, ἀπισχε δὲ φάσγανον ὀξὺ,
αἱματος ὄφρα πίω καὶ τοι νημερτέα εἴπω.—Odyss. XI, 90.

truth. Just such a "*hocus-pocus*" as the entire rite is; a pompous specimen of the stupidities and abominable cruelties of those heathen forms of worship so justly denounced in the Ebrew sacred books.

Among the numerous visitors in Hades had come also the mother of Odysseus. She, too, was very hungry, and eagerly had asked for the blood-offering; but her son warded her off with the sharp sword until first the soothsayer, Teiresias, had taken his share. Then only came her turn. She did not stand upon ceremonies. She came again, after the prophet, drank of the blood and at once recognized her son.(¹) Before partaking of the food she did not; she then gave him her motherly advice.

Herbert Spencer's hypothesis appears to be strongly confirmed by such passages, viz: the dead were simply persons sleeping in their tombs, shadowy and weak, trembling and shaking their heads for want of food.— As soon as they drank of the blood of the victims they felt refreshed, remembered their friends and gave them good advice. Most pathetically Odysseus' mother closes her long discourse with the thrilling words: "I did not die of sickness, but from longing for thee, musing about thee, Odysseus. My tender love for thee has deprived me of sweet life."(²) Here again is an honest word of nature, which finds a thrilling response in our souls. It is not artificial, no mythology. One passage more and our Greek parallels will be at an end. Among the many pale visitors came also Elpenor, one of Odysseus' companions. He had been, as all of them, entertained at the house of Kirke, the

---

(1). "Ὡς φαμένη ψυχὴ μὲν ἔβη δόμον Ἀϊδος εἴσω
Τειρεσίαο· . . . . ἐπὶ μήτηρ
ἤντε καὶ πίεν αἷμα κελαινεφές· αὐτίκα δ' ἔγνω,
καί μ' ἔπεα προσηύδα· —Odyss., XI, 150.

(2). οὔτε τίς οὖν μοι νοῦσος ἐπήλυθεν, ἥτε μάλιστα . . . .
ἀλλά με σός τε πόθος σά τε μήδεα, ...
σή τ' ἀγανοφροσύνη μελιηδέα θυμὸν ἀπηύρα." —Odys. XI, 200.

famous witch, drank too much, fell down from the roof,
died, was left there unburied, and hence, according to the
ideas of those times, could not be admitted into Hades till
his body was inhumed. He pleads for such a burial, and
finds us sympathetic. "I pray thee, now, on my knees, by
those thou didst leave behind, by thy wife, by thy father,
who reared thee, by Telemachus, whom thou didst leave as
thy only son in the palace, . . . I pray that thou
rememberest me. Going away hence, don't let me remain
there unwept and unburied; that the gods should not be
wroth at you on account of me; but bury me with my arms
and make me a hillock at the shore of the gray sea; for
me, the unhappy man, that future generations should
remember me."( )

Thus the unfortunate Elpenor prays for burial and a monument "that he may be remembered by future generations."
Just as in the Bible: "The first son of the Levirate marriage shall represent the deceased kinsman (the widow's first
husband), that his name shall not die out." (²) Is that not
wonderful! Seemingly there is such a vast distance between
Greece and Judæa; so much prejudice, so much misunderstanding.—Yet after all, the genuine tones of nature, at the
very spring of the soul, before they are overlaid with the
varnish of superstition and hypocrisy,—such tones are identical! In Homer and in the Bible we find the same cravings,
same hopes and aspirations, viz: The dead wish to be

---

(1). νῦν δέ σε τῶν ὄπιθεν γουνάζομαι, οὐ παρεόντων,
        πρός τ' ἀλόχου καὶ πατρὸς, ὁ σ' ἔτρεφε τυτθὸν ἐόντα,
        Τηλεμάχου θ', ὃν μοῦνον ἐνὶ μεγάροισιν ἔλειπες· . . . .
        ἔνθα σ' ἔπειτα, ἄναξ, κέλομαι μνήσασθαι ἐμεῖο·
        μή μ' ἄκλαυτον, ἄθαπτον, ἰὼν ὄπιθεν καταλείπειν,
        νοσφισθείς, μή τοί τι θεῶν μήνιμα γένωμαι,
        ἀλλά με κακκῆαι σὺν τεύχεσιν, ἄσσα μοί ἐστιν,
        σῆμα τέ μοι χεῦαι πολιῆς ἐπὶ θινὶ θαλάσσης,
        ἀνδρὸς δυστήνοιο, καὶ ἐσσομένοισι πυθέσθαι—Odyss., XI, 65-76.

V. M. 25, 6.—יקום על שם המת, ולא ימחה שמו מישראל. (2)

remembered to posterity. The living feel piety and tenderness for the dead. Homer bespeaks for them a grave and funeral rites and a monument. The Bible legates to them, children to bear their name, cultivate their acre, and occupy their cottage. Here we find the source of the immortality-idea with Heathen, Jew, Christian and Mohammedan. The Hindoo sage aspires to *Nirvana*, or absorption in God. The biblical nations crave for posterity, and shudder at annihila-tion. Curious! Semite, Turanian and Arian now coincide in the West in this instance.

BIBLICAL REVERENCE.

This, apparently, wonderful coincidence between Arians, Turanians and Semites, between Christian, Mohammedan and Ebrew peoples of to-day, having the same hopes and aspirations to commemorate the past generations, and be remembered by the future ones, this fidelity to the dead and to the living, equally entertained by present nations of divers creeds and origins, is most naturally and easily explained. We have but to remember that all those three sets of races have been nursed at the breast of the same *Book*, and that piety to the departed, and those unborn, is one of the leading traits of that book. The Bible does not expressly teach the doctrine of human immortality. But it does more; it conceives mankind as one huge tree, the different races as its branches, and the different generations as the blossoms, leaves and fruits of the divers seasons and crops of the one and the same arbor. Therefore is each and every individual person part and parcel thereof, and each is in duty and reality bound to consider himself as such, and constantly act as such, viz: to have regard for the past and the future, and be faithful to those gone by and those to come,—that is the law of the biblical solidarity; solidarity not only within the limits of the same State and genera-tion, but solidarity and responsibility between the mem-

bers of the generations present, and those of the past and
the future centuries.

This feeling of unison of all mankind and all centuries,
vaguely pervading the civilized and refined of all times,
found its most solemn expression in the Decalogue (II. M.
20, 12), where it stands forth in grand relief. After the
solemn declaration of the unity and spirituality of the
Deity, connected with and revealed to man through the
Sabbath, the day of rest and sanctification, the lawgiver
solemnly enjoins *parental reverence*. "Honor thy father
and thy mother, that thy days may be long upon the land
God is giving thee."—Now, parental reverence is filial piety,
is piety for the dead and fidelity to the unborn. To respect
the ancestors is taking into consideration the unborn generations. Again, reverencing our fathers is the pledge of being
considered by posterity. Parental piety affirms the family,
secures the nation, establishes the country, and thus secures
the offspring. Hence, reverence for those preceding us safeguards the coming generations; it is the connecting bridge
between past, present and future.

This fifth commandment, passing over from the natural
religion of antiquity to the positive religion of Sinai, sunk
deeply into the human heart. From the Ebrew it passed to
the Christian and the Mohammedan, to the civilized in
general. For long centuries it was specially established
among the biblical people. When that people lived yet in
the European and Asiatic *Ghetto*, in the gloom of poverty
and wretchedness, during long ages gone by, this precious
family solidarity, this noble fidelity to the dead and the
living, this reverence for parents and love of kindred, was
the only sunshine of that ghetto, the only redeeming
feature of that social Tartarus, invented by popular stupidity and priestcraft. Parental reverence was the mystic gem
illumining and cheering that night of the Ebrew middle-
ages. It was that love, devotion and adherence to prede-

cessors, kindred and posterity, the reverence of the children to parents, the love of parents to descendants. At a time when everything Ebraic was decried, hooted and derided, parental reverence and fidelity to the dead and the living was its redeeming feature, was respected and admired by the entire world, and slowly it was learned by the world; it was acquired by Arian and Turanian. Slowly the Teutonic nations, the Latin, Slav and Mongol races, made it their own. And that plant, nurtured with tears and kisses at the Ebraic ghetto, became the brightest flower of civilized mankind, an organized feature in man's physiognomy, adorning the halls and the drawing-rooms of the Latin and German count, the English earl and the Slav *boyar*, as well as the peasant's hut.

JULES SIMON.

May this ever be its crowning glory, and may this gem never be plucked from civilized man's diadem; but I fear recent nihilism has partly, already, tarnished it. Sometimes it appears as if the fragrance of that costly flower be already evaporated and its colors faded. There is something in our modern way of understanding liberty and equality which tends to fade and rot that flower, to uproot all reverence and love for, all veneration and devotion to past or future, to parent or descendant; to scoff at the wrinkles of the mother and the tears of the babe, which creates impatience and insubordination, coldness and indifference, selfishness and self-sufficiency,—the doctrine of: "*After me the deluge*," concentrating all upon the Ego and the present, and caring for nothing but the dear self and the gratification of the hour. That is the nihilism of the family.

Mr. Jules Simon, the well-known French Minister of education, a great statesman, philosopher and writer, is of the opinion that the sense of reverence for the noble and the good, that parental respect, filial piety or fidelity to the

13

dead and the living, with the solidarity of the family are strongly on the wane. And, mark it well, reader, he claims that this process of family-deterioration is having its focus in our beloved United States of America, and that from here it is invading Europe.

The *Baltimore Sun*, of the 14th April, 1892, brought out the weighty utterances of Mr. Jules Simon in this regard. I quote here the following verbatim. After having unfolded the sweet picture of the adherence, cohesion and mutual respect of the family members of by-gone times, Mr. Jules Simon says: "Again I fancy to myself a family of persons, pressed and busy, who disdain everything that is not new, and trample upon everything which might interfere with their 'progress.' The father and mother have merely consented to marry one another as a business of convenience; finding marriage too heavy; . . . they go to the magistrate . . . . declaring that they love in other places. The children do not bear the yoke of obedience, as in that age when it was absolutely necessary that they be guided and protected. Being yet supported—by the parents—this is the only band binding them to the parents. The strong and holy bond of former years has given place to the marriage of adventure, facilitated by the divorce . . guardianship . . . boarding-house and emancipation from family control. . . . The family is further deserted for the club, the games of chance, the out-door meals, . . · the Exchange, the fine hotels, the dinners. . . . Emancipation is good, but too much is not good." . . . So far Jules Simon on Nihilism in the family.

THE CAVE OF MACHPELAH.

From this picture of *"brilliant wretchedness"* and the neglect of family-piety, let us pass to its reverse, the solemn, yet inspiring scene, in Genesis, 23, of a model family; still suggesting all the purity, nobility, affection and mutual self-sacrifice of the conjugal ideal, as expressed in the legend of Eve cut out from the side of Adam, with the pointed moral of: "Therefore shall man leave his father and mother and cling to his wife and become one person." (Gen. II. 24).

There—I. M. 23—we read: "And the life of Sarah was a hundred and twenty and seven years; and Sarah died at *Hebron*, in Canaan; and Abraham came to mourn and shed tears over Sarah; then he arose and bought an hereditary burial-place, the *Cave of Machpelah*, paying its full price, acquiring it for ever, as a burial-place for the family." Look how weighty and solemn, yet quiet, serene and manly are these words and verses, as if to impress us with the import of this model pair and model family picture, this paragon of suave and manly piety for the dead. One hundred and twenty-seven years she had lived at his side—first as a child and kindred, then as his consort; had clung to the chequered fortunes of an innovator, an initiator; had shared in his battles and struggles, obloquies, failures and poverty; shared in his exile, wanderings and vicissitudes of fortune; slowly rose with him to affluence, wealth, renown and greatness, thus fighting his battles, ever cheering, smiling, hoping, inspiring, persevering.—She now breathed her last in his arms. . . . Well deserving his tears, his respect, a place for her dust to mingle with his, the worthy consort of a providential man.

The ancient Syrians, Canaanites and Egyptians knew no more sacred duty of the living than to provide for the dead; and their precautions were indeed extraordinary. They built their graves as if for eternity. Kings and princes built during lifetime their residences of hereafter. Towers and gigantic structures they erected over their last abode. The Pyramids, the most astonishing works of ancient times, seem to have had for their chief aim the security of the rest of the dead. The greatest misfortune

that could befall an individual or a nation was to have the
rest of their dear ones rudely interrupted.   The mass of the
people had their burial-place in subterranean caves.   These
were either naturally or purposely hewn in the rock, in
order to defy destruction.   These catacombs generally
consisted of one spacious chamber or hall, lit up only by
an aperture at the top, giving to the whole a mysterious
half-darkness, fit for the sacred repose of the dead.   Alongside the walls there were niches, each containing one. sarcophagus.   Sometimes the hall led into another chamber
or a long corridor, the walls of which were lined with
coffins, each standing upon pedestals.   Sometimes the cave
had again another cave beneath, accessible by a staircase,
having thus one burial-ground upon another.   Perhaps the
" Cave of Machpelah " was such a double cave, *kafol*
meaning double.   The door used to be closed by a huge
stone, requiring several persons to remove it.   The original
meaning of such massive tombs may have been to preserve
the body for resurrection.—The Bible never taught it,
though allusions may be claimed for it.

MOSES AND THE TWO ARKS.

But the most beautiful instance of fidelity to the living
and the dead we find in Exodus 13, 19 : "And Moses took
the bones of Joseph with himself (to bring them into the
Promised Land), for Joseph had earnestly enjoined upon
the Israelites, 'When God will remember you, then take
my bones with you hence.' "—Thus, when Moses had
matured his scheme of redemption, when he had vanquished
the numerous obstacles on his way, those of the despotic
Pharaohs and of the inert Ebrew masses, then, in the
moment of departure and of liberation, what occupied his
attention in that crisis?   The care for the ashes of the
patriarch!—What a noble piety for the dead!   Again,
Joseph, the juvenile shepherd, sold into slavery, a captive in

Egypt, and there becoming the viceroy, when dying, at the foot of the throne, prayed his brethren—those who had wronged him so much—"God will remember you; you will return home, then take my bones with you, that my ashes may mingle with yours."—What a noble piety for the living!

Think! Joseph, the Egyptian prince, prefers a humble mound near his kinsmen to the proud mausoleum of the Egyptian Pharaohs. Centuries later, Moses, starting a new nation, a new era, fulfills that wish. The sarcophagus of the dead patriarch had been buried under a stream, turned away for that purpose. Legend claims that, at the voice of Moses, the sarcophagus arose and came swimming across the waves to share in the redemption and return from exile to the ancestral home. Legend and history both, what fine ideals of fidelity to the living and the dead!

In classic times it was customary (says Dr. Yellinek), when a general returned victorious from his campaign, to receive the honors of a triumph. Gorgeously clothed with the imperial purple, a rich, golden wreath around his brow, he made his entrance in a magnificent chariot, bands of music and numerous decorated guards, the war-prisoners, the captive, chained princes, the booty, following; the people hilarious and shouting, the banners gaily waving, the names of battles gained, of cities taken, exhibited to the admiration of the vociferous multitude. Such was the triumphal march of a Roman imperator. Moses, having conquered the successors of Raamses, liberated his clansmen, and leading them forth to independence—what was his trophy? what his triumphal pomp? The sarcophagus of the dead chieftain, Joseph, who wished his ashes to mingle with those of his posterity!

What a noble example of fidelity to the living and the dead.

A legend claims that Moses was preceded on his march by two arks, one containing Joseph's remains, the other destined as the future ark of the covenant. And the nations wondering at that, were answered: "Why, one ark is containing the ashes of the dead and the other the spirit of the Ever-Living;" the one representing the past, the other the ever future; those ashes had been inspired by that spirit—that spirit is but the unfolding of history past and future.

SERAH B. ASHIR.

Who discovered the place where Joseph's sarcophagus had been buried under the stream? A legend tells that it was *Serah b. Ashir*, a woman. She had lived and waited, since Joseph's demise till the liberation by Moses. She pointed out to the latter the watery grave of the viceroy. Thus a woman was made the symbol of hopefulness to bridge over and connect the past bondage with the future redemption! The Greek myth claims that *Pandora* frivolously opened the fatal box with the fatal locked-in ills; the ills got out to the ruin of man; hope alone, at the bottom of the box, remained, thus precluded from solacing man. Thus the Greek myth insinuates woman as disappointing man's hopes. The Ebrew legend makes woman the bearer of solace and hope to man. Here is another contrast between woman in Greek myth and Ebrew legend. (¹)

Reader, am I wrong in saying that Homer and Hesiod, Virgil, Edda and Niebelungen, are eclipsed by such simple narratives, and such sweet legends as just mentioned from Pentateuch and Agada? And wherein lies their charm, their thrill, their superiority? Simply in their truthfulness; fact and fiction have their gold grain of truth; they mirror nature in their crystal waves. Both their conceptions and their feelings are honest and genuine; they touch us, because they touch a corresponding chord in our bosoms, ever ready to respond to what is really great and noble.

---

(1) Jalkut be-Shalah.

POSITIVE BENEVOLENCE AND POOR-LAWS.

We have discussed, above, many institutions and enactments of the Pentateuch, which we may denominate as negative benevolence, laws that remove obstacles in the way of the needy to recuperate and rise in the economic scale. Let us now have a survey of the *positive* ones. Those by which they shall actively be helped to stand again upon their feet. (V. M. 24, 19-22): "When thou reapest thy harvest and hast forgotten a sheaf, do not go back to fetch it, but leave it to the stranger, the fatherless and the widow."—"When thou beatest down thy olive tree do not go over the boughs again, but leave something for the stranger, fatherless and widow."—"When thou gatherest in thy grapes, do not glean over again, but leave some, etc., etc., that God may bless thee. . . . Remember, a slave and poor thou hast been in Egypt." . . .

These divers gifts are by the Talmud denominated pickings—leavings—margins and gleanings.(1)

(See Maimonides—*Yad*—"Gifts to the poor," I. 1, and Peah. I. 2): "Remember, thou hast been a bondsman in Egypt; therefore do I command thee." This is the law's constant keynote. Thus the most helpless of mankind are placed under the special protection of the Deity, the king of the biblical State. According to III. M. 19, 9, the products of the margins of the farm belong to the poor, too. In the Release-Year the spontaneous field-growth belonged to the same. (III. M. 25, 6).—Three yearly festivals are instituted, during which the whole nation should, possibly, be at the capital to worship and unite in the same national bond and feel happy.—"But," adds the law, (V. M. 16, 11) "thou shalt rejoice with thy children, thy slave, the Levite, the stranger, the widow and the orphan." Thus the holidays, too, were benefits for the poor. So was especially

---

(1) לקט, שכחה, פאה, עוללות.

the weekly Sabbath. Even in the Ghetto, the darkest days of the Mosaic people, this hospitality to the poor was a standing virtue with them. It was a privilege to take home a poor traveling guest for the Sabbath.—In V. M. 14, 28, we read: "At the end of every third year thou shalt collect the tenth of thy field-produce and leave it in thy storehouses, that the poor, the Levite, the Gentile-immigrant, the orphan and the widow shall eat and get enough—that God may bless thee in all thy handiwork."—In V. M. 26, 12, this law is repeated, preceded by another of a similar nature, according to which the firstlings of the produce of the land were consecrated to the national gatherings in the capital, the above-named poor to participate in. According to tradition (Bikkurim III.) the people met in the leading places of the districts, and, accompanied by music and a wreathed ox for sacrifice, they pilgrimed to Jerusalem and the temple mount, each with his provisions and his friends. After a solemn temple service and a most touching special prayer, remembering the common lot of troubled mankind, the feeling of national unison and solidarity, they enjoyed the humble feast in the presence of the Deity, extending the conviviality to poor and stranger, etc. The wreathed ox in the procession is remembered in the "Mardi Gras." These festivals are frequently alluded to in S. Scrpt., a beautiful trait intertwining and fusing religion, nation and mankind, body and soul and their solidarity, as they really are in nature.

It is not easy to decide whether the lawgiver instituted for such purposes one-tenth of the crop or several tithes, since they are mentioned several times.

Of course, critics have claimed to find here different hands and divers epochs. The Rabbis try to settle matters in the following way: From all field-produce the Ebrew farmer had to bring two from one hundred to the priests; next the *first tenth* to the Levites; next a *second tenth* to be consumed in Jerusalem during the holidays (V. M. 14, 23). Of this second tithe *every third* and *sixth year* the produce was set apart for the poor, etc. (Maimonides, *Yad*, Poor-gifts and second Tithes—Talmud Peah. 8, 5) ([1]).—Nor must we forget that the Sabbath is especially instituted for the poor serving classes, as expressed with special emphasis in the second Decalogue, V. M. 5, 14.—These popular gatherings in the capital during the holidays Maimonides justly thinks "to intend keeping alive the feeling of sociability and fraternity." (More Neb. III, 39). Moreover, L. Philipson adds: "They were to conform to the mode of the ancients, to unite religion and joy; whilst in modern times, people are given to either the stern earnestness of religion or to unbridled sensuality."—I think, they were intended as an especial bond of nationality and consanguinity, coupled with the desire to interconnect life and religion, as is the case throughout Mosaism.

BIBLICAL TITHES.

These tithes were levied upon the produce of the soil, and the flocks of clean and unclean animals. The first-born son, too, had to be redeemed. The firstlings of animals belonged, too, to the Temple. The question now arises: "Were not all these taxes exorbitant, and were they really paid?" Some claim, they were not paid; some, that there was but one and the same tithe, differently applied in divers epochs and circumstances. Yet, according to Tobias I, 7, and to Josephus, (Antiquit. 4, 8 and 8-22), such tithes were actually paid! Let us not forget that the tribe of Levy had no lands, and hence needed some safe income for subsistence. Again we must remember that these tithes covered the expenses of State, church and school, of temple, priests, Levites, police, etc., representing all of our modern government, divine worship, public instruction and justice;—

---

(1) תרומה, מעשׂר ראשׁון, מעשׂ״ שׁני.

then it would not seem to be exorbitant. Nor must we forget that these were not taxes, in our sense of the term. They were rather moral duties, ordained by law, the payment of which was left to individual good-will and conscience. The Levites were always classed with the poor, the widow, the stranger and the orphan; that proves sufficiently that the Levites and many of the priests were not overpaid for their spiritual services. Judging from different hints in *Mishna* and *Gemara*, we feel justified in thinking that the farmers were believed not to be overscrupulous in the payment of tithes. They were often termed "*ignoramus,*" "*idiot,*" and naturally presumed as "*unclean boors.*" (¹)

BIBLICAL CHARITY—UNSECTARIAN.

In the above-mentioned verses we find the classic sources of the so-called "Jewish charities," the "Christian charities," the "Moslem charities," etc.; all these are but the developments of the Mosaic teachings on benevolence and universal solidarity. The Rabbinical law, the New Testament, the Koran, are but expounding and applying those principles to actual circumstances. When, in later times, the Jews had become less an agricultural and more an industrial and commercial people, especially those out of Judæa, money was raised for charitable purposes called *Quppa,* charity-box, wherewith it was prescribed to assist Ebrew and Gentile poor indiscriminately; in conformity with the biblical prescriptions, where the Gentile stranger or immigrant was recommended, side by side with the native poor, the Levite, the orphan, the widow, etc.

Thus does the Bible provide for the less-favored of fortune, not by begging and modern pauper-rates, but by right of sympathy, human solidarity or national community of interests; to such an extent that it became an Ebrew saying:

---

(1) עם הארץ, הדיוט, דמאי, טמא.

(Prov. 14, 31): "Who wrongs the poor, blasphemes his Maker; and who befriends him, worships God;" identical with our English expression: "Worship to God is love to man."

RABBINICAL CHARITY AND NEW TESTAMENT.

In Talmud Shekalim, V. 6, we read that the ancient temple had a room called "room of the silent"([1]), where those needy persons were remembered that refused public charities. Here we have the parallel of the New Testament saying: "In giving alms, let your left hand not know what the right one is doing."—Our modern charities must be stimulated, if not provoked, by the public press. Closely seen, certain people become philanthropists solely as a paying means of advertisement. Many things are undertaken ostensibly for the public interest, really for self-glorification. Let it pass, if the public at least profits by it. The New Testament is especially severe on ostentatious alms-giving, denying it any merit whatever. It closely follows its predecessors. The prototype of such views on the delicacy of charity is found exactly so in Talmud Chagiga, 5 a : "Better no charity than for ostentation's sake."

In Mishna Tanith 4, 5, we read of peculiar and unique festive days (the 15th Ab and 10th Tishri), instituted for matchmaking, called the "pretty ones," when the maidens took the initiative in courting the youths. "All of them alike were dressed in white, plainly and humbly, in order not to shame the poor girls, and let each of them have their good chances."([2]) Here is the origin of our leap-year free courtship and sociable, at least as to the privilege of feminine initiative. As to the magnanimity of dressing plainly in order not to shame the humbler rivals, I know of no instance in modern times. Competition now-a-days seems to be of a hardier stuff, even among the gentler sex.

---

(1) לישבת חישאים.

(2) לא היו ימים טובים לישראל כט״ו באב וכיה״כ.

Here is another sweet emanation from the biblical solidarity and charity laws:—(Peah, I., 1). The following have no limits (¹): "The gifts to the poor of the corner growth of the field; of the firstlings of the fruit; of festivities during the national gatherings in Jerusalem; free benevolence and study or learning."—To the question whether wordly or Greek learning, too, is included, the answers and opinions are varied, according to the school and the epochs of the expounders.

Thus we read in Talmud, Menachoth, 99 *b*: "Ben Doma, nephew of R. Ismael, inquired of the latter: 'I, who have learned the entire law, can I study the Greek science?' The uncle quoted thereat the verse: 'This law-book shall not be removed from thy mouth, and thou shalt ponder thereover day and night.' Now go and look out for an hour that is neither day or night, and learn the Greek science." Again in other places it is mentioned eulogistically of Rabbis, strong in Greek and in science. So it is claimed that every member of the great Sanhedrin had to know many languages, as the examination of criminals had to be held without an interpreter. Liberality produced liberality, and intolerance intolerance, with Jew and Gentile.

The same Mishna continues: "These (²) are the things whose fruit a man enjoys in this world, whilst the principal remains for the hereafter, viz: Filial respect to parents; benefactions to the needy; peacemaking; whilst learning outweighs them all."—It is interesting to remark the high esteem in which the Rabbis held learning. Their education began with morality and closed with mentality. They based the latter upon the former. Mentality without morality they likened to "a large tree with huge, wide-spreading

---

(1) הפאה והבכורים והראיון וגמילת חסדים ותלמוד תורה·

(2) כבוד אב ואם, גמילת חסדים, שלום בין אדם לחבירו, ותלמוד תורה כנגד כולם.

branches rising to the sky,—but with slender roots ; such a tree tumbles down at the least storm."—The Rabbinical moralists enjoin on all public occasions benefactions to the poor, as in dangers and sickness, at funerals, births, weddings, etc.

And whilst they so much and so often enjoin to give, they at the same time enjoin the needy to refuse public *assistance* as long as possible. Only actual starvation allows that; only in extreme cases alms were acceptable. Here are some Talmudical proverbs to that effect : " Skin a carcass in the street, but ask for no alms."([1])—" Whosoever neglects teaching his son a trade is as much guilty as if he had raised him for robbery."([2])   R. Simon says : " It is written, ' Choose life.' " (Deuteronomy, 30).— That means a trade.—" Work honors the workman." ([3])— " Cherish work and hate assumed gentility." ([4]) " Make thy Sabbath a week-day and apply to nobody for help."— " Upon three things stands the world : upon instruction, work—others, prayer—and benevolence."—(Aboth, I).— Another version thereof is : " Upon truth, justice and peace stands the world." Many other passages there enumerate the leading human virtues : For the mass of the people they extol practical work as the highest of virtues. For the professional scholar learning is the highest. Many Rabbis combined learning with a humble trade.([5]) " A scholarly bastard is above an ignorant high priest," is a significant Rabbinical proverb.—All these teachings are staunch supporters of work, menial and mental. " For six days shalt thou work," was just as sacred a commandment as the Sabbath-rest. They stand up for property, for mine and thine. They were no communists. They recognized the knighthood of both labor and knowledge. They aspired to both whenever possible. Says a teacher in the same *Aboth :*

(1) Pesachim, 113 a.   (2) Kidushin, 29 a.   (3) Nedarim, 49 b.   (4) Aboth 1, 9. (5) Aboth II, 2.

"That is the way of study."—"Eat bread with salt; drink water in moderate quantities; sleep on the bare floor and go on studying."—"Well goes learning with work. The first alone will not thrive."—"*No meal, no learning.*"— "There are in the world three crowns: that of learning, of priesthood and of royalty; yet a good name is the highest." Others say: "Learning is the best."—"Seek for no other honors than learning."—"Seek not for prince's favors, since thy table is more honorable than theirs and thy crown is above theirs," etc.

The Rabbis understood well the delicacy of charity. So *Yoreh Deah* (Charity, 249,) says: "We must give charity with a friendly, smiling face, sympathetically conversing with the poor one and encouraging him. If you have not to give him, do not speak harshly, but rather by kind words, show him, anyhow, your good-will.—There are several grades of charity, each one higher than the other: First encourage a man who is impoverished, by a loan, a partnership, etc.; *i. e.*, offer no degrading alms. Next give charity without letting the poor one know who gave it to him. Next give without waiting for being asked. Above all, do not speak and boast of the charity bestowed."— *Ibidem*, the poor scholar is especially recommended. His work, his goods, etc., shall first be considered by buyer or employer.

We read in Hagigah (5 *a*) a Rabbinical discussion concerning sins deriving from simple, indelicate, indiscreet dealings. As such are quoted, persons that "give alms in public," for "better is not to give, than give and shame the poor;" or to "give alms to a poor woman secretly, on account of the evil tongues." In Kethuboth, 67 *a* and *b*, we read: "A male and female orphan in need, the female comes first to be assisted. When such are to be married she is first in order; he shall wait."—We are bid to assist the poor, not to enrich them. Yet it is told of Hillel I. that he gave to such an effeminate one even a horse and a slave. When the poor refuses alms, a loan shall be given him.— A Rabbi used to give, *incognito,* a small alms daily; once upon a time the poor detected him; the Rabbi ran away, hurting himself on the occasion—"*for better is to run into a fiery furnace than shame a fellow-man.*"

TALMUDICAL CHARITY METHODS.

There is no denying that the Talmud once started in assuming that the biblical word "*Guer,*" in connection with gifts to the poor, originally denoting immigrant, foreigner, meant only the "*Guer Zedek,*" a proselyte, a Gentile having adopted the full Judæan faith, trying to deduce this from a verbal analogy. Yet their solid sense for truth, propriety and morality made the Rabbis soon abandon that position, and declare that "the heathen poor are not to be deprived of those gifts, *for the sake of humanity*" (darkai Shalom.) There is not, etymologically, a shadow of doubt that the biblical, original sense of *Guer* is a non-Israelite, an immigrant stranger, the distinction between "*Guer Zedek*" and "*Guer Shaar,*" or "*Thoshab*" being of later date (Maimonides Yad—Poor-gifts I, 9.)

Beautiful, indeed, are these teachings. (Ibid. VII): "It is a positive commandment to be charitable to the poor as much as we can. Whosoever closes his eyes to the destitute, transgresses the law.—We must give according to their needs and habits—clothing, dwelling—a wife, too."—Malthus' misgivings concerning "*over-population*" never disturbed the minds of those teachers, whose maxim was, "*Who gives life, will give bread.*"

"If the poor was bred up with the habits of a riding-horse and a servant attending on him, he must be provided with them."—A Rabbinical hyperbolical anecdote narrates that Hillel I. having provided such a fastidious poor with a horse, and not being able to give him a servant, put himself at his disposal as such.—"A fifth part of one's income should be spent in charities. Heathen poor shall be fed and clothed together with Jewish poor, for the sake of humanity. Sensitive poor refusing charity, shall be assisted in some other honorable manner. The city authorities are entitled to compel every one to contribute to the public charities. The redemption of captives is a special and privileged duty. Woman has the privilege over man concerning food, clothing, marriage and ransom from captivity. The scholar has the privilege before all. A learned bastard comes before an ignorant high priest."—Ibid. VIII.

Maimonides, following the Rabbis, continues: "Every Jewish community is bound to appoint a charity-board, who shall make collections of money, eatables, etc., and distribute them among the poor, the money-distribution was called '*Quppa*,' and that of eatables: '*Timchui*.'" Never have we seen or heard of a Ebrew community not having such an arrangement. Especially on fast-days such distributions should be made; a fast-day without charity is hypocrisy, is almost homicide. The collections and distributions are carefully to be done, to prevent fraud by the busy-bodies, etc. (Ibid. X): "More than any other commandment must we practice active charity, charity being the *criterion of the seed of Abraham*. The import of Israel and his faith aro established solely by acts of benevolence. Always is benevolence bringing blessings, for *whosoever loves, is loved*, whilst who is hard-hearted, is of doubtful blood and origin. God is love. The sages gave without being known; they first gave and then prayed. Whosoever spends to the poor with an unfriendly mien, even a thousand gold-pieces, has forfeited all his merit. We must give with a kindly, smiling, beaming countenance, showing compassion and true sympathy by word and deed, with the object of our charity; if you have nothing to give, give kind words, anyhow; be not harsh to him who is heart-broken. Woe to him who

shames the poor!—There are different grades of charity.
The usual, dry, cold almsgiving is the very lowest. The
highest is to procure employment, give encouragment,
utilize the sinking man's capacities in a manner as to render
him above anybody's charities."—Here is an outline of the
Talmudical charity teachings, emanations from the biblical
ones, models for all civilized nations, finding their echo in
New Testament and Koran. The New Testament reader,
especially will now see whence derive those fine pithy,
pointed, sharp sayings of Jesus about true and false charity,
about hypocrisy and genuine goodness; they come from
a disciple of Hillel's school. That treatise concludes
(Ibid. X, 18) "Ever shall a man toil and bear everything,
and not throw himself upon people's charities."—" Make thy
Sabbath a week-day, and apply to nobody for assistance."
"If even a distinguished man, nevertheless, rather skin a
carcass in the street, and say not: I am a nobleman and
can't work. Some of the great sages actually did chop
wood, draw water, work as smiths, etc., and never asked
for charity."

HERBERT SPENCER ON PUBLIC ALMSGIVING.

In modern times economists and scientists have decidedly pronounced themselves against indiscriminate public
charity. From Adam Smith to Herbert Spencer and John
Stuart Mill, they have declared poor-laws and poor-rates,
etc., as inadequate, futile and even hurtful. Herbert Spencer especially, [1] is pretty near condemning it as misguided
and cheap philanthropy. With pointed arguments he questions the feasibility and the right of the government to
interfere in such a way on behalf of the poor. The government's office is, he says, " To protect the citizen in the
exercise of his rights, to shield him against wrong, not to
confer boons upon him at the cost of a fellow-citizen."

----

(1). Social statics on "poor-laws" and elsewhere.

14

He shows that, looking at the bottom of things, the poor has been wronged somewhere in his struggle for existence; that society has somehow ostracised him and robbed him of his chances; that the government ought *there* to step in and protect him and open him the avenues of subsistence, not to make him a pauper, not to give him poor-rates and petty endowments, which may, at best, save him from starvation, but chain him down to the galley-bench of the .proletariat. He shows, for instance, that the appropriation of the soil by a minority to the exclusion of all rests upon a very doubtful title. With Karl Marx and others, he points to the fact " that property in lands originally rests upon violence, cunning, fraud, force and prerogative; that its title-deeds are written by the sword, with blood, and paid with blows."

He claims " that such title-deeds can never confer legitimate ownership, however many hands have changed and however much time has elapsed since." . . . " There is the source of wrong, and many more social wrongs may have been committed against the poor in the struggle for existence. Here is the place for the government to interfere, and to see that one person should not *accapparate* all, and ten to live on sufferance." So poor-laws and rates are now almost universally condemned as a burden to the tax-payers, and useless, yea, dangerous, to the beneficiaries. That criticism refers especially to alms-giving and indiscriminate charities, as practiced whilom at the doors of abbeys and mosques and old-time synagogues. Again, such indiscriminate alms-giving, considered from another standpoint, is the outcome of heedless philanthropists and doubtful pietists; for such poor-laws rather breed than diminish pauperism. They are a heavy burden upon, and an unjust taxation of, the honest worker, a premium for laziness, vice and improvidence. They take away the well-earned comforts of the first and bestow them upon the latter, as if to foster and indulge them. They often rob the producing honest to feed the dishonest drones; being thus an actual premium for laziness and vice, they propagate and breed vicious drones and criminals, and stint the growth of honest, laboring families. . . . How, then, treat that class of people? The answer to that is: "Well, do not actually drown them, but do for them as little as possible; do not let them starve, but, anyhow, keep them from breeding. For pauperism is hereditary, just as any other vice is."—This is Herbert Spencer's idea concerning governmental and public charity; and that of most of modern, economic thinkers. Indeed, who is not aware of the many abuses and drawbacks of many charity institutions! How often are not the most heartless and worthless hypocrites at their head, as if to cover their own ill-gotten wealth by the veil of public sympathy! I know many men and women, thrilling with true philanthropy, occupied with public benevolence. But I know, too, others, wolves in sheep-skins, using it as hypocrisy's cloak.

But we must not "turn out the baby with the bath." We must not confound and condemn the two sorts of persons, nor the two kinds of charities, nor put pretense alongside of genuine goodness. Hypocrisy is a parasite, fastening itself just upon the noblest and holiest. Indeed, what sacred things have not been desecrated and profaned by such *Tartuffes*! Even so the English poor-laws may be laws poor indeed, and Herbert Spencer may be right in his strictures upon them. No doubt indiscriminate alms-giving, as practiced in the Middle Ages at the abbeys and churches, or in the Orient in mosque and synagogue, or even to-day in certain quarters, may be an abuse—may rather foster pauperism and vice than diminish it, an opportunity for pretense, rather than philanthropy.

But there is, too, another kind of benevolence, a benevolence which is but justice masked. Let us look to that other kind and its criteria.

MOSAIC SOLIDARITY.

The benevolent and solidary laws of Mosaism are of that kind. They are not degrading; they are not begging opportunities; not easy alms-giving and alms-taking, requiring no effort from the rich, and from the poor none except cringing or showing a contrived, "crooked arm," or a stolen "shivering baby." Those laws were simply reservations of the State, held in store for the less endowed. As we have in modern times "commons," or large lawns, grounds, tracts of land and parks, belonging to all the citizens, as common property, which the State reserves for and utilizes on extra occasions, even so did the Pentateuch make its reservations. The Sabbath-rest, the seven yearly festivals, the Year of Release and Jubilee-restitution, the corners of the field, the forgotten sheaf, the gleanings, the firstlings, the tithes, the holiday-gifts, etc., were such reservations for the poor, the scholar, the stranger, the widow, the orphan, etc. They were reserved in right, not as an alms, not degrading the needy, but uplifting them, giving them a backing in extreme cases, placing them under the especial protection of God, the king and proprietor of the State, not depriving them of any of the rights of men or of citizens, leaving them all the chances and room to recuperate and reconquer an economical independence. Whilst the English poor-laws, poor-rates, poor-rents, poor-workhouses, poor-gifts, etc., used to give the destitute but a poor resource—a dog-kennel, with a bone and a rag, bedding them upon vice and filth and contempt, beyond the means of resurrection, considering them as pariahs, lepers and outcasts, the Bible treats them as "*brothers*" in momentary difficulties and reserves for them rights and sympathies, not alms and contempt. Why this? Because the political and social fabric of the Bible is based, not upon property, or conquest, or birth, but upon solidarity; upon liberty, equality, equal economic chances and community of interests; because of the principle of one humanity, "children of one God." (¹)

Indeed, never was a lawgiver so free in his legal promulgations as the Mosaic one. He led his people out of Egypt under the guidance of God, all alike, unfree and poor; he gave them a country, conquered by God, the sole king of . the State.

He portioned out among them that territory, dividing it into equal shares, and declared them all free and equal; he did that upon his own terms, emanating from a superior source. "Mine are the Israelites, my servants, redeemed from Egypt." "Mine is the land, ye shall not sell it forever." Person and soil were thus declared inalienably free. This being the case, he could prescribe the one God-worship, the Sabbath-rest, the Septennate and Jubilee, the Release from debts, the leaving of parts of the crops, of the flocks, the tithes, etc., to the Levites, the poor, the stranger, the widow and orphan. Never was a lawgiver so untrammeled and original; not Manu, Lycurgus or Solon, Buddha, Zoroaster or Rome's Decemviri and their *Twelve Tables;* nor any of the modern leaders.—Hence the originality, the impartiality, the universal justice of the Bible legislation. Nor was there any injustice resulting therefrom, not even in the course of long centuries of Judæan occupation; no injustice to the occupants, nor degradation to the beneficiaries, for these benefactions were from the start granted as rights, not as gifts and alms. For the thrifty, the intelligent and lucky always profit by the stupid, the lazy and the wasteful ones; they get their own share and moreover, that of the luckless ones. Hence it is but fair to let them give a pittance of their own superfluity, arising out of the missed share of the luckless. It is a kind of "ransom to the poor," as Mr. Chamberlain says. Or better as the Bible puts it, *"that thy brother shall live with thee;"* an admir-

---

(1) .בנים אתם ליהוה אלהיכם

able phrase, seldom met with in modern poor-laws. Thus, the Bible considers them, and the New Testament, with a special, thrilling sympathy and warmth, as *brothers* and *fellow-citizens*, and does all it can to rescue them from pauperism, and help them to a competency. All in all, the Mosaic poor benefactions, State-school—and temple—contributions may have amounted to some twenty per cent. of the national produce; a pretty fair share it was. But the ancients wasted less in silks and in cards, and in wines and cigars; hence they bore it patiently.

RETROSPECT ON STATE CHARITY.

We started from the proposition that the Biblical State and Society are built upon four cardinal principles: Personal liberty, social equality, equal distribution of the national wealth, and, lastly, solidarity or community of interests; hence mutual assistance as a right, not an ideal. As a branch of this last-named, we considered the Mosaic laws on benevolence. We have compared them with the English poor-laws, the most elaborate of Europe, beginning with Elizabeth, in 1563, and developing steadily and continually to this very present. We have seen the scathing criticism of Herbert Spencer, Huxley, etc., upon these latter, claiming that they are rather means for propagating pauperism than alleviating it; that England has probably the largest and most helpless pauper-class in the world—nearly a million of English-born subjects—and that emigration is their only means of escape; that in spite of poor-rights and poor-rates, and colonies and work-houses and endowments, etc., they are kept down and riveted to pauperism, as with an iron grip, by social ostracism, disfranchisement and contempt—kept from starvation for eternal degradation. Quite otherwise the Bible. It begins with the ideal of " Ye shall be unto Me a kingdom of priests and a holy nation," *i. e.*, all alike and of the same caste—all educated; no mob. " To

Me is Israel subject."—"To Me is the soil subject." God alone is King; all persons are free, equal, obeying the same laws and enjoying the same rights. The soil is equally divided out, and inalienable. There is but little of high industry, little of high internal commerce; all subsist upon the produce of the original family-lot. Hence, equal distribution of the national wealth. No proletarians, no paupers and no nobles. The poor are protected, encouraged, helped up to rise again. Can we detect in that system any kind of communism? No. It consecrates property, work and profit, individuality, emulation and effort. It rewards the virtues and talents, and punishes vice, laziness and improvidence. Thus, the Bible contains the best of scientific socialism. The State superintends, directs and prescribes all—"God is King;" laws govern; the State originally owned all; to that reverts all. The citizen is but the freeholder—the tenant of the soil. Every seventh year, and especially the fiftieth, there is a readjustment of persons and property; a return to the original conditions; universal equality in rights, duties and wealth. The law intentionally discourages internal high commerce and external, unjust wars. It is moderating and curbing cruel competition; it tries to keep every citizen on a par with his neighbor. Thus it establishes the solidarity principle, or community of interests. For him crushed in the battle of existence, it provides, first, by negative protection. He cannot be enslaved; his acre can't be alienated; he can't be crushed by debts; nor by usury; nor his bread endeared by *rings* or monopoly; nor can he be ground down by overwork; nor mutilated; nor harshly treated. He is in every respect a citizen, with special care protected by the State; he is "*a brother*." "Let thy brother live with thee," is a leading maxim.—Next comes a group of laws of positive benevolence, of active assistance in his behalf, as loans, portions from harvest and flocks, exemption laws, punctual payment

of wages, Sabbath and holiday boons, tithes and gifts on all
solemn occasions.—Withal, he has not lost caste, he is not
disfranchised, not dishonored; all avenues are open to him,
to rise again and become an independent member of society.

Thus whilst the ancient State generally consisted of
rulers, ruled and slaves; the Mediæval State of rulers, ruled
and serfs or conquered; the modern one of wealthy, well-
to-do, proletarians and paupers; the Biblical Society was
unique in having but one class, but one mass of citizens, all
alike by law and fact, legally, socially and economically
equal; no aristocrats, no plebeians, no proletarians and no
paupers. As to the accidentally impoverished individuals,
the law looked intently to it that they should not become a
pauper class; by provisions, negative and positive, which
gave them all the necessary means and deprived them of
no means to rise again and become self-sustaining, independent individuals, just as the rest of their fellow-
citizens. Thus the Biblical State put forward a scheme,
which granted to each and all of its members all their
natural chances in the struggle for existence; granting no
privileges to some and allowing no drawbacks to others.
This the Biblical State did, without recurring to any of the
far-fetched, unnatural, yea, impossible means of ancient
Sparta or of modern communism. It consecrated family,
inheritance, property, individual effort and emolument;
generous emulation, thrift, economy, etc. Yet it chained
down fierce and soulless competition, and left full scope for
altruism by constantly appealing to man's moral sense.
" *That thy brother may live with thee,*" including all races,
creeds and tongues in the term "*thy brother.*"

DIVINE LEGISLATION.

These are the Mosaic solidarity laws, so vastly different
from modern poor-laws; they are elevating and human-
izing; not pauperizing and degrading; calculated for the

classes and masses, impartial to strong or weak—to all.
And this universally is the grand criterion, the touch-stone
of a truly divine legislation; a legislation made to create a
great nation, and through that nation to spiritualize and
ennoble mankind. This democracy and this sanctification of
the law is the real and secret principle which makes out
the strength of the Bible and renders it invulnerable to the
tooth of time, the havoc of conquerors and the prejudice of
the vulgar. The Bible system is a theocracy, but in the
noblest sense of the term. It never became a hierarchy.
Priestcraft was always put down. State and Church there
are one. So they are in nature; so they are in body
and soul: for good use, not abuse. Egypt and India, too,
were theocracies, but hierarchies, and full of abuse. The
Mosaic form, surely, is calculated for a *certain* epoch and
people, in a special land under given circumstances. But
the spirit of Mosaism is universal and boundless; no clouds
of sect, race or country obscure its vision. It is for all
times and circumstances, and hence divine. It is calculated
to slowly gain over mankind and make all man one large
·brotherhood. Israel is intended there as mankind in miniature, and mankind considered as Israel in *extenso*.

CHURCH AND STATE.

Church and State are simply identical in the Bible. So
they are in nature. In our text-books and in their practical
administration they are divided, but in fact, they are one;
one thing looked upon from different standpoints, as the
one ray of the sunlight, broken by the prisma into many
colors. Both aim at right living. What we believe, we
must realize, or our faith is hypocrisy. The creed is the
theory, life is the practice, the necessary outcome of the
first, just as the fruit is of the root. If not, there is pretense and sham. Hence, the indissoluble interfusion of
Church and State in that system. In our times, where

often Church means dogma and ceremony, mostly artificially taken up from tradition, whilst there are many such Churches and various dogmas, ceremonies and traditions, which but little influence actual life, we feel their burden and try to lighten it by clamoring for *separation* of Church and State, to avoid spiritual or political despotism. Not so at the formation of religions; life and principle there are intertwined; they belong to each other, and as little separable as body from soul. They are simply the two poles of the same being. This is the Mosaic theocracy. God rules, and His just laws are the rules of the State government. The human rulers were but the spokesmen. The Mosaic, or Abrahamic, religion was originally most simple and rational. God, the creator of all, was sole and absolute authority. To Him alone belonged worship. Worship was: actual, virtuous, humane life; the realization of the commandments of justice tempered by charity.

SACRIFICIAL SERVICE AND CEREMONIES.

Slowly the temple-worship was elaborated, supplemented and adjusted from materials extant and believed in by the generality of mankind. But they were closely examined, sifted, selected and adapted from what would the least conflict with the original *Jahveh* worship. The masses could not and cannot grasp abstract ideas and principles. The *Jahveh* religion was too sublime for them. Hence, were added thereto necessary and adequate forms and observances. Slowly many more forms accrued, mostly from the general stock extant at those times, and consecrated by venerable ages past; forms to keep alive the sense of history and nationality; as the holidays, the gatherings in the capital, etc., or to nurture the sense of nationality and country, as the one capital and the unique temple; or the sense of solidarity and community of interests; as the tithes, poor-gifts and national banquets, etc.; or to give an

external expression to the recognition of our sinfulness, of
duty, of obedience to God and his laws; as sacrifices, the
universal mode of worship in ancient times; that mode—
sacrifices—came down, no doubt, from pre-historic, barbarous times, when God was but the ancestral ghost or an
idealized fetich. But that crude notion had been obliterated
and more refined ideas evolved, not only with the Jews, but
even with the Egyptian and the Asiatic priesthoods, at
least in their select *mysteries*, where the Deity was nearly
as nobly thought of and taught as in the Bible.

Homer's Gods.

The sacrificial service, the least congenial, of all modes
of worship, to the modern mind, was then not so repugnant.
In the Bible it was so refined and purified as to represent the
idea of expiation, or the eradication of sin, discarding the
notion that the Deity were dependent on man for food,
drink, smell, etc. Compare, for instance, the Homeric and
the biblic systems concerning the sacrificial service, both
composed at about the same time,—and you will find an
immense advance in the latter. In *Hesiod* and *Homer* the
gods are really in need of food, drink and luxuries; likewise
they need habitation, sleep, sport and eulogies. Man offers
them their wants, under the express condition that they
should grant him favors, protection, victory; not even
shrinking from asking miracles of them. The gods, besides,
are above all the rules of either reason or morality. Even
the great Zeus himself, sometimes described nearly as
sublimely as Jahveh, often acts as a paltry tyrant, being
moved in different directions, as a puppet by strings, or by
small motives and personalities, like a petty potentate is
by his favorites. Here are a few examples about the needs
and greeds of the gods.

We read in Homer's Odyssey, I, 59 and 66, about
Athenê praying to Zeus in favor of Odysseus being

allowed to reach his home, concluding with : (¹) " Does not
thy heart thrill with sympathy, Olympian?   Did not
Odysseus serve thee well and bring thee sacrifices in the
Greek ships, in the vast land of the Trojans?   Why, then,
art thou so wroth with him, Zeus?"   To which Zeus replies,
affirming that he would never forget Odysseus. . . .
" Who did bring most of offerings to the gods?" (²)   So
again (IV. 351) : " The gods desire '*hecatombs*.' "   Ibidem,
IV. 473, the same is claimed for services rendered. (³)   So,
again we read (Odyssey, VII. 201) : (⁴)—" On many occasions
the gods appear to us bodily as soon as we offer fine
hecatombs ; they dine with us, sitting down where we, too,
are sitting.   When one of us, travelling alone, meets with
them on his journey, they do not hide themselves, since we
are their kindred, just as the cyclops and the wild generations of the giants."   In Odyssey, VIII, 266, we are treated
to a scandalous story among the gods, as never reporter of a
sensational daily could offer better to his scandal-thirsty
readers, viz: " The love of *Ares* and the beautiful
Aphroditê, when they first met secretly in the house of
Hephaistos. . . .   Many presents he had given her, etc.,

(1).   . . . . οὐδέ νυ σοί περ
    ἐντρέπεται φίλον ἦτορ, 'Ολύμπιε. οἰ νύ τ' 'Οδυσσεὺς
    'Αργείων παρὰ νηυσὶ χαρίζετο ἱρὰ ῥέζων
    Τροίῃ ἐν εὐρείῃ ; τί νύ οἱ τόσον ὠδύσαο, Ζεῦ ;"—Odyss. I, 59.

(2). πῶς ἂν ἔπειτ' 'Οδυσῆος ἐγὼ θείοιο λαθοίμην,
    ὅς . . . . περὶ δ' ἱρὰ θεοῖσιν
    ἀθανάτοισιν ἔδωκε," . . . .—Odyss. I, 66.

(3). ἀλλὰ μάλ' ὠφέλλες Διΐ τ' ἄλλοισίν τε θεοῖσιν
    ῥέξας ἱρὰ κάλ' . . . . ὀφρα τάχιστα
    σὴν ἐς πατρίδ' ἵκοιο . . . ."—Odyss. IV, 473.

(4.) αἰεὶ γὰρ τὸ πάρος γε θεοὶ φαίνονται ἐναργεῖς
    ἡμῖν, εὖτ' ἐρδωμεν ἀγακλειτὰς ἑκατόμβας,
    δαίνυνταί τε παρ' ἄμμι καθήμενοι ἔνθα περ ἡμεῖς.
    εἰ δ' ἄρα τις καὶ μοῦνος ἰὼν ξύμβληται ὀδίτης,
    οὔτι κατακρύπτουσιν, ἐπεὶ σφίσιν ἐγγύθεν εἰμὲν,
    ὥσπερ Κύκλωπές τε καὶ ἄγρια φῦλα Γιγάντων."—Odyss. VII, 201.

etc. How, then, her *fiery, lame* husband caught them together, in a trap, having given out that he was leaving on a journey. . . . His own wrath and the immense laughter of the gods finding the lovers entrapped. That is most comical—but speaks very badly of the ideas of the Hellens about their Deity and of their own loose morals and models.(¹) Of similar sensualities of the gods is narrated there, XI. 240.—Whilst in Odyssey XII, 383, Apollo brings complaint to Zeus about Odysseus' friends having killed his oxen, threatening that: "If they would not give him an equitable indemnity he might go down to Hades and spend his light to the dead." (¹)—An exceedingly puerile threat from a first-class god.

Again, there we find the loud disputes of Zeus, Herê, Aphroditê, Athenê, etc., concerning Troy. Everywhere it appears that the vagaries of the Greeks about mundane government were brought home to the gods.—Nowhere do we find there that sublime conception of the Bible regarding the Deity, the *holy* God, who "takes no bribes and favors no persons, needs no sacrifices, dwells in the sublime heights and looks down into the hearts of the meek and the contrite, pleading for the widow and orphans, giving bread and raiment to the stranger," etc. The utterances of Homer and Hesiod respecting the gods show that Max Muller's views about mythology

---

(1). Αὐτὰρ ὁ φορμίζων ἀνεβάλλετο καλὸν ἀείδειν
ἀμφ' Ἄρεος φιλότητος ἐϋστεφάνου τ' Ἀφροδίτης,
ὡς τὰ πρῶτα μίγησαν ἐν Ἡφαίστοιο δόμοισι·
λάθρῃ· πολλὰ δ' ἔδωκε, λέχος δ' ᾔσχυνε καὶ εὐνὴν
Ἡφαίστοιο ἄνακτος· . . . .
Ἥλιος, ὁ σφ' ἐνόησε μιγαζομένους φιλότητι. . . . .
οἱ δ' ἀγέροντο θεοὶ ποτὶ χαλκοβατὲς δῶ . . . .
θηλύτεραι δὲ θεαὶ μένον αἰδοῖ οἴκοι ἑκάστη. . . . .
ἄσβεστος δ' ἄρ' ἐνῶρτο γέλως μακάρεσσι θεοῖσιν
τέχνας εἰσορόωσι πολύφρονος Ἡφαίστοιο.—Odyss. VIII, 266 and 320.

(2). εἰ δέ μοι οὐ τίσουσι βοῶν ἐπιεικέ' ἀμοιβήν,
δύσομαι εἰς Ἀΐδαο καὶ ἐν νεκύεσσι φαείνω.—Odyss. XII, 382.

must give way to those of Herbert Spencer. Those gods are not idealized bodies, stars or personified forces of nature. No, they are mostly idealized and apotheosized real persons, patriarchs, heroes, sages, conquerors, male and female, who were transplanted to heaven and Olympos in pre-historic times. There they were believed to talk, eat and live as before, on earth. This theory alone explains the fables about them.—They were sublimized men and women—an apotheosis later yet in use among the Roman emperors. The biblical Deity, especially with the epoch of Moses, is almost invariably delineated with all the sublimity and purity asked even now by a fastidious metaphysician. Once or twice only a phrase still reminds us yet of the ancient cruder conceptions of the divine essence. (See the verses in Exodus XXIV, 10-11.) (¹) Generally the sublimity and spirituality of the Deity is maintained in S. Writ.

THE PENTATEUCH AND THEOLOGICAL CRIMES.

Remark, again, with all the rigor of the Bible against idolatry, the theological crimes and transgressions there are very limited. At certain observances of great historic and national bearing, the law pronounces a curse upon the transgressor thereof—"His soul shall be cut away from among his people."—But the Rabbinical tradition is perfectly right in not understanding there a judicial condemnation to be put to death. Michaelis (see his Mosaische Gesetzge-bung), not always well acquainted with the inner spirit of Mosaism, claims that it means a judicial death-warrant. He is mistaken. I decidedly believe that tradition here has more correctly grasped the lawgiver's sense. Such extermination is pronounced, for instance, for eating leav-ened bread on Passover, the law prescribing unleavened bread as a reminiscence of the Exodus. Michaelis construes this into a death-penalty. The Rabbis think it implies a

(1)   ויראו את אלהי יישראל ותחת רנליו.

strong vituperation, and they are right. Hence, about the only theological crime entailing death is *idolatry*—active public worship of Baal, Astarte, etc. And whosoever knows well that worship, how even among the refined Greeks and late Romans, it was full of licentiousness, cruelty, murder and superstition, will acknowledge that the Mosaic rigors were here in order, and that these rigors do not constitute a proof of sectarian bigotry. Monotheism was not theology; no, it was morals, it was the ethical and social basis; hence the political foundation of Judæa. . . . We can, therefore, abide by our theory that the Bible, originally, is broadly tolerant, humane and unsectarian. A salient proof of the correctness of this view is the fact that it allows the Gentile immigrant (Guer Toshab) all the privileges of civil citizenship when he does not practice idolatry and has but adopted the general moral law of mankind. (¹)

RABBINICAL EXUBERANCE.

I can not claim the same for the Rabbinical laws. There we do find a huge multiplication of forms and observances, as also, ostensibly stringent punishments for transgressing them (²). Intolerance and sectarianism can not be denied there. But upon the correct cognition of facts and motives thereof, we can hardly condemn them. During the long period of Talmudical jurisprudence, the Ebrews had no country of their own. They lived scattered in all parts of the globe, from Mesopotamia and the Tigris regions to Asia and Africa, Spain and all the European countries. Immense, cruel, vulgar superstitions hovered over those regions; whilst the dominant religions were in some sense a form of Judaism, close issues and varied patterns thereof, yet not identical therewith. Christianity claimed to be a rejuvenated Judaism, having adopted the one God-belief, the Decalogue,

---

1) ‏"טבע מצות ב"נ.‏

2) ‏מלקות, מכות מרדות.‏

the prophetic morality, etc. But in fact, as the Gentile races had but lately emerged from crude polytheism, they had brought over into new Christianity a great deal of practices, phrases and even dogmatic symbols that nearly obscured the noble Monotheism of the Bible, with its rationality and luminous morality; even the status of man was obscured by words brought over from foreign systems and theories.—Whilst in the *Islam* religion, the Biblical God-idea was fairly well kept up; unfortunately the prophetic morality and humanity, etc., were not; the universal indiscriminate justice of the Decalogue, its moral purity, the sacredness of property, of life and chastity, of word and desires were strangely contrasted by the Arab polygamy, roving propensities, conquests, enslavements and conversions by the scimetar. The intelligent observer will therefore understand, that the Rabbis were excusable in not recognizing either of those daughter-religions as perfectly identical with the Synagogue, and that they deemed it their duty not to give in and fuse, but to continue the unequal contest, at any cost and any price. But now arose the question, the Jews not having an inch of land as their own, how could they keep up their identity in an age where religious toleration was simply unknown? This they answered by counter-sectarianism and counter-intolerance. The few rational, luminous, religious ideas were hedged in by a profuse forest of forms, ceremonies and observances. The Biblical Monotheism and prophetism, so simple as hardly to require any creed or text-book, were elaborated and built out and up into a vast, complicated and impenetrable religious system, with forms and observances that first counted by the hundreds, but soon by the myriads. They are encompassing the orthodox Israelite from morning to eve, from the cradle to the grave, and beyond it, beginning with the hoary past and reaching to the farthest future. These myriads of forms and observances were

to be the bulwarks, fences and citadels of the faithful
and the safeguard of Monotheism. They were of such a
construction as to form around each individual a Chinese
wall; to isolate him in the very midst of the Gentile
world, each and everyone to form a centre, a nucleus, an
independent being, a people and country in miniature.
In the market, the Exchange, the palace, he was a unit
of the Gentile community he lived with. At home, with
his family, his books, his festivals, his ceremonies, his
worship, he was again a Judæan, an Ebrew, an Oriental,
living and dreaming in his old by-gone surroundings.
Rabbinism is perhaps the unique historic example of a
small, broken, infinitesimal minority, treated for centuries as outlaws and pariahs that knew to keep up the old
identity, patiently waiting for recognition. Rabbinism
kept up these claimed-to-be pariahs as a nobility, as
an aristocracy of mind and morals, "as a light to the
nations." It was the first bold trial to upset the usual laws
of majorities and those of the crude times, and to show for
once, that the minority, too, has a right to be, and that the
genius of history, of God, often moves in the minority,
working out by it the salvation and the advance of the
majority. When the Greeks of the time of Antiochus
Epiphanes challenged the Judæans to adopt Greek life, and
these refused, that was, no doubt, then thought foolish and
foolhardy. And, nevertheless, the philosopher now admits
that it was magnanimous. Why, then, should not the
philosopher now, perhaps, admit the same line of reasoning?—So, some years ago, St. Hilaire, the great Frenchman
and writer of the Thiers government, declared that, "Should
present Israel yield to the onslaught of anti-Semitism and
give up its biblical Monotheism, that would be one of the
greatest misfortunes to mankind at large."

15

KABBALAH.

For long centuries the Rabbis went on increasing the ceremonial and ritualistic bulwarks and fences, which served the Jew as his armor and coat of mail, to isolate and strengthen him, even in the midst of danger and temptation. At last these observances began to weigh heavily upon the votaries. The masses not knowing them as simple armor, but as a part of divine teachings, began to doubt them as such, and to murmur against them, as heavy shackles in the battle of life. But the Rabbinical leaders, aware that that armor was not yet superfluous, contrived a new mode of spiritualizing and re-enlivening those forms. It was the system of the *Kabbalah* that did revive these myriads of observances. With the advent of the *"Sohar,"* this spirit awoke and infused new life among the mystic Jews. It was now admitted that these forms would be useless and even burdensome, if not for their symbolical value and their connection with the supernatural world! All the stars and angelic hosts were believed to be set in motion by these apparent forms! They ceased to be forms, or historical, or symbolical remembrances, and began to be charms, mysterious powers, to dictate to the laws of nature, yes, even to the Lord of nature Himself. The *"Zaddiq,"* the mystic saint, took up the Messiah-role of ancient times and became omnipotent. But that exalted spiritualism broke its spell by its own exaggeration. When the followers of *Sabbatai Zevi,* the Palestinian Messiah of the seventeenth century, boldly passed into the Moslem religion, and the Polish *Frank,* with his followers, into some sort of Trinitarianism, claiming thus to reunite the three religions into one Kabbalistic Judæaism, the Rabbis shrank back from that dangerous and extravagant mode of spiritualizing the forms, and fell back into the enigmatic, old and cold Talmudic formalism, hardly knowing where to stop; until with Moses Men-

delssohn, the new school arose, coming back to the study of
the Bible and the origins of tradition, and began to find their
way in that labyrinth of *thirty* centuries, slowly discover-
ing the luminous traces of original Sinai, as the religion for
Jew and Gentile, for all mankind and all times.   The
Renaissance of the ghetto-Judæaism began.   With that
Mendelssonian epoch opened a new chapter in the history
and the activity of Israel.   The career of mysticism was
closed; so was that of formalism.   And the master minds
undertook that other task of critically studying the Bible at
the torchlight of conscience and science, and to square it
with the just needs of the times.

RESUME OF THE FOREGOING.

One glance more at the chapters on "Laws and Ordinances" (Mishpatim II, 21, etc.), and we shall recognize the
universality, the divinity thereof.   "The male citizen can
hire out for six years; on the seventh year he must go
free."—"The female citizen sold becomes the master's wife,
or goes free."—"The heathen male slave must not be
maltreated, or he goes free."—"The heathen, conquered
female slave, when cohabited with, becomes the master's
wife, or goes out free.   *Ipso facto,* since she was his wife,
hence, she can no longer be his slave."—"The punishment
for murder is death, no difference whether native or
. foreigner, rich or poor, free-born or slave."—"There is no
pecuniary compensation, no privileged ranks nor refuge
places for murder."—"From the altar take him to die. "—
"One law is there for native and stranger, Ebrew and non-
Ebrew."—"Eye for eye and tooth for tooth."—Even so,
"Money for money and value for value."—"The thief,
fraud and robber are punished in purse, not in body."—
"The stranger, *guer*, non-Israelite, in Judæa enjoys all the
protection of the law.   If permanently located, *toshab*, he
has all the civic rights."—"The poor stranger, just as the

orphan, widow and poor Israelite, are under the special protection of the law."—"A portion of the crops, the flocks, etc., is
reserved for them by right, not as a degrading charity."—
"Benevolence is not an ideal merit, but a duty prescribed.
Those benefited by it are not degraded and disfranchised;
they continue as citizens and brothers."—"The poor are not
crushed by debts, for these lapse every seventh year; nor by
interest and usury, which are never allowed; nor by rings
and monopolies enhancing the price of his bread, butter,
meat, etc., for all commerce for profit's sake is prohibited."
—"The family-lot goes down to posterity; it is not alien-
able; it is free as the citizen."—"The freed Ebrew servant
gets a portion; the freed Ebrew girl an establishment or
dower." The entire fabric of the Biblical State is built
upon the solid rock of personal liberty and social equality,
and these are real and tangible, not simply *de jure* and
ideal. They are built upon the original equality of wealth,
kept up by equal chances to improve, by the safety-valve of
Sabbath, Jubilee and the Release-Year, the three great
Septennate institutions.

The Jubilee is tantamount to a radical social renovation;
the Septennate to a partial one. Internal commerce and
foreign wars are discouraged. Thus all possibilities and
opportunities for sudden unequal acquisition or loss of
wealth and property are reduced to a minimum. Hence
plutocracy, proletariat and pauperism are nearly impossible.—Now, these three pillars of the Bible State are
sustained by the necessary fourth one, solidarity, the consciousness of the people that they are but one large family,
that the welfare of each depends upon the welfare of all,
that their interests are common, that altruism, not selfishness, is the sound social base, and that, "love thy neighbor
as thyself" is there a fact, not an ideal.

The Pentateuchal legislation being universal, humanitarian, aiming at the elevation and the happiness of all, the

divine character thereof, as emanating from the eternal wisdom, the source of truth and reality, is established. For what is good for all classes and for all times and all circumstances can emanate but from supreme wisdom and truth; from Him who created all with eternal fitness and inherent harmony.—Whatever is purely human, is partial, temporary, exceptional; all things eternally good and just are divine. And this is the secret strength of the biblical legislation; the Samson's hair of that grand historic monument, old as the pyramids, young as the United States; a legislation long since without a special country, nation, armies or defenders.—Yet it conquers. It conquers by its inherent force, by the spirit of truth and goodness pervading it, by the genius of mankind moving in it. Like the famous Parthian hosts that conquered whilst apparently fleeing, so is the biblical legislation; it conquers whilst migrating from country to country, from continent to continent, everywhere scattering the seed of its divine truth, everywhere proclaiming: " Peace, peace to those near by and those far away."

RETROSPECT—CARDINAL PRINCIPLES.

We have started with the proposition, in the second chapter of this work, that the biblical State and community rested upon four cardinal principles, viz:

I. *Personal Freedom.*—Every Israelitish inhabitant of Judæa, male, female, and child, poor or rich, lay or priest, were born and remained absolutely free, and could, under no condition, be robbed of their inherent liberty. We have seen that personal freedom is, thus, not of modern origin, deriving from the speculations of J. J. Rousseau and A. de Voltaire or Kant and Descartes, nor from modern Holland and Switzerland, nor from old Rome and Greece. No; that principle has been first clearly stated in the Biblical Legislation.

II. *Social Equality.*—Whilst not only India and Egypt, but even Greece and Rome, had their classes and masses, patricians and plebeians; even whilst Germany, Holland and Switzerland had their different strata of society, separated by difference of rights and duties, an abyss not to be filled up, except by civil war and blood—Judæa had no such castes; its citizens were absolutely equal, participating in all the emoluments, honors and burdens of the State, capable of all employments, dignities and charges.

III. *Equal Distribution of Wealth Among the Members of the Community.*—Originally the conquered Canaan belonged to the entire people. That land was parceled out into equal shares and then divided among the grown male members, the heads of families; and that farm or lot remained in the family from generation to generation. It could never be sold nor wrested from it. Thus, every child born in Judæa was a free-holder. No land-grabbing, no great landlordism was allowed, and no proletariat possible.

IV. *Solidarity, or Community of Interests*—The altruistic feeling as link of the one body politic.—That bitter rivalry, that fierce competition, that venomous, economical envy, the curse of modern society, was not known nor possible in the Biblical State. The citizens felt that, as members of the same body, their interests were common; that happiness and calamity is in store for them equally and conjointly; that the fate of one is the fate of all. Hence was, in all critical cases, mutual assistance, benevolence and active charity not simply an ideal, a moral recommendation. No, it was a duty peremptorily ordained by the law, just as paying one's debts; because all were mutually interdependent; all interested in the welfare of each. Hence was there the modern, chronic, inherited pauperism impossible.

Contrasting the Biblical State with the modern ones concerning government and rulers, peace and war, conquests, dominant and serving races, militia, taxation and exploitation, etc., we have seen that the principles of personal liberty and social equality settled those questions at once and for ever. Once these two principles admitted as fundamental, the long and bitter civil strifes and quarrels, internal and international wars on account of freedom and equality, as in modern and in ancient times, could not take place in the Mosaic community. Had there existed several such communities, peoples really governed by the same law, but in different States, they could not have gone to international war. The wars between Judæa and Samaria were constantly denounced by the prophets as fratricidal, and had at last to be stopped. Nor could a biblical monarch or an oligarchy ever practice usurpation and tyranny, the people having the right of rebellion as a protection. Hence, our last century's revolutions could not have taken place under a biblical *regime;* nor could the present European struggle occur.

Applying further the principles of *equal distribution* of wealth and *solidarity* of interests, the present all absorbing, *social problem* is likewise solved by the Bible legislation. Equal distribution of wealth disposes of plutocracy and of proletariat. Community of interests, not soulless competition, not force and taking advantage; generous emulation, harmoniously combined with humane, mutual assistance; sympathy and charity as a right and duty, not an alms, a degradation, a dog-kennel for the poor; benevolence to eradicate poverty, not the poor, to uplift and make him independent; community of interests at the base of the social structure that disposes of pauperism and of proletarianism. Thus equal distribution of national wealth and the feeling of national unity or solidarity of interests settles our social problem.

Now the Mosaic State, as the Platonic Republic, has never existed; both have remained ideals.—But should it ever be

a possibility of founding a State and a society on the grounds
of the Bible, there would be no civil strifes and revolutions,
no international wars, no plutocracy, no proletariat, no
pauperism, no aristocrats, no mob, no masters and no slaves,
serf or wage-labor or its "*iron law.*" The social question
would be settled in a natural, rational way.

It would be settled without the utopia of communism
or of exaggerated socialism. Property, individuality and
family would continue to be sacred. Personal effort, talent,
genius, thrift and wisdom would be fostered and rewarded,
whilst vice, laziness, wastefulness, and imprudence would
have their due and necessary rebuke. A rebuke, necessary
not only as a healthy encouragement to virtue and wisdom
in general, but as a stimulant and corrective for the vicious
themselves; the only remedy left them for improvement;
punishment being the last salvation of the vicious.

GENERAL PRINCIPLES REVIEWED.

The principles of the biblical legislation are first to be
looked for in the hoary Sinaic Ten Commandments. The
base of that entire legislation is the God belief. God is the
Creator of the universe, the Redeemer and Liberator of His
people. He is the conqueror of Canaan, the liege-lord and
king of the redeemed, and He is the authority of that legislation. That theme runs through Pentateuch, Bible, Talmud, New Testament and Koran.

As such, God consecrated the Sabbath as the symbol of the
new nation. It is the emancipation day of all the enslaved.
It is remembering the Ebrew redemption from Egypt. He
further consecrated filial piety, human life, chastity, property, the sacredness of our word and our feelings. This
decalogue is the organic law of the biblical State and society.
That community is a theocratic democracy. God is king, His
law rules. The magistrates are but the servants; the people
are the aim. It is a theocracy; it is not a hierarchy. Not

the priests reign—they but apply and execute the supreme law.—They hold their authority from the people in whom resides all authority. That authority is the reflex of the law, of eternal reason. The people are the judges whether the priests apply the genuine law of God or their own caprice, and whether it is correctly applied.—Later crept in royalty; but that was half a rebellion, God alone being the rightful sovereign. The king was at best but the executive officer, judge and general. He was but a "brother;" he could have no guards, no seraglio, no exorbitant wealth. The Supreme law was ever binding upon him (Deuteronomy 17, 15). What a vast difference between him and an Asiatic or Egyptian monarch, himself a god or descendant of the gods, himself law-maker and yet above the law!

The community was a democracy. No born aristocratic classes and no oligarchies; rigidly all equal in social rank and economic wealth; all alike educated, all free, equal, with same laws, duties, rights, chances, burdens, charges, imposts, honors and emoluments. The model was: "Ye shall be unto me a kingdom of priests and a holy nation."—"Mine are the children of Israel, I have redeemed them from Egypt."

Status of land: "Mine is the land, ye shall not sell it forever."—Every citizen had a farm, detailed to him from God's own property. That acre descended to his posterity, could never be alienated nor wrested from the family. This was the economic base of liberty and equality.

All taxation and imposts were made by law. About one-fifth, it appears, of the produce of the soil and of the flocks, the sole Judæan wealth, went to defray the expenses of government, divine worship, public justice, schools and sustenance of the poor.

In the preceding chapter we have sufficiently reviewed the laws about freedom and slavery. We have seen that the Ebrew could be hired out, but never enslaved. So was

freedom inherent in every and each man and woman of
Judæa.

Every seventh year all debts were cancelled. Every
fiftieth year man, soil and houses returned to their original
families. Thus was all social and economic inequality
remedied.

Justice was freely and gratuitously administered. Special
protection was given to strangers, widows, orphans and the
poor.—The children suffered not for the parents' sins, nor
parents for the children's.—Justice became less cruel.
Excepting the Canaanites, is toleration and forbearance
enjoined towards all, even the Egyptian and the Edomites,
hereditary foes of the Judæan people.—The dead, too, have
their rights of an honorable burial and a family remembrance; even the criminal was protected from undue cruelty.

Woman was the equal of man, his helpmeet, born in the
image of God, "the mother of life," to work and toil, to
rule and enjoy, as the companion of man and at his side,
as part and parcel of man. She was not a mischievous
toy, a Circe, a Pandora, to beguile and ruin, but to bless
and assist him.

War was discouraged and sufficiently humanized.—No
wanton destruction of useful things. The yielding enemy
had his life spared. The captive enslaved was protected in
life and limb.—The captive woman could be *married*, not
abused, and her issue was legitimate. So were children
anxiously sheltered and under the ægis of the law.

The ideal of social harmony is, "Thou shalt love thy
neighbor as thyself."—It is founded upon that other idea
of one parental stock and one origin of man. Thus God,
sole king, the people a unit, one country, same patriarchs,
same interests, rights, duties, chances and equal wealth, all
deeply moored in the emancipating Sabbath, the inalienable
family-lot, the ever nivellating and renovating economics:
the Year of Release and the Jubilee—these are the leading
ideas of the biblical legislation.

REFLECTED IN THE TALMUD.

These principles have been fairly kept alive by succeeding ages, leaders and teachers, on the whole. The Talmudists, the Casuists and the Moralists have fairly elaborated that biblical ideal of State and people, not in its minute practical details, but in its ethical features. In spite of their vicissitudes of fortune, the amount of hate and suffering, unparalleled in history, they have never deserted their task nor their people. That noble example of adherence, of unflinching perseverance, through a long line of centuries and generations of martyrs, is as unparalleled as that of their sufferings. It will remain a theme of admiration to posterity. This seems to have been the secret of their strength. Why their followers remained true to them? It was their unflinching trust in the cause; and next, their self-sacrifice, which won the respect and adherence of the masses. In our times both, cause and effect, have disappeared; will they ever reappear?—

By that phalanx of martyrs the leading ideas and ideals of Mosaism have been fairly kept up, often times, pure and unalloyed—a marvelous phenomenon in the history of two thousand years' legislation. Pure Monotheism has been retained to this day at such an enormous sacrifice and under such tremendous temptations.—So has been the belief in the unity of the human race, its doctrine and its final goal, in spite of mountains of prejudice. "Thou shalt love thy neighbor as thyself," prominently culminating as the climax of the noble 19th chapter of Leviticus, was duly emphasized and conscientiously declared by them as the central doctrine and "essence of the law."—So it was by Hillel, adding: "What thou wilt not be done unto thee, do not unto thy neighbor." (Sabbath, 31 a.)—It was repeated by Akiba (Sifra Kedoshim IV, 12.) It is declared such in the New Testament by Jesus. It is so by all later moralists.—

"All men are in the image of God; hence their lives, dignity, rights, duties, are holy, all men being but one race, all brothers," (Ibid.) is deduced by an old teacher from the verse: "This is the book of the generations of men." [1] This he declares "the first cardinal principle."—"All the righteous among the Gentile nations will share in eternal bliss," is a well-known Talmudical doctrine.—All practical duties, as respect, love, benevolence, justice, truth, etc., the Talmudists, in *Halachah* and *Agadah*, without exception, enjoin upon their adherents to practice toward Gentiles, without asking for their creed or race or country.—From Jeremiah[2], who enjoined it upon the Babylonian exiles, to this day, patriotism to country, just as love, forbearance, justice, etc., toward our fellow-citizens, are emphasized and taught by Jewish moralists and Talmudists. The proofs are given above in all detail.

Thus has been upheld the great prophetic Messiah-ideal concerning the eternal progress of the human race, that once the nations will stop their wars and jealousies, that through knowledge and wisdom united they will form but one people, practice one right and worship one God. This is the combined sense of the identical ideal in Isaiah II and XI and Michah IV.

AIMS OF THE BIBLICAL SCHEME.

The biblical scheme is vast and profound; it is both practical and theoretical, realistic and ideal. We have but to take as an instance the great Decalogue and the nineteenth chapter of Leviticus, and we shall soon be aware of this. First, it lays down the rule that the laws are simply for practical good. (III M. 18, 5): "Ye shall observe my statutes and judgments which a man shall perform, and *live by them*."—It has little or no dogma, no special creed,

---

[1] Genesis V, 1.
[2] Jeremiah 29,7.

no mystic teachings—though a great deal of practical symbolism, as in the Orient. It lays all stress upon active morality, upon purity and sincerity, justice and right-living. But it aims just as much at the practical well-being, at individual, bodily happiness. It promises earthly, divine blessings for right-living. Right conduct will insure a joyous, long and happy existence. The rights of the mind and of the flesh are equally noticed. It goes so far as to make even external, physical nature depend upon the morality of its votaries. It promises (V M. 2.)—"Rain and sunshine, peace and plenty, as the reward for obeying Jahveh." Thus, the aim of the Bible religion is in first instance, morality and happiness. They appear to Mosaism but one thing, one and inter-dependent; neither can exist alone.—A life pleasing to Jahveh will be moral at one pole and happy at the other. The Roman stoics cared alone for correct conduct; virtue was their *"summum bonum."* The neo-Platonic philosophers aimed at ecstacy, or absorption in God. The Greek popular ideal was military glory; the Greek philosophers' ideal was knowledge and truth. The Roman ideal was patriotism. The Mosaic scheme labored for morality and happiness; for health, peace, plenty, progeny, etc.; these were the necessary results of a noble and pure life; worship of God was chiefly love to man. So psalmists and prophets seem often to imply religion as wholly absorbed by justice and charity, by purity and modesty; and these go with happiness.

Yet it is not wholly so, when deeply looked into the system. The Bible religion is more than morality. It has its own and proper sphere. Not practical equity and happiness is its final goal; no, it aims higher, at *"Holy shall ye be, for holy am I, your God."*—Here is the noble idealism, the hoary, oriental mysticism, ever rooting at the bottom of human hearts. Religion is the striving for God; to imitate, to reach, to identify ourselves with the

Divine, to achieve perfection. Behold! Frail, shortcoming, one-day creatures that we are, we yet dream of and labor to know all, embrace all, reach all: happiness, glory, beauty, wisdom, holiness, perfection. "To be as God." (I. M. 22).— This ideal is the grandest, the noblest, the divine in the human, the image of the Deity in our soul, the reflex of the Creator in the individual creature, the universe mirrored in man, its thinking miniature. This is the higher ideal, the mysticism of religion, self-perfection in the highest degree; this is: "*Holy shall ye be, for holy am I, your God.*"

This is elucidated in chapter XIX of Leviticus, first as practical right-conduct, next as ideal goodness, culminating in God-likeness, in striving to reach divine perfection, divine holiness. This ideal is further elaborated by psalmists, prophets and later teachers. Read each of these literatures carefully, and you will find this manifold character reflected; very realistic and yet sublimely ideal. From Deuteronomy it runs through prophets, Halachah and Agadah undismayed at the havoc of times. Will that idealism outlive the present "*blood and iron policy?*"

Some such ideal apparently is depicted in the mystic personality of the Messiah, or *Adam Kadmon*, born before creation, the Demiourg of Talmud and Midrashim and Kabbalah; next in the hoary patriarch, Abraham, his efforts, his results, his doctrine, his worldly success and his family happiness; that is expressed in: "Jahveh blessed Abraham with all" (1) on which the Midrash expatiates in that sense; such an ideal, God-like man is to the Jew Moses who died with all his faculties unimpaired; who passed over to immortality with his glance intent upon the promised land, from the sublime Pisgah-height (2); or Elijah, after a formidable struggle against idolatry and sensuality, disappearing in the clouds, snatched away to ethereal life.

---

(1) Genesis XXIV, 1.
(2) Deut. 34, 1 to 8.

Socrates was thought such in Greece, cheerfully drinking the cup of hemlock, unjustly forced upon him by the State; such was the Sage of Plato's republic, alone entitled to rule in the name of the gods; such does the pious Christian imagine Jesus, his sublime and ideal God-man, dying with the prayer upon his lips: "Pardon! O father, thy children, they know not what they are doing." Such do thinkers imagine Spinoza, living and bearing without a murmur, and dying without regret; ever even-tempered and cheerful. "For all must be; 'all that is, is good.'" "All comes from God; *and God is the Ever-good.*"

The neo-Platonic *ecstacy* and the Hindoo *Nirvana*, we commonly conceive as identical with self-annihilation. The biblical *"Holy shall ye be"* seems to be more self-conscious. And even so is the Rabbinic ideal of the highest beatitude, or paradise. They say: "The righteous are sitting there, radiating with glory and beholding the splendors of the *Shechinah;*" to which Maimonides adds: "They recognize truth in all its reality."—Thus, highest mentality, embracing all, based upon morality and happiness, seems to be the ideal and aim of all Biblic and Talmudic religion. That is·termed: holiness and perfection. The *Sohar*, the leading book of the Kabbalah, often spreads out its bright-colored wings towards that ideal. But it is such already in the Psalmist, 15: "Who is to ascend the mount of the Lord?" answering: "The pure. the good, the truthful, the unflinching, etc., etc."

There are some claims and discussions about differences in the systems of Abraham, of Moses, of Prophetism, Talmud, etc. Such claims have a scant foundation. All the above-mentioned ideas and ideals are but one continuous development, without any real break or discrepancy, less yet a contradiction, or even antagonism. They are developments from Abrahamism to Mosaism, to Prophetism and to the best of Rabbinism. Any discrepancy there is not the conscious result of the teacher's change of front, but rather a sad echo of the times and conditions. Barbarous times and treatment had their counteraction among the Ebrews, and such times emphasized more creed and ceremonies within and prejudice without. The Ebrew nationality harshly treated, most naturally thought harshly of its persecutors; and the more it was attacked, the more it had to intrench itself behind forms and observances. Liberal times laid most stress upon deeds and principles. Thus, there is no real break in those systems. They are but the natural evolutions of one from the other.

THE BIBLE AND THE PRESENT.—*Conclusion.*

Having carefully studied the legislation of the great Book, let us now examine what does the present State and Society owe to that system and what to other sources; what elements of the present civilization derive from Judæa and what from Greece and Rome and their predecessors, Assyria, Persia, Phœnicia or Egypt; what modern manners, feelings and views come from classical and what from biblical impressions.

No doubt our present society rests upon a solid biblical foundation. The ideas of God, duty and righteousness underlie our community, at least as an ideal. That God-ideal is Monotheism; and righteousness, not force, is the sequel; both are biblic. Our modern religions are monotheistic. Polytheism, apparently, is dead among educated people.

The next principle is morality, or the doctrine of the golden rule, "Thou shalt love thy neighbor as thyself."—In theory that is the base of our society, and it is biblical, Old- and New-Testamentary.—But in reality, in grand outlines, in politics, statecraft stands upon egoism, force and taking advantage.—The present condition of Europe, its huge standing armies, its late and its latent wars, its

" Pan-Latinism, Slavism and Germanism," as well as our own would-be " Pan-Americanism " and our "silver" dilemma, prove it sufficiently; and that hails from heathen Rome and Greece.

The best part of our present religions derives from the Sacred Writ.—Regular worship, or popular yearning for the good and the holy, with the Sabbath and holidays, epochs of great moral, political and historical import, utilized for ideal and refining purposes, come from that same source. The pattern thereof we find only in Judæa. Elsewhere public worship was a State contrivance.

Next our idea of pan-humanity can originate only in that of pan-deity and unity of creation, with their sequels of justice, philanthropy, fraternity, freedom, equality, human dignity, one race, one interest, same rights and duties; no poligamy, no slavery; woman the equal and companion of man; no ruling and no serving-races,—all these are the logical outcome of Monotheism, never of Greek, Roman or Oriental Polytheism.

From the Bible is next hailing our " sweet home," family, marriage, conjugal and filial piety; because there woman is an *Eve*, not a *Pandora*. There she is the "helpmeet," the mother of life, to bless man, not to ruin. The pattern of womanhood was low, even in Greece and Rome, not only in Babel and Assyria. Force was there, yet the measure of worth and VIRTUE was a manly epithet. Woman and family rose alone with the Bible.

The full idea of property I must likewise vindicate to the great Book. There alone is work consecrated and rendered noble. In Greece, Rome and the East, with Arabs, Teutons and Mongols, was conquest the supreme source of acquisition, and conquest is shifting; it is a poor foundation for property. Work alone is its solid base. With property and work, Mosaism consecrated thrift, effort and individuality.

16

So it is with truthfulness, sincerity, honesty, veracity, pity.—The Greek gods and heroes were not distinguished for any of these qualities.

So are our noblest social features biblical; democracy, or popular government, the citizen as the aim and object, not the pedestal of the State; the magistrate as the brother and officer, not the despot, of the people; enjoyment, happiness and education at the reach of all, is biblical.

So is the best and soundest part of socialism. Land is the property of all; each is entitled to his share—his family-lot. No one is born for pauperism, nor for proletarianism; equal chances for all, and for none privileges; no over-reaching, nor taking advantage of the distressed; no land-grabbing and no plutocracy; no born nobles and no mob; solidarity and community of interests among all the members of the community; altruism and not crushing competition—all that is biblical doctrine. Whilst it is united there with religion, family, property and individuality, which some socialists unreasonably repudiate.

From the ancient Greek philosophers and sages present society derives the noble tastes and cravings for exact knowledge, careful study, close observation, discrimination and criticism; to learn by experiment and trial, to follow the steps of nature, to search for each effect its adequate cause, not to rely upon authority and blind imitation, not to account by an *a priori* hypothesis or *"deus-ex-machina"* assumption, but rather by inductive methods, by watching the workings of nature and generalizing its laws. Hence all exact sciences, all fine arts, all practical trades and crafts, nearly all about mechanics, solidity and beauty in forms and esthetics, all accurate mathematical knowledge, the method of beginning with doubt, advancing by observation and arriving at knowledge by verification, that adhering to scientific truth, above all authority and preconceived theories, all that is of Phœnician and Egyptian, especially of

Greek origin; the modern elements thereof may be retraced by derivation to Hellenic methods; Aristotle coming before Bacon and Darwin.

The useful elements of present society coming from Rome and her predecessors are government and legislation. To assimilate and form divers units and petty tribes into one compound, political society, to turn clans and masses into organized civilized bodies, by persuasion or by compulsion, by cunning or by wisdom, by law or by force, by good means or by foul means, to show the useful (?) part which *"blood and iron"* play in human affairs; the art of government, State-craft, war and legislation, we moderns have learned from Rome and Nineveh, Babel and Persia.

From Greek and Roman and Asian paganism, we have yet our lingering remnants of Polytheism, our very numerous, popular superstitions and our dogmatic crudities; further, the present unprincipled politics; cynicism, private and public; hypocrisy in State and in Church, bloody dynastic ambitions, heartless competition, tyranny of race and creed; selfishness, violence and over-reaching; reckless sensuality; demagogism, small and great, careless of consequences; civil, social and international wars; altruism in church and egoism in the world; "Love thy neighbor" in theory, and "Ruin thy neighbor," in practice, they hail from that quarter, decaying Greece and Rome.

It is not easy to classify all the present social features. It is harder yet to weigh their import. But it seems that most of our communities' best moral and social elements derive from the Bible, and most of its worst traits hail from declining Hellas and Italy and their Asiatic predecessors.

It appears that duty, righteousness and morals, men learned from Judæa; exact knowledge was imparted by Greece. The first ever points to supernatural guidance. The latter teaches self-reliance. Noble inspirations, and great moral thoughts mankind derived from Jerusalem;

exact scientific truth and methods from Athens; bold initiative from classic Rome. Our head turns towards refined
Hellas; our bold hand towards Patrician Rome, and our
heart and feelings towards Judæa. As our feelings have
the strongest hold, as the heart is most concerned in our
deeds, even such is the hold of the Sacred Book upon
present society. Believers or not, it influences them. It
is the ethical pulse thereof, though not by far yet the norm
of deeds. There is no doubt that the leading moral aspirations and noblest instincts of our modern civilization, in
Church, State and home, mankind has derived from the
Bible; and there is merit enough.

True, we Americans, have yet our "silver question," and
Europe its "Pan-Latin-Slav—and Germanism." True the
forum and the *curia*, the market and politics are yet
heathen, selfishness being there dominant. Yet we may
fairly hope that common sense and exact science, that
nature's promptings, ripe reflection and the advancing influence of mankind's great Book, will succeed in making the
doctrine of "Thou shalt love thy neighbor as thyself," a
full and substantial reality.

THE END.

COMMENTS ON THE AUTHOR'S PUBLICATIONS.

The Baltimore *Sun* in last June, brought out the prospectus of this work. So did other papers in the East and West. Among the first encouraging letters with subscriptions were those from his Eminence, Cardinal Gibbons, Honorables Attorney-General J. P. Poe, Charles J. Bonaparte, L. N. Hopkins, Baltimore; Attorney-General S. N. Rosedale, Jacob H. Shiff, New York; leading ministers and laymen, booksellers, congregations followed.

Advanced sheets have been submitted to leading scholars, and their opinions were unanimous that: "The book is highly interesting and important, fully deserving public attention." Such are the replies, among many others, by the Rev. Drs. EDWARD A. LAWRENCE, Eutaw Congregational Church; J. T. WIGHTMAN, McCulloh Methodist Episcopal Church; H. M. WHARTON, Brantly Baptist Church; C. A. FULTON, North Avenue Immanuel Baptist Church; R. H. PULLMAN, Guilford Avenue Universalist Church; Dr. CLAMPETT, Druid Hill Avenue Episcopal Church, and Dr. A. FRIEDENWALD, Physician, North Eutaw street.

The Cincinnati *American Is.* published in 1888, two lectures by the author on that theme, delivered at the H. Union College, with *Resolutions of thanks* voted him. The Book will prove interesting and useful to the general reader, as well as to professionals. The author and proprietor's address is:

REV. MAURICE FLUEGEL,

2041 DIVISION STREET,

Baltimore, Md.

The Author's "*Thoughts on Religious Rites and Views*" received the cordial acknowledgment of many scientists, writers, divines and leading Universities in America and Europe. So writes:

President W. H. GREEN, of Princeton. "The book seems to embody, in an interesting way, the results of extensive reading, study and careful reflection."

President ANDREW D. WHITE, of Cornell: "It interests me very much in my hurried examination of it."

President DAY, of Yale, had a continued correspondence on it, desiring the author to write on kindred themes.

FRIEDRICH VON BODENSTEDT, German poet: "I have read your thoughtful tract with lively interest, and marked many passages to talk over with you. I find in it so much instruction and suggestion."

Professor FRANZ DELITZSCH, of the Leipsic University: "It is likely to prove a real enrichment of *science:*" and later: "It is a little book, rich in contents, and offering much material for reflection."

Professor W. WUNDT, of the same University: "Taking great interest in the history of manners and customs, your historical researches are calculated to vividly interest me." Again: "I shall utilize your remarks in my studies on Spinoza, with reference to Maimonides."

Professor A. NEUBAUER, of Oxford University, England: "Hearty thanks for your interesting work, which I have just finished reading. I shall lend it to DR. MILLS, of New York, who is writing on the Avesta and the Vedas, etc."

The Right HON. W. E. GLADSTONE, London: "It appears to be of great interest. Examining into the character of the Mosaic system, compared with others, all that throws light on this subject is *very welcome to me.*"

CARDINAL GIBBONS, Baltimore, sent his good wishes for its success.

The Chief Rabbi, DR. ZADOC KAHN, of France: "I have read your charming little book with as much pleasure as with profit."

DR. SCHWARTZ, Land-Rabbi of Baden: "With great pleasure have I read already many fine things therein."

The Author's "*Mosaic Diet and Hygiene:*" "Attracted considerable notice, in Germany especially."

PROFESSOR DR. GRÄTZ, of Breslau, writes: "It pleases me very much . . . and I request you to let me keep the copy."

DR. H. ADLER, Chief Rabbi of England; DR. ISADORE LOEB, of Paris; DR. G. GOTTHEIL, New York, and others cordially approved of it.

Many European and American periodicals reproduced or epitomized the above.

Smaller publications, as "*Belus' Tower,*" and the "*Two Philosophies,*" were cordially endorsed by PROFESSORS D. FRICKE and FRANZ DELITZSCH, of the Leipsic University.

PROFESSOR GRÄTZ writes: "Your polemics: 'Shylock' and 'Prejudice,' are beautiful. In our country one can not speak so plainly."

In 1877 HON. W. E. GLADSTONE wrote: "Rev. Fluegel's articles, 'The Ottoman Empire,' gave me unqualified pleasure. . . I am desirous of expressing my gratification to him."

Two letters by LORD BEACONSFIELD (1878), acknowledge the receipt of his articles on that topic.

PRESIDENT GARFIELD and SECRETARY EVARTS sent thanks for interesting articles on the same.

AD. CREMIEUX, the French statesman (1877): "Your articles on the Oriental Question have been much remarked by our committee."

Rev. Henry W. Beecher (1869): "I congratulate you upon your having acquired such a command of the English language. Your work might make many a native proud."

Rev. Dr. S. Adler, New York (1887): "I gladly acknowledge your earnest sense of research."

Rev. Dr. Hübsch, New York (1875): "Your *Hyksos* article proves your profound studies. I am ever ready to listen to your excellent remarks."

Dr. L. Philippson commented, flatteringly, in the *Allgemeine Zeitung*, on "The United States' Credo."

Hon. Carl Schurz, recently: "Your sketches of 'Germany' are most instructive and interesting."

So was the "*Reply to Prof. Fr. Delitzsch*," cordially received by scientific and laymen.

Spirit of the Biblical Legislation, single copy...... $2.00
Thoughts on Religious Rites, " " ...... .75
Mosaic Diet and Hygiene, " " ...... .50

Address:

Rev. M. FLUEGEL,
Baltimore, Md.